STUDIES IN AFRICAN AMERICAN HISTORY AND CULTURE

edited by
GRAHAM HODGES
COLGATE UNIVERSITY

A GARLAND SERIES

WHAT PRICE ALLIANCE?

BLACK RADICALS CONFRONT WHITE LABOR 1918–1938

KEITH P. GRIFFLER

GARLAND PUBLISHING, INC.
NEW YORK & LONDON / 1995

Library of Congress Cataloging-in-Publication Data

Griffler, Keith P.
    What price alliance? : Black radicals confront White labor,
1918–1938 / Keith P. Griffler.
        p.   cm. — (Studies in African American history and culture)
    Includes bibliographical references (p.) and index.
    ISBN 0–8153–1921–5 (alk. paper)
    1. Trade-unions—United States—Afro-American membership—
History—20th century.   2. Afro-American communists—History—
20th century.   I. Title.   II. Series.
HD6490.R22U647   1995
331.6'396073—dc20   94–32944
                                                                    CIP

Printed on acid-free, 250-year-life paper
Manufactured in the United States of America

Contents

What Price Alliance?

Introduction

In truth, the "racial" nature of the Negro problem in the United States has been greatly exaggerated. The orthodox racial approach to this vital problem tends to put the cart before the horse and blinds itself to factors in the problem which are far more significant than those of mere "race." This is due to a widespread misconception concerning the true position of the Negro in society. If it be said that the Negro population constitutes a "racial" minority group in the United States, it must be clearly understood that this is true only in the narrow terms of a socially imposed artificial status, having no scientific basis. In every other respect than that of this all too simple racial interpretation, the Negro population, rather than being a closely knit minority group, is subject to the same divisive influences impinging upon the life of every other group in the nation. In the economic sense, the Negro, in the vast majority, is identified with the peasant and the proletarian groups of the country, which are certainly not in the minority.

--Ralph Bunche, *A World View of Race*, 1936

The words of Ralph Bunche, one-time Black radical and later American diplomat, quoted above could only have been written in one period of American history and could only bear one interpretation. Contained within these words, the understanding of what radicals called the "Negro Question" they entail, and the policies that follow logically from them, are the key to understanding not only an epoch in African-

American thought, not only the development of African-American political economy consequent thereon, but nothing less than the changes in the American proletariat's class structure that began prior to the Depression but reached fruition only with the postwar expansion of the middle class. Concealed within the Depression decade and shrouded within the continuity of American development in the 20th century is a fundamental discontinuity--a fork in the road. Nowhere is that discontinuity more visible than in African-American thinking on the "Negro Question." Bunche's words could be reprinted again and again, but they could never represent the programmatic convergence of African-American radicals, Black political groups, and white labor and left-wing parties that they did in the mid-1930s. Never again would African Americans consent to policies that were so entirely in the interests of the relatively privileged layer of white workers on which the American labor movement rested, and never again would white labor need them to do so. The period in which Bunche wrote *A World View of Race* is unique in American history, and it is this uniqueness which makes the understanding of it so crucial to the study of 20th century American history.

By all appearances, the 1930s signaled the beginning of the end of the relegation of Black workers to the margins of working-class existence. To be sure, the barriers to be overcome were substantial. An estimated 36 percent of Black male industrial workers were unemployed, compared to 28 percent of whites.[1] For the three-quarters of all working Black women normally engaged in domestic labor, the unemployment rate was estimated as high as 56 percent. Moreover, being employed by no means guaranteed Black workers a living wage. In the laundry industry, to cite just one example of an industry employing mainly Black workers, the fourteen cents per hour minimum wage was so low that even the head of the New Deal government's National Recovery Administration, General Hugh Johnson, admitted it was not enough to live on. Meanwhile, the agency's compliance division documented that the legal rate was seldom put in practice. The situation was still worse for those Black workers, men and women, who worked in domestic and personal services. Some took home as little as $2.75 per week for as much as 14 hours of work per day, a wage one-tenth of that of the *average* white factory worker of the period, for a working day of nearly twice the length.[2]

Nevertheless, there seemed to be cause for optimism. During the Great Depression, the demand that African-American workers be organized came forth as never before. The self-professed working-class parties inaugurated unprecedented interracial agricultural workers' movements in the rural South early in the decade, the communists in the form of the Share Croppers' Union and the Socialist Party with the Southern Tenant Farmers' Union. By mid-decade, the newly-formed national labor confederation Congress of Industrial Organizations (CIO) initiated massive drives to enlist industrial workers, white and Black, in the ranks of labor. Even the old-guard conservative American Federation of Labor (AFL), prodded by Black radicals and spurred by CIO competition, began organizing some of the Black workers it had barred from membership for decades. At the same time, the beginnings of a Black-labor alliance took shape, as African-American organizations, most notably the middle-class National Association for the Advancement of Colored People (NAACP) and National Urban League (NUL), and the upstart left-wing National Negro Congress, either endorsed the unionization of Black workers or were well on their way to doing so. By the end of the decade, progress of a sort had been made: the number of Blacks with union cards soared more than tenfold in barely four years of concerted efforts, reaching more than half a million. For a time it may even have appeared to some that the union hall had replaced the courtroom and the legislature as the vehicle of change for African Americans.[3]

Two decades and two wars later, however, a new generation of young Black militants would take up the fight again, having grown up in economic conditions not essentially different from those faced by their parents and grandparents. America had certainly changed in the interim, with a shrinking working class and growing middle class, but African Americans remained (and remain) on the economic bottom. The "Black Revolution" would encompass the political changes of

the Sixties instead of the economic transformation for which
the Thirties held so much promise.   And while the events of
the Sixties have lived on in the popular memory, the same
cannot be said of the mass movement of the Depression decade
which had seemed to so many Black political leaders of the
time to represent the coming of a new era.   How could such
apparently sweeping changes have altered so little?
Answering this question requires the examination of the roots of
the Black-labor alliance that emerged in the mid-1930s; for it
was in the later Twenties and early Thirties that each
participant in the alliance formed its program.[4]

The legacy of organized labor had been its exclusion of
African Americans, not their avoidance of it.   In its most
profound essence, of course, this policy traced its roots to the
southern economic system that had enslaved African Americans
for centuries on American soil.   Even after the formal end to
that system with emancipation, African Americans in the
South remained but a small step from that form of bondage,
with new forms having arisen on the ashes of the old.
Organized labor, however, had been an exception to the general
American record.   Taking its cue from the steadfast opposition
to both overt and disguised slavery on the part of the European
working-class   movement,   led   by   the   International
Workingmen's Association under the leadership of Marx,
American unions had made some strides toward extending a
genuine hand of class solidarity to African Americans.   The
early post-emancipation years saw the formation of a union
movement that accepted, and sometimes even encouraged,
African-American membership.   All of that changed, however,
when the United States took up, around the turn of the century,
the "white man's burden" of the imperialist domination of
peoples of color.   The largest national trade union federation,
the AFL, from that point forward, conditioned the admission to
its ranks upon the color of the skin of the applicant.   A half
century of progress, however halting, was abolished.

As the trade union movement grew more conservative,
opting for "business unionism" that put the rise of wages before
all else, and certainly before class solidarity, it became more
and more the province of the most privileged layer of workers,

the "labor aristocracy." Skilled, highly-paid, American-born, white, and largely male, these workers felt little kinship to the "huddled masses" who poured into Ellis Island, New York, from all parts of Europe--and none to those who came from anywhere else. The AFL was, perhaps, the most ardent supporter of the exclusion of all people of color from the borders of the United States--and had it had any say in the matter, it would also have prevented the migration of African Americans from the South to the northern industrial centers that took place in the first decades of this century.

If the trade union movement had thus severed its connections to its own beginnings, neither had the working-class political parties made much attempt to maintain them. Although the largest of these by far, the Socialist Party, continued to proclaim its allegiance to the doctrine of Marx and the International, its practical policies were directed more toward supporting the aims of the AFL, of which it constituted a significant faction. Toward African Americans it continued to profess sympathy, but refused at the same time to recognize their plight as pariahs of the working class. They were free to join, except in the South, but they would not be permitted to espouse their cause within party bounds. To be sure, the socialists in their great majority were certainly not going to permit African Americans to come between them and the trade union movement, that is, the AFL.

Rather than either the union movement or the left bringing about any change in the conditions of the working class, it would be the changed conditions of that class that altered the unions and the left. The epoch of imperialism proved to have profound effects upon the working class. With the coming of World War I, the United States called a halt to the flood of European immigration and the working class rapidly lost its international flavor, becoming, as it was called then, "Americanized." At the same time, wages rose steadily. The U.S. Bureau of the Census recorded that the "real wages" of the average factory worker increased from $576 dollars in 1914 to $805 in 1927, allowing for unemployment over part of the year. In absolute terms, an average fully-employed worker took home $1612 in 1927, three times the figure of 1899.[5] Even the lowest of the workers, at least the lowest of the white workers, shared in the post-war prosperity.

When the trade union movement and the left awoke with the onset of the Depression in 1929 to discover the thoroughgoing alteration in the nature of the working class wrought by the seemingly gradual rise in wages, they inaugurated what they heralded as the most important development in working-class politics since the International: "progressive unionism." The organization to which it gave birth in 1935 was perhaps the most celebrated of all working-class organizations in American left folklore, the CIO. At the head of the CIO stood John L. Lewis, schooled in the "business unionism" of the AFL, and as conservative a labor leader as even the United States could produce. Behind the AFL rival, however, stood the entire American left, unified on this formation as they never were before and never would be again.

The basis behind this "new unionism"--as its advocates referred to it--was "new" only in purporting to consummate a "revolution" on the basis of the form of organization of the unions. As a federation of skilled workers, the AFL had traditionally been organized along craft lines, that is, according to the occupation of the workers. This suited the largely independent lines of work of the turn-of-the-century labor aristocrats. But it rendered virtually impossible the organization of large industries like steel, in which a dozen or so trade union organizations asserted jurisdiction over the various kinds of workers in the industry. The attempt to organize the steel industry after World War I, culminating in the Great Steel Strike of 1919, had come to grief over precisely this problem. The alternative, unions organized by industry, was no novelty even in America. The first large union federations had opted for an essentially like basis of organization, as had the syndicalist Industrial Workers of the World in the first decades of the twentieth century. But those movements had put forward labor solidarity and revolution, respectively, as the path to the working class's emancipation. The CIO "progressives" were unique, perhaps, in asserting that the form of trade unionism alone was to work miracles.

The object of the progressives' crusade were the mass production workers that the AFL had traditionally despised. But these mass production workers now stood in an entirely different relation to the old labor aristocrats of the craft unions. The latter were no longer the strong force they had once been. The rapid strides of the mass production industries had cut the ground out from under their aristocratic feet. The workers of those new industries, the markets for which expanded in geometrical fashion, were quickly replacing the skilled craft worker as the new labor aristocracy. By the 1930s it had become an imperative of both private industry and the government to rid these workers of their traditional affinity, however weak, to radical politics and revolutionary unionism. A form of governmental unionism ushered in by the Wagner Act in 1935 provided the solution. Henceforth, workers would be granted higher wages (which the ever-more "capital-intensive" industries could withstand) in return for labor peace and an end to worker radicalism. After a stormy period of labor strife, this solution was foisted upon both workers and industrialists, to the immediate material advantage of both. In this struggle, the left and the federal government under Franklin Delano Roosevelt played the role of seemingly unlikely allies.

The results for the white mass production workers, the new labor aristocracy, were significant. By the decade after the Second World War, they bore little resemblance to the ethnically and linguistically heterogeneous broken masses of the turn of the century. Nor did they any longer seem to have anything in common with the masses of extremely poor workers and peasants in the colonies, whom only a short time ago they had called brothers and sisters. Like the impoverished "Third World" workers, African Americans did not share the promised benefits of this new era, and its benefits extended almost not at all to those left in the South. Clearly, American workers (and their Western European brethren) no longer believed in the principle of "labor unity" with which they had lured Black workers into the CIO. They could not recognize in the oppressed people of color of the world the occupiers of the social position from which they had so recently emerged, and they were

certainly in no mood to take any part in the anti-colonial wars
and revolutions. Never again would a worker simply be a
worker. To American workers, the old slogan, "Workers of the
world, unite," belonged to an era in the already distant past,
along with the ideas which had helped to launch the new era
of "progressive unionism."

During the initial phase of the CIO organizing drive,
however, "unity of labor" was precisely the slogan federation
supporters adopted in their dealings with African Americans.
The reason is not far to seek. As a result of the "Great
Migration" of African Americans from the semi-slavery of the
South to the industry of the North, Black workers were
strategically placed in industry. Industrialists, such as Henry
Ford, the automobile manufacturer, had deliberately brought
in African-American workers to foil any attempts at organizing
unions in their industries. Given AFL policy, the strategy was
impeccably sound. Out of narrow self-interest, therefore, the
"progressive" unions easily surmised that without Black
workers on their side, their cause was lost.

"Progressive" legend has it that the CIO was "racially
egalitarian" from its outset.[6] Facts prove otherwise. So
strongly entrenched was racism, fed by imperial chauvinism, in
the aristocracy of the working class by this time that even in
the face of self-interest "progressive unionists" found it
difficult to generate any enthusiasm for organizing Black
workers. Black radicals would make up for that deficiency by
their enthusiasm for "progressive unionism," at least at the
crucial moment. How Black radicals came to be accomplices in
this cynical betrayal of Black workers forms the substance of
the present work.

To be sure, African Americans appreciated the need to turn
labor into a vehicle to take the part of all workers, that is, to
make it what it purported to be. It cannot be denied, however
much it is generally ignored, that the efforts of African
Americans were directed above all toward combating racism
within the left and converting it into a force for workers of all
races. Furthermore, the unfolding of this struggle by Black
radicals to convert the left had naturally to be concentrated in
the arena of the labor movement. The unions, as literally the

mass movement of workers, held the key to the direction of the struggles of the working class and, therefore, of the overwhelmingly working-class African-American people.

If it is not, then, the alliance itself that is in question, it can only be the terms upon which it was to be concluded: Were Black workers simply to do their part in bringing about the "progressive revolution" of white workers-turned-middle-class, or were white workers, at least a section of them, to forsake the privilege of race to join in the struggle for the emancipation of all workers? A battle of sorts would indeed take place over this question, but, in the end, Black radicals would never take their fight out of the cover of the back room negotiations. The Depression decade would produce its mass movement, but certainly not one aimed at or capable of attaining the aims which "progressive unionists" proclaimed and Black radicals set themselves out to accomplish. There would be no sustained effort to convert organized labor to a representative of the interests of all workers. Black radicals would settle for a Black-labor alliance founded upon African Americans' unqualified support for labor and the CIO's token support for "symbolic" reformist legislation which, for the most part, mild though it was, never got out of the congressional committees to which it was submitted.

The reasons behind the shallowness of the "liberation struggle" of the 1930s must be sought in the examination of the understanding of Black radicals of the place of African-American workers in the American working-class structure. The "Negro Question" provided the theoretical form in which the struggle over this understanding would unfold, and constitutes, therefore, the necessary point of departure.

II.

The cycle of the development of Black radicalism that culminated with the formation of the alliance between Black radicals and labor progressives began during the aftermath of the Bolshevik revolution of 1917. That epoch-making event permanently altered the terrain of American radicalism, setting the American left into a ferment that lasted for more than a decade. Having come to power in the multi-national, multi-ethnic and multi-racial remnants of the tsarist empire, the Bolsheviks would place the "national question" squarely at the center of the international communist movement. And it was in this climate that the "Negro Question" would come to occupy the theoretical place of honor among the Black radicals who gravitated to the American communist movement in the late 1910s and early 1920s. In the spirit of the internationalism of the times, the leading Black communists of this period consisted mainly of West Indians, at least somewhat to the chagrin of Black socialists such as A. Philip Randolph. Joined by a promising crop of U.S.-born Blacks, these radicals would combine to make the communist movement the focus of an intense debate on the "Negro Question," a debate in which Black communists would make extraordinary use of the climate of internationalism to combat the insular thinking among most, if not all, white American communists. Before their struggle got caught up in international Stalinist politics, Black communists had succeeded in such a decisive break with the old socialist approach to the "Negro Question" that even Black socialists would feel the effects.

The traditional socialist position was known as "Debsianism," after the most prominent socialist leader of the period, Eugene V. Debs. He most forcefully advanced the notion that class exploitation alone rested at the foundation of the oppression of African Americans, and that the solution of the "class question," the overthrow of capitalism and the establishment of socialism on the basis of the struggle of the working class, particularly its favored sections that opted for socialism at the time, was alone necessary to rectify any and all social and class-based ills. In the 1920s Black radicals challenged this standpoint, putting forward an understanding of their own, which I will call the "internationalist" position, to emphasize its roots in the division of the world into imperialist and subject nations. The latter explicitly tied the "Negro Question" to the world struggle between international capitalism (imperialism) and the workers of the world, particularly the most exploited. The struggle between these two opposed views of the path to working-class emancipation would decide the course that Black radicalism was to pursue.

The decade following World War I displayed a vibrancy in Black radicalism in the United States that no decade before or since could match. There were three main radical camps during this period: the members of the African Blood Brotherhood (ABB), a Black nationalist organization formed after World War I, composed mainly of the West Indian radicals, and allied to the communist movement--the progenitors of the internationalist position; the small group of Black socialists, adherents of Debsianism, led by A. Philip Randolph and Frank R. Crosswaith; and a group of independent radicals led by W.E.B. Du Bois and Abram Harris, and joined by John P. Davis and Ralph Bunche, all of whom were middle-class intellectuals working within or around Black political organizations such as the NAACP and NUL. It was this latter group which would decide the contest in favor of the socialists, ironically, by joining the communists, as it were. They accomplished this unlikely "synthesis" by taking the intellectual content of Debsianism and giving it the theoretical form of ABB radicalism. The new doctrine, which I call "neo-Debsianism," was no longer the advocacy of a "class-only" approach by default, but a positive program, self-consciously put forward in the name of Black workers themselves, and put into effect through means the Debsians proper would never have considered: a separate Black political organization ostensibly representing Black workers, the National Negro Congress. It is from the elaboration of this doctrine at the hands of Ralph Bunche that the quotation that opens the present work is taken. And it is this outlook that would provide the theoretical justification for the most one-sided of "alliances"--that between the Black radicals and the progressive unionists of the 1930s. The complex course of development that brought about such a "synthesis," and with such results, can only be grasped in the course of its exposition.

III.

In the pages that follow, I use the term "radical" in its original sense: representatives of the extreme left-wing of liberalism. By this definition, the vast majority of socialists (in European terms social democrats) qualify, while communists in the true sense of revolutionaries determined to overthrow the liberal-democratic regime do not. Yet communists are included in this study under the term "radical." There are two reasons for this inclusion. First, the communist movement has always attracted a greater or fewer number of radicals, people who by conviction are not more than extreme liberals but who for various reasons, from sheer opportunism to the most genuine of false conviction, momentarily or permanently throw in their lot with the revolutionaries. The great majority of the American Communist Party (CP) throughout its history, and certainly its decisive elements, fall into that category. There have been few genuine revolutionaries in its ranks. Second, I include them because the leading Black communists included themselves there. No doubt many of them for a short time, and perhaps a handful for longer, became revolutionaries and deserted the radical camp. But they represented the exception. What follows is essentially a story of radicals, Black and white, which is to say, the most consistent liberals in America in regard to questions of race. Whatever potential ever existed in America for anything other than a liberal, gradualist "solution" to the "Negro Question" (a "question" which, for all the intervening years and struggles and "progress" remains to be "solved") has never been realized.

Chapter I
The African Blood Brotherhood and the Development of the Internationalist Position on the "Negro Question"

That the "Negro Question" would ever come to be a topic of concern to the American left seemed remote in the first decades of American socialism. Old roots there were. Marx and Engels had attached great importance to the "Negro Question" in America, with Marx commenting on more than one occasion that the liberation of white labor could not occur without the liberation of Black labor. Engels had pointed out that "race privilege" in America had triumphed over class privilege at the inception of the republic, leaving the clear implication that the "class question" would never be posed alone in America, that the "Negro Question" would ever come along with it. And early socialists, both Marxists and non-Marxists, had supported the idea of the radical reconstruction of the American South (and North) along lines that would spell the end of racial oppression.[1]

But by the time the main branches of American socialism had been established, these roots were buried well underground. The Socialist Party (SP), following the thinking of its most important exponent, Eugene V. Debs, was to develop by the turn of the century a class-only approach, or "Debsianism." In Debs' well-known phrase, the SP had "nothing special to offer the Negro." In other words, socialism would approach the "Negro Question" as part and parcel of the "class question," requiring no independent solution. Instead,

Debs said, Black workers must be "arouse[d] . . . to the necessity
of taking their place and doing their part in the great struggle
that is to emancipate the workers of all races and all nations
from the insufferable curse of industrial slavery and social
degradation." But as to gradations in that degradation, Debs
saw none. He did not, as did most other socialists, believe that
African Americans needed no particular attention. But neither
did he do or suggest doing much more than expressing his
general solidarity with them.[2]

The classic statement of Debsianism was expressed, not by
Debs himself, but by the socialist periodical New Solidarity.
Under the title "There Is No Race Problem," it declared,

[T]he problem of the workers is not a race problem.
There is [sic] no white or brown races. All have but one
problem to solve, and that is the problem of how to
overthrow the system of slavery under which all are
bound to the employing class. When this one problem
is solved there will be no race problems.

According to this view, a worker was simply a worker, and a
Black worker who faced racism and social oppression required
no more from socialism than the white worker who got double
his salary and the choice of jobs from which his Black brother
was barred. This outlook proclaimed that socialism and
socialism alone would solve the problems of African Americans
and all the oppressed, whether of nations with colonial slaves
or whether of nations of colonial slaves. Nothing could be
painted in terms more black and white than this view that
denied any difference in the essential conditions of Black and
white. With such an outlook, it is hardly surprising that in a
nation as thoroughly imbued with racial consciousness, as
permeated by racism and racial oppression, as the United
States, the SP found few adherents among the Black
population. W.E.B. Du Bois, an early convert to socialism, gave
up on the Socialist Party as a vehicle for the revolutionizing of
the conditions of African Americans, even while he maintained
an active sympathy for the goals of socialism. As Du Bois put
it, the SP lacked "the political courage to face up to the race
problem." A drastic change would be required before socialism
could become a movement behind which African Americans

could throw their support.   What it took, in fact, was a revolution.[3]

The Bolshevik revolution in Russia first put the "national question" squarely on the agenda of international socialism. With its very first declaration to the world the Russian revolutionaries signaled their intention to take up the cause of Africans and Asians, subject to both class and national oppression.   With its launching of the Third (Communist) International, the Russian revolution thrust Lenin, who had long held that African Americans were an oppressed national minority, to the center of international socialism.   The results upon the status within that movement of the peoples of African descent were both profound and immediate.

Lenin distinguished himself among socialists, and communists, of the period by his steadfast insistence that distinctions within the working class be recognized.   Lenin argued that benefits could accrue to the group of labor aristocrats within the working class because of the extreme degradation of its lowest sections.   For Lenin, this fact could not be separated from the imperialist subjugation of entire nations:

> The exploitation of *worse paid* labour from backward countries is particularly characteristic of imperialism. On this exploitation rests, to a certain degree, the *parasitism* of rich imperialist countries which bribe a part of their workers with higher wages while shamelessly and unrestrainedly exploiting the labour of 'cheap' foreign workers. . . .   [T]he exploiters in 'civilised' countries always take advantage of the fact that the imported foreign workers have no rights.

Moreoever, Lenin draws precisely the same conclusions for this state of affairs that, as will be shown subsequently, Black communist Richard B. Moore and some of his African Blood Brotherhood comrades would later:

> It would be expedient, perhaps, to emphasize more strongly and to express more vividly in our [the Bolsheviks'] programme the prominence of the handful of the richest imperialist countries which prosper parasitically by robbing colonies and weaker nations. This is an extremely important feature of imperialism.

> To a certain extent it facilitates the rise of powerful
> revolutionary movements in countries that are subjected
> to imperialist plunder, and are in danger of being
> crushed and partitioned by the giant imperialists, . . .
> and on the other hand, tends to a certain extent to
> prevent the rise of profound revolutionary movements
> in the countries that plunder, by imperialist methods,
> many colonies and foreign lands, and thus make a very
> large (comparatively) portion of their population
> *participants* in the division of the imperialist loot.

Hence, Lenin insisted that the privileged workers of the
imperialist nations had a certain stake in the oppression of
workers of other nations and races, within the "home country"
or not, and that this interest had its effects upon their outlook
and commitment to the class struggle of the workers.

Moreover, Lenin would apply precisely this general
understanding to the specific circumstances of African-
American workers. As early as 1913, Lenin had shown an
especial interest in the condition of African Americans,
although he would never set foot in North America. He noted
that their social position in the American South, where before
the migrations, the vast majority resided, were entirely
parallel to that of the Russian serf, except that grafted onto
the grinding class oppression that African Americans faced was
an all-pervasive racial oppression. Later research and
reflection on African Americans led Lenin to conclude, in 1916,
that African Americans "should be classed as an oppressed
nation." Lenin carried this conviction to his leadership of the
Third International. At its second congress in 1920, the
Comintern took up the "National and Colonial Question,"
which Lenin considered of the greatest importance and for
which he took the responsibility of drafting a set of theses. In
them he made special reference to "American Negroes" as
included among the "dependent and underprivileged nations."
Hence, Lenin directly linked the Black liberation struggle with
the struggle against imperialism, according it thus a place of
honor in the communist movement. In addition, he signalled to
the members of the national and colonial commission (the only
one which he chaired), who were charged with discussing and

amending the resolutions his particular desire for more information on African Americans, and he made the acquaintance of Otto Huiswoud, a Black delegate from the American party.[4]

The second-ranking international communist leader at the time, Leon Trotsky, displayed a similar interest in the plight of African Americans. Having lived for a time in the United States, Trotsky had perhaps a more personal knowledge of American race relations. Whatever the reason, he was to take as great a theoretical interest and an even greater personal interest than Lenin in the "Negro Question." In the "Manifesto of the Communist International to the Workers of the World," which he authored, Trotsky called attention to what he considered to be perhaps the most important result of the First World War: "Never before has the infamy of capitalist rule in the colonies been delineated so clearly; never before has the problem of colonial slavery been posed so sharply as it is today." And Trotsky sounded a clarion call which would reverberate among people of African descent, particularly those from the West Indies: "Colonial slaves of Africa and Asia! The hour of proletarian dictatorship in Europe will strike for you as the hour of your own emancipation!" Never had socialists proclaimed this intention so clearly and so openly.[5]

After the Fourth Comintern Congress, Trotsky initiated contact with the West Indian communist Claude McKay during the latter's stay in Russia in the early 1920s and commissioned him to write a treatise on the "Negro Question." In his response to a letter from McKay, Trotsky wrote of the "exceedingly urgent and important revolutionary task" of recruiting Blacks into the communist movement. He also called attention to the relationship between the "labor aristocracy" and racial oppression:

> In North America the matter [of uniting white and Black workers] is further complicated by the abominable obtuseness and caste presumption of the privileged upper strata of the working class itself, who refuse to recognize fellow-workers and fighting comrades in the negroes. [AFL president Samuel]

> Gompers' policy is founded on the exploitation of such
> despicable prejudices, and is at the present time the
> most effective guarantee for the successful subjugation
> of white and colored workers alike.

Trotsky implies here that African Americans stand in the same
relation to white American workers that the colonial masses
stand in relation to those of the imperialist nations: white
workers benefit from the increased exploitation of Black
workers based on the lower wages paid them because of their
race.   Lenin, for example, wrote, "The English
bourgeoisie . . . obtains larger revenues from the tens of millions
and hundreds of millions of the population in India and of her
other colonies than from the English workers. . . . In these
conditions, a certain material and economic basis is created for
infecting the proletariat of this or that country with colonial
chauvinism." Neither Trotsky nor Lenin, however, would ever
do more than make this the clear implication of their thinking
on African Americans and "white chauvinism." But Trotsky
still proceeded to the logical practical consideration of this
standpoint: "One of the most important branches of [American
class] conflict consists in enlightening the feeling of human
dignity, and of revolutionary protest, amongst the black slaves
of American capital. . . . [T]his work can only be carried out by
self-sacrificing and politically educated revolutionary
negroes."[6]

Both Lenin and Trotsky expressed their contempt for the
racism of white Americans workers, which they saw as akin to
national chauvinism by the citizenry of imperialist powers,
and both insisted that it could not be tolerated in communist
ranks. Unfortunately for Black communists in America, neither
would remain in the leadership of international communism
beyond the mid-1920s, and their replacement, Stalin, did not
hold the national question in nearly such high regard.

Brief though it was, the tenure of Lenin and Trotsky as the
leaders of the world communist movement sufficed to weld the
most vital trend within Black radicalism to the Third
International and its American affiliate. Black communist
Cyril Briggs later revealed that he had declined to join the
Socialist Party because of "its refusal to recognize the special

character of Negro oppression in the U.S.A." So, attracted by "the solution of the national question in the Soviet Union," Briggs joined the American Communist Party, "confident that the American Party would in time take its lead on that question from the Soviet party. . . ." For W.A. Domingo, Briggs' fellow West Indian radical, the case was the same. White American radicals paid only lip service to the plight of oppressed Blacks, whereas, Domingo declared not long after the Russian revolution, the "Russian Bolsheviks understand [racial oppression] very well and use [this understanding] to good effect by supporting and encouraging the oppressed of all races, creeds and nationalities." As another Black communist, Otto Hall, put it, "We had faith in Lenin and the Russian comrades." Lenin's and Trotsky's thought, backed up by the Bolshevik revolution, provided Black communists with the starting point of their quest for an approach to the "Negro Question" to supplant Debsianism.[7]

Besides the leaders of the international movement, there were some white American socialists who, on the basis of their experiences in America, had come to something of the same understanding on the "Negro Question." John Reed, shortly before his death in 1921, separated himself from standard American socialist thinking both in referring to the "oppressed Negro people" and in advocating full social equality as the only possible communist policy. But what most distinguished Reed, perhaps, and what would have made him an invaluable ally to Black communists if he had lived, was the attention that he insisted African Americans be given. At the Second Congress of the Comintern in 1920, Reed voiced his strong conviction that African Americans could not be ignored by the communists, but that the latter must embrace the mood of rebellion developing among African Americans and convince them that "social revolution . . . [is] the only effective means of liberating the oppressed Negro people." Briggs did his best to call attention to Reed's assessment of the necessity of appealing to Blacks, but in the factional atmosphere of the early years of the Communist Party the thinking of a former leader, even one buried with Lenin, carried little weight if he was not there to defend it in person. Moreover, Briggs and other Black communists must have felt a certain ambivalence toward Reed, who refused to accept Lenin's view that African Americans were subject to exploitation on the basis of their race added to that of their class.[8]

Of more significance, William "Big Bill" Haywood, a founder and leader of the Industrial Workers of the World (IWW) and a supporter of the Bolshevik revolution and communist goals, not only advocated social equality, and not only helped to put it in practice in the IWW, but had even taken a giant step toward the understanding of the "Negro Question" at which Black communists arrived. He asserted in the early 1920s that "the conservative trade union spirit, the spirit of the [labor] aristocracy, . . . has built its welfare [in part] on national and racial prejudices"; far from Black labor dragging down white, the privileged position of the white labor aristocracy in America rested in part on the base of the extreme degradation and exploitation of Black workers. The loss of these two outstanding champions of Black liberation-- Reed to premature death and Haywood to exile--no doubt injured the cause of the Black communists in struggling for the implementation of their program on the "Negro Question."[9]

The IWW deserves mention in its own right. Its policy of admitting Black workers at a time when the AFL and the independent national federations of railroad workers refused them admission caused the IWW to be praised widely among African-American leaders, from James Weldon Johnson of the NAACP to the socialist A. Philip Randolph, in the late 1910s and early 1920s. Although it did not go appreciably beyond Debsianism, it did make reference to the importance of the African-American freedom struggle. It acknowledged that African Americans would have to "force the white race to grant [them] equal treatment," and urged them to struggle for their "rights as . . . human being[s]." In an act of unparalleled solidarity (one that has not been equalled by either the left or organized labor to this day), the IWW called upon white workers to make the following their slogan within capitalist society: "If you do not stop discrimination against the colored race, we will stop working for you." In fitting with the general tenor of the IWW, it maintained the strong conviction that society must be revolutionized to end racial proscription. The IWW also launched the career of Black trade unionist Ben Fletcher, an early advocate of a Black trade union confederation.[10]

Within the Communist Party itself during the 1920s, only two white thinkers showed any consistent inclination to abandon Debsianism. Nationally-known political cartoonist and party leader Robert Minor, following in the footsteps of Black communists, with whom he maintained close contacts, concluded that the CP could not afford "to ignore the question of a caste system" in the United States. In assimilating the understanding made official Comintern policy at its second congress fours years before, Minor noted that "a vast majority of the world's population . . . are peoples more or less marked with color, and all are held under subjection of a white-skinned minority." Following in Reed's footsteps, Minor highlighted the importance of the communist commitment to "social revolution": "Not a mere change in the surface of life, but the deepest social overturn, with the uprooting of every kind of inequality and every trace of class division, is our distinguishing purpose." If such a determination did not actually distinguish the white American communists, it did distinguish Minor among them, at least until his submersion in the factional sea of American communist life.[11]

The other white communist to go substantially beyond Debsianism was the former socialist Scott Nearing, who had been trained as an economist. After touring the South in 1928, Nearing felt compelled to write about the overwhelming oppression he saw there, the results of which are found in his book *Black America*, probably the first such volume by a white leftist. Since Nearing himself confessed to being rather isolated from the intellectual life of the party, including its Black members, the book represents conclusions developed largely independently. While it meant that Nearing could have no real influence on the fate of the "Negro Question" in party circles, it does speak to the possibility of a white radical to attain something beyond the Debsian outlook on the basis of the general principles of socialism.[12]

Although Nearing never asked himself whether African Americans constituted a nation of one type or another, even his unsystematic observations revealed to him that their race lay at the root of the horrors, including lynchings, that he witnessed. As such, he commented, "*Black America* deals with the American Negro, not as a 'social problem' but as an oppressed race." This term Nearing used interchangeably with "subject race" and "exploited race." In transcending the pie-in-sky optimism and unbounded naivete that has always characterized American liberalism in matters of race, he had gained the firm belief that "the white exploiters of the United States [would] keep the Negroes in subjection as long as the Negroes are willing to stay there." The only solution Nearing could see came in the form of "economic reorganization," by which Nearing probably meant to indicate what Reed and Minor had called "social revolution." Moreover, to a degree far greater than any white American thinker had ever formulated the question, Nearing explicitly tied the oppression of African Americans to the domination of other peoples of color at the hands of American imperialism. Not only, he believed, could African Americans benefit from an examination of the fate of other oppressed peoples--Filipinos, Puerto Ricans, Nicaraguans, Haitians, and so forth--but these peoples could learn invaluable lessons from studying the position of African Americans. All must conclude that "an imperial ruling class such as that which now dominates public policy in the United States needs subject races to work and sometimes to fight. The imperialist rulers will take any necessary steps to hold the subject race in its subordinate position."[13]

Moreover, Nearing began the work of applying this understanding to the economic position of African Americans. He was one of the first to see the connection between race and class in the U.S.: "To be black, in the United States, is to be proletarian." And he recognized in African Americans the "largest single reserve of mass labor power." He also saw through the Debsian myth that Blacks were exploited solely on the basis of class:

> [African Americans] carry the normal burden of workers
> under capitalism. In addition they must shoulder the

> special burden of economic discrimination which the
> exploiting whites of the United States have laid upon
> the shoulders of Negro workers in industry.

In other words, not only are African Americans subject to class
exploitation, but they "are exploited as a race." He noted that
this had effects on whites themselves, that they maintained
"a definite consciousness of whiteness" as members of the
"exploiting race." In the same measure, African Americans
would "be forced" to maintain an "equally definite
consciousness of blackness." But Nearing could see no
implications for political policy in the relationship of race
and class in America. He called only for white workers to
establish "working-class solidarity across race lines." And
though he declared that there was "no more vital task before
the American workers today," Nearing did not gain the insight
that such solidarity could only be truly founded on a definite
basis. Besides, Nearing was soon removed from the contest
within the party, when he broke with it over an entirely
separate issue. That he did not feel strongly enough to do so on
the basis of its attitude toward the "Negro Question" indicates
something about the level of his commitment to its proper
solution.[14]

But the absence of white allies in the communist movement
affected only the chances for the acceptance of the
internationalist view of the "Negro Question," and not its
development. For it would be, in America, the product of the
thinking of Black intellectuals, not white. While statements
in the internationalist spirit by white American communists
are occasionally to be found, no white American communist
played an appreciable role in the development of the
internationalist position, although several played prominent
roles in the transformation of Debsianism into neo-Debsianism.

The former task was left to Black communists, who grouped
themselves around the African Blood Brotherhood (ABB) from
its founding in 1919. Behind the ABB were such West Indian
Blacks as Cyril Briggs, Otto Huiswoud, Claude McKay, and
Richard B. Moore. While the ABB would later all but merge
with the Communist Party, its organizational independence in

the early Twenties provided an important early base for the development of a Black radical (and revolutionary) program.[15]

If the pursuit of the "class question" had led such thinkers as Reed and Haywood (not to mention Lenin and Trotsky) inexorably to the "Negro Question," for Black communists it was quite the other way around. Unlike their white comrades, their first and in most cases primary devotion was to the liberation of the peoples of African descent. And these Black radicals were unanimous in their condemnation of the American left for its lack of a program for what the ABB radicals referred to as the "Negro people of the world." Claude McKay, for example, commented that the CP "must establish a completely clear program on the Negro question."[16]

W.A. Domingo was even more forthright. He declared, "One can boldly say that in America the Negro question is the touchstone, the measure by which the sincerity of American radicalism can be measured." But Domingo recognized that it could not be left to white radicals to come to any kind of profound understanding of the "Negro Question" on their own. It would be up to Black "revolutionaries [to] have an ear cocked and attentively watch each practical step of revolutionaries on the Negro question." Black communists "absolutely must indicate to white comrades the root problems of the Negro working class and turn their attention to snares which capitalist tricksters set while playing on racial inequality."[17]

But criticism of American socialism's lack of a program was one thing, developing such a program on their own another. Still, Black radicals had "inherited" none of the Debsianism of the socialists, and they (particularly as their most important representatives were West Indian) did not suffer from the illusions of American democracy or the "white man's burden." In fact, it was entirely outside of the communist movement (and for that matter, outside the milieu of American radicalism in general) that they would begin their work. And so, even if "classical Marxism" offered nothing (i.e., nothing but a general framework) to American communists toward the "Negro Question," as has been asserted, "classical" Black radical thought did. Its earliest and most important theoretician was Cyril V. Briggs.[18]

Briggs, whose complexion and temperament earned him the appellation "Angry Blond Negro," seemed the least likely figure to play his historical role. Born in 1888, he hailed from the small Caribbean island of Nevis. Light-skinned enough to pass for white and born on the fringes of white society, but removed from the poverty of Caribbean Blacks, his early education, as he later described it, "aimed to turn out Black Anglo-Saxons, glorify whites, [and] and denigrate Africans." In 1905, Briggs followed his mother to the U.S., settling in Harlem, and within a short time had taken up a place on the *Amsterdam News*, a Black newspaper. Briggs' journalistic career soon led him into radical politics.[19]

When circumstances chanced to put Briggs in the editorship of his own "race" magazine in 1918, a tremendous intellectual force was let loose to concentrate its efforts on the "Negro Question." For while Briggs' *Crusader* was neither the first nor the most widely circulated of Black radical organs, it was certainly the most intellectually vibrant and original. In the four years of its existence Briggs laid the groundwork of the internationalist position on the "Negro Question" in America, codified in the program of the African Blood Brotherhood, and gave other Black radical thinkers a firm base to stand upon.[20]

At the time of the founding of *The Crusader* in September of 1918, Briggs was on the threshold of being revolutionized in his thinking by the course of developments. He understood that World War I portended great changes, though he was less definite on the source. Certainly he recognized that the participation of Black troops (American and African) would signal a new era in the Black liberation movement. But as yet he still held to the contradictory views that, on the one hand, the people of African descent would have to liberate themselves, and that, on the other, Africa might gain its independence as a result of an Allied victory--since Wilson had promised, or at least intimated, as much in his Fourteen Points. Briggs was at this point sympathetic to the Socialist Party, but by far the greatest influence upon him was Wilson's promise of self-determination. Ironically, it would first be Wilson, rather than the Bolshevik revolution and workers' government, that would point Briggs toward communism. When Wilson reneged

on his promise of self-determination for all peoples of the
world, Briggs, in his fury, cast aside the duality in his
thinking: henceforth he would be a determined champion of
self-determination for the people of African descent by
revolutionary means.[21]

Yet if Briggs had harbored some ambivalence as to the
means of African liberation, as to the goal itself he had never
wavered. In contrast to W.E.B. Du Bois's assertion that Africa
was not yet prepared for self-rule, Briggs adhered to a belief in
the "Race genius" of the African peoples that predetermined
their successful civilization. They had, however, been robbed
of the knowledge of this genius through the falsification of
their history, and a restoration of it, one of the primary goals
of *The Crusader*, would help bring about the cherished aim of
redemption of the continent. Exactly what African liberation
entailed varied with the wide-ranging exploration of Briggs'
mind. From the first he put forward the slogan "Africa for the
Africans," which would for a time make him favorably
disposed to Marcus Garvey. But sometimes Briggs would speak
in favor of merely a "Negro nation," the location of which
changed from the West Indies to Africa and once even landed in
the southern United States. Other times he advocated the
building up of Liberia or Ethiopia into a war machine capable
of fending off European encroachment in Africa, and even
perhaps giving birth to a liberation army for the African
peoples.[22]

On one point, however, Briggs was perfectly consistent: the
inability of Blacks and whites to live together peacefully and
fruitfully. He was convinced that racism was innate and as old
as civilization itself. Blacks disliked whites as much as
whites Blacks, and thus it would ever be. The solution, then,
though Briggs only occasionally put it so bluntly, was
permanent separation. More and more, however, Briggs began
to change this to "government of the Negro, by the Negro, for
the Negro," and he always insisted upon full equality for
Blacks in the United States.[23]

Once the bitterness of Wilson's "betrayal" of Africa, as
Briggs called it, wore off, Briggs found himself more and more
drawn to the Russian revolution and less inclined to view the

world purely in terms of race. Far from the victorious "democracies" having freed the German colonies, let alone their own, they had simply divided them among themselves. Briggs concluded more forcefully than ever that imperialism was the enemy of the "Negro people." As such, then, the white working class was, or at least could be, their ally. In late 1919, Briggs joined the Communist Party, just in the process of formation out of the remnants of the shattered Socialist Party. At around the same time, Briggs founded the African Blood Brotherhood (ABB), mainly as a base for propagating his views of the "Negro Question," but also as an independent base from which Black communists could work and for armed self-defense in the face of racial violence. And while the ABB accepted the Communist Party's basic program, the Communist Party was far from accepting the program of the ABB.[24]

For Briggs took with him into the CP several principles which were anathema to the white communists. One was that the Black workers had every right to be suspicious of the white workers and to demand from them concrete proof of their solidarity. Hence, even as Briggs first proclaimed his allegiance to the cause of the working class and placed the Negro question squarely in the domain of class struggle, he refused to be part of a one-sided relationship. In an editorial, "The Negro's Place Is With Labor," in the June, 1919 edition of *The Crusader*, Briggs included the proviso that this was so "providing white labor does its share toward erasing the resentments raised by its unwise attitude in the past. . . ."[25]

And while Briggs came to accept that socialism (or as he called it "the Socialist Co-operative Commonwealth") was necessary to solve the class content of the "Negro Question," he was adamant that it alone was not enough: "The Negro has been treated so brutally in the past by the rest of humanity that he may be pardoned for now looking at the matter more from the viewpoint of the Negro than from that of a humanity that is not humane. And again, he may prefer that his rights and immunity from oppression be based upon his own power rather than upon the problematical continued existence of the Socialist Co-operative Commonwealth." In other words, Briggs retained at least the spirit of Black self-determination in his vision of the future socialist world, including, perhaps, the socialist U.S. Briggs tried to interest the communists in an open discussion on the "Negro Question" through the pages of *The Crusader* in early 1921. Not surprisingly, none of them took him up on it. One white socialist, Edward J. Irvine, however, did. This rank-and-filer had come by his socialism and his respect for African Americans as a marine in the Dominican Republic (where, as he put it, he was unwittingly upholding the "dictatorship of the bourgeoisie" and "guarding American interests"). And although, as we shall see subsequently, he far surpassed other white radicals in one aspect of his understanding of the "Negro Question," he undoubtedly reflected the prevailing sentiment in white radical circles when he declared that "the only thing I hate as bad as race-prejudice is race-consciousness." Briggs, however, would not budge from his position of old. He replied, "As to race-consciousness: that is a weapon with which the Negro race cannot very well dispense so long as it remains one of the most important factors in the rise and fall of nations and of races, and is so utilized by other people."[26]

The culmination of Briggs' thought on the "Negro Question," and the substance of his contribution to the internationalist position, is to be found in the program of the African Blood Brotherhood, which bears Briggs' unmistakable stamp. The ABB program was built around two central principles: (1) that Blacks the world over constituted a "people" dominated by imperialism which could only gain its freedom by the revolutionary overthrow of the "Big Capitalist Powers"; and (2) that the basis for the "liberation" of people of African descent (referred to as the "Negro people") was an alliance with the class-conscious white working class. The first principle proves that this program could not have originated in the CP, which until the late Twenties gave only token attention to African Americans and which gave no credence to Black nationality. But the program identified one "outstanding fact" that drew the ABB toward the communist movement: "Soviet Russia is opposing the imperialist robbers who have partitioned our motherland and subjugated our kindred." On this basis, the ABB would seek an alliance with the Communist International, which attracted the ABB's leading members to the nascent Communist Party--Huiswoud, for example, being a charter member.[27]

In addition to the conception of the "Negro people" of the world, Briggs' ABB also brought two other ideas with it when it fused with the CP that together would form the basis of the conflicts that would characterize their relationship for more than a decade. First, the ABB program put forward the notion of African Americans as the vanguard of the Black revolution. Through the "knowledge" gained by virtue of "being a part of the population of a great empire," American Blacks--"whether native or foreign born"--were "destined to assume the leadership of our people in a powerful movement for Negro liberation." Hence, the ABB explicitly linked the destiny of African-American workers to that of all people of African descent. They did not speak only as a group within the American working class, as did the various ethnic components of the multinational Communist Party, but as representatives of a people dispersed throughout Africa, Latin America, and North America. As such, they constituted not a peculiarly "American problem," as did for example the presence of so many ethnic groups melded into the American nation--a problem upon which American communists could claim expertise through unique experience--but part of a much larger question that could only properly be understood in a world context by the communist movement as a whole. In short, African Americans were not the specific domain of the American communists.[28]

Second, while the ABB program designated "class-conscious" white workers as "actual allies," it emphatically declared that, contrary to the views of the leadership of the American CP, "The non-class conscious white workers who have not yet realized that all workers regardless of race or colour have a common interest, must be considered as only potential allies at present and everything possible [must be] done to awaken their class-consciousness toward the end of obtaining their co-operation in our struggle." In other words, white workers were not allies of African American workers by virtue of being workers but only insofar as they overcame their racism.

An alliance with them could not be concluded on just any terms, but solely on the condition that it advanced the liberation struggle of Black people the world over. Moreover, the duty for conducting a struggle to combat the influence of racism among workers devolved upon all revolutionaries.[29]

Claude McKay was the other Black communist to take up the task of a positive program on the "Negro Question" at this early date. McKay was born in 1890 in Jamaica into a middling peasant family. After an abbreviated trade school education, he became a factory worker, and then held down various other jobs in Jamaica, before he left for the U.S. in 1911 to acquire agricultural expertise which he intended to bring back to his homeland. After a stint at Tuskegee Institute, he transferred to an agricultural college in Kansas, where he began his career as a poet, and also gained introduction to socialist circles. McKay decided to remain in the U.S., and in 1914 transferred his residence to Harlem, supporting himself as a waiter and later, again, as a factory worker. In this capacity, in 1919, he joined the IWW and soon entered the ABB and CP.[30]

Like Briggs, McKay advocated that the peoples of African descent cast their lot with the communist movement. And like Briggs, he complained of the racism within the American and British communist parties, the two with which he had experience. In 1922, he wrote, "The Negro radical wants more than anything else to find in the working class movement a revolutionary attitude towards the Negro different from the sympathetic interest of bourgeois philanthropists and capitalist politicians." He noted that "Some friendly radical critics think that my attitude toward the social status of the Negro should be more broadly socialistic and less chauvinistically racial as it seems to them." He added that they believed that "the pretty parlor talk of international brotherhood or the radical shibboleth of 'class struggle' is sufficient to cure the Negro cancer along with all the other social ills of modern civilization." Like Briggs, McKay was adamant that Blacks the world over could not afford to ignore the "Negro Question," but must insist upon its resolution over and above the "class question."[31]

Moreover, McKay did take some steps beyond Briggs, however tentative. He asserted that not only did the "Negro Question" require treatment on its own behalf, but that its correct solution was needed for the solution of the "class question." As he explained in a letter to white communist Max Eastman: "[T]he Negro question is an integral part and one of the chief problems of the class struggle in America." In this view, McKay was probably influenced by Domingo, whose writing on the subject McKay held in high esteem, and who had declared that socialism would not come to America without a correct understanding of the "Negro Question" on the part of American revolutionaries. McKay charged white radicals and labor leaders with "a shameful, half-hearted struggle against capitalism," because they did not "extend a fraternal hand to the black working force."[32]

But McKay's most important step forward was his assessment of the place of Black workers in the American class system. In his book *Negroes in America*, commissioned by Trotsky on behalf of the Comintern during McKay's sojourn to Soviet Russia, McKay said of African Americans, whom he had previously identified as a "subject race," that they constituted "historically the most exploited class in American life." And he began to approach the implications of this in terms of the relations of white and Black workers in America. The original Russian translator of McKay's work, who had talked at length with McKay, recorded that McKay believed that

> the workers' aristocracy in the United States will either turn into shareholders and coupon clippers of private capital in order jointly to exploit the working masses, or Wall Street will continuously sabotage the bank interests of the workers' aristocracy and compel it to return to the masses. But in either case the revolutionary leaders of the masses must be prepared for all possibilities.

McKay began here a justification for the ABB radicals' insistence that white revolutionaries in Europe and America prove their solidarity in action. The privileges associated with their relatively better position gave them, implicitly, a certain stake in the relatively worse conditions of the most

oppressed, and, as noted, McKay placed African Americans at
the top of the list of the most exploited. McKay indicated that
the next logical step would be the inclusion of the most well-off
workers (who must be white, although, it is true, McKay did
not apparently state that directly) in the exploiting classes
who made their fortunes on the backs of the workers of the
world. As such, McKay put the "Negro Question" squarely in
the domain of the development of imperialism, and its solution
in imperialism's overthrow. Indeed, he took exception to those
"American revolutionaries who suppose that the Negro
question in all its ramifications can not be solved by relying on
the international workers' movement." McKay believed that it
could only be solved in this international context. It was
McKay himself who gave the name "internationalist" to the
ABB approach to the "Negro Question" by insisting that
African Americans would only find their salvation by becoming
"internationalists" in their outlook.[33]

Another Black communist whose thought deserves
attention is Lovett Fort-Whiteman. Unlike the other early
Black leaders of the communist movement, Fort-Whiteman was
born in the United States. But like McKay, Fort-Whiteman
spent a considerable period in the Soviet Union, which had a
profound impact on his thinking. Even if it is true, as Black
communist Harry Haywood later claimed, that Fort-
Whiteman's stay there seemed to have left him out of touch
with African-American life and mores, he nevertheless
expressed many of the same ideas as his more overtly
nationalistic comrades. Fort-Whiteman declared at the Fifth
Comintern Congress in 1924 that "The Negroes are destined to
be the most revolutionary class in America." And although he
probably used the word "class" loosely, he gave other
indications that his thought had moved along the same lines
as that of Briggs and McKay. He declared that African
Americans were "historically of the most oppressed and
exploited group in America." He insisted that African
Americans be approached differently from whites, and he
proclaimed the growing nationalistic mood among African
Americans to be nothing new: "The Negro has always regarded
his social problem as a world problem. . . ."[34]

The recognition of the world context of the "Negro Question" led Fort-Whiteman, like Briggs and McKay, directly to the question of imperialism. Fort-Whiteman was most emphatic about the point, insisting that "It is probable that no colonial people suffer the weight of imperialism to the extent that the Negro does, whether he is in the New World or in Africa." Fort-Whiteman also moved toward a positive recognition of the effects of this upon relations between white and Black workers:

> The extent of the power of any given imperialist state over the darker races may be a fine measurement of the extent to which problems obtain within that particular state, for in the very nature of imperialism the working class of the dominant race assumes an attitude of arrogance and racial superiority towards the colonial peoples in that state.

Having gone that far, it only remained for Fort-Whiteman to examine the material basis for that "attitude." But he apparently left that for others.[35]

It would be wrong to say that Briggs, McKay and Fort-Whiteman in their early explorations had quite solved the "Negro Question" from the theoretical point of view--but they had certainly laid the groundwork. At the least, they had emphasized that, like the national question, it was not one that could simply be disposed of by white radicals. It was a question of crucial importance to the international proletarian revolution on which they pinned their hopes of eventual Black liberation, and it was, moreover, the *sine qua non* of Black participation in the communist movement. Hence, Debsianism was laid to rest in its original form. In addition, both Briggs and McKay had closely tied the "Negro Question" to imperialism, and its oppression and exploitation of the peoples of color of the world. What still remained was to dispose of the notion that a worker was merely a worker, that there were not class distinctions within the working class itself.

There had been early hints of an understanding of the relationship between African Americans and the class structure of American society. As noted earlier, William Haywood advanced a long way toward this by recognizing that the labor aristocracy rested at least partly on the base of racial and national discrimination. Even Edward J. Irvine, the white socialist who criticized Briggs' adherence to the importance of the "Negro Question", still insisted, "I regard the American Negro as the genuine industrial proletarian of this country." The West Indian communist Otto Huiswoud called the position of African Americans "fundamentally an economic problem but intensified by racial antagonism." Claude McKay hinted at a substantially deeper understanding in his *Liberator* articles and the book he wrote in Russia. And Briggs' logic pointed in the same direction, particularly his criticism of the "white proletariat" for its role in helping to subdue Africa and Asia, in which the white proletariat was "a not unwilling factor," and his vague threat that "tomorrow" it might be "called to account." None of this was calculated to be to the liking of leaders of the American white labor aristocracy.[36]

But it was still Richard B. Moore, another West Indian ABB communist,[37] who became the first to explicitly propound the doctrine that African-American workers were subject to super-exploitation, exploitation above and beyond the lot of the white worker, *and that the white workers (at least the privileged sections) benefited from this situation.* Nothing could be more baneful to the white communists, and perhaps it is more than a coincidence that soon after Moore openly proclaimed this for all to hear, the reaction against the internationalist position set in within the American communist movement.

This thesis was no more than the logic of communist internationalism applied to the American "Negro Question," yet Moore gave it its first explicit expression, at least in America. As early as 1927, Moore had already stated that "the vicious system of suppression operates to reduce this race to an inferior servile caste, exploited and abused by all other classes of society." He advocated for the "peoples of Africa and African origin" "Unity with all other suppressed peoples and classes for the fight against world imperialism." He also warned the white workers of the imperialist nations that "they will no longer occupy a privileged position in the mother countries." In 1929, after pressure from the Communist

International had forced the American Communist Party to open its journals to debate on the "Negro Question," Moore put the matter squarely at the door of white American workers:

> The condition of the Negro masses in America grows steadily worse as the racial caste system spreads more and more into the North and West, becoming daily more deeply intrenched in the life of the nation. Large sections of the white workers of Europe, America and Africa are bribed with a share of the imperialist spoils drawn out of the toil and degradation of the Negro masses, and are filled with white imperialist propaganda against these workers.

Now, not only were white communists and workers being asked to accept Blacks into their ranks on the basis of full equality (including social), but they were also being told that they had to renounce (and denounce) the privilege that the color of their skin provided them in order to be true internationalists. Moore appended onto the traditional statement that "The Negro problem cannot be solved save through the solution of the labor problem" the addition that "The labor problem cannot be solved unless the race problem is solved." The workers were no longer simply workers, their class interests no longer identical and inseparable. If white workers (and their white Communist Party) did not renounce caste privilege, not only were they not revolutionaries but actually enemies of the revolution. Moore had sounded the tocsin against the white labor aristocracy. Its leaders, however, would not go down without a fight.[38]

Chapter II
Black Radical Politics in Prosperity, 1919-1928

If the Bolshevik revolution had set off the evolution of thinking of the "Negro Question" that brought about the ABB's internationalist position, so, too, had it wrought significant changes in the Black radical movement. Within a decade of the Bolshevik Revolution, the process of differentiation of the various currents of Black radicalism that it had sparked had reached its fruition. By 1925, Black radicals had divided into three camps, with the communists and socialists forming their own Black labor organizations and Du Bois and the young Abram Harris standing outside and sniping at their efforts. A radical consensus seemed the remotest of prospects, with the lines strictly drawn and the viewpoints apparently irreconcilably opposed. On the one hand, the Black communists attempted to put into practice their "internationalism." And on the other, the Black socialists clung tenaciously to the Debsian position of old, allying themselves with old-line socialists and the racist AFL. Between them, and at the same time operating outside the context of the American left, a group of independent Black radicals led by W.E.B. Du Bois put forward a program of middle-class nationalism that refused any contact with white workers. This chapter will trace the evolution of the Black communists, the socialists, and the independent grouping behind Du Bois.

The Du Bois-style radicals placed matters almost purely in a racial context. For them, the "class question" had no application and represented simply the delusions of, equally,

the socialists and communists. In their close attention to the
interests of African Americans, they resembled the Black
communists. But in their rejection of a revolutionary solution,
they sided with the socialists.   This connection would
ultimately pull them in the socialist direction.

The Black socialists considered the Du Boisites
representatives of the elite interests of the Black bourgeoisie,
who did not want to dirty themselves with the problems of the
Black masses. They considered the communists fearful
terrorists and anti-democrats and the Black communists racial
chauvinists in the vein of the Du Boisites. But without a
national or racial justification to stand upon, they were to find
it exceedingly difficult to spur their white comrades,
notoriously neglectful of and uninterested in African Americans,
to action. Their efforts to form a socialist trade union
organization toward the securing of the interests of African
Americans would not prove the resounding success they had
hoped. They would have to await the compelling force of the
recognition of self-interest on the part of these white radicals.

In contrast, Black communists, who began with precisely
the same problem, hit upon a solution that would eventually
clear the path for all Black radicals, if only indirectly. Black
communists found that their "internationalist" position, by
placing the "Negro Question" in the domain of the
international communist movement, provided them with a
powerful ally in the Comintern, backed, as it was, by the
prestige of the only nation which had accomplished a
successful socialist revolution. In the short run, however, the
intransigence of the white factional leaders of the CP blocked
the road. This stalling tactic allowed them to weather the
storm and await circumstances in international communism less
favorable to the Black communists' internationalism.

II.

Although the ABB had effectively merged with the CP,
its program had by no means been accepted by that party.
Indeed, the main body of white communists in America was

very far from even consistent liberalism. The Workers (Communist) Party adopted at its second congress in 1922 a resolution supporting "the negroes in their struggle for liberation," but such a struggle meant to the vast majority of American communists only economic, political and educational equality. According to a reporter for the *New York Times*, "Efforts by some delegates to make a fight for the social equality of the negro were overwhelmingly defeated." As Claude McKay commented with bitter irony, "President Harding. . . stands a little more to the left on the Negro question than the Workers' party convention. . . . Every Negro worker knows that, whatever the party, when it refuses to take a stand on social equality to that extent, it also refuses to approach the Negro question." And far from an "inheritance" from the socialists, William A. Domingo puts it in its true perspective: such thinking comes right out of white "American psychology."[1]

The white party leaders also expressed their pointed opposition to the Great Migrations of southern African Americans to the industrial North. Cyril Briggs later explained that their justification for doing so relied upon "the rotten social democratic and A.F.of L. argument that the coming North of these workers would hurt the economic position of the northern white workers and result in the sharpening of racial antagonism with resultant race riots." Briggs also revealed that the punishment meted out to him and the other "older Negro comrades" for opposing this "gargantuan stupidity" included denying him the five dollars per week that it cost to put out his weekly Crusader News Service, which fed the Black press with the ABB perspective. In addition, he asserted, he and his ABB colleagues were "absolutely ignored" in the later formation of the American Negro Labor Congress. He described this policy as amounting to "The bourgeois trick of utilizing the least militant of the oppressed race," giving, at the same time, something of an assessment of the class partisanship of white party leaders.[2]

Black communists fought back by taking their case to the Communist International, much to the distaste of the white American communists. The CP, as a section of the Communist

International, was subject to its discipline, and from the very beginning Black communists sought to use this to push the party into action. In the leaders of internationalism, the Black radicals found an effective ally, since Lenin had taken an especial interest in the cause of oppressed nations and nationalities. Hence, the faction-ridden American party, which so often had to turn to the Comintern to settle its infighting and power struggles, would find itself the subject of ringing criticisms and numerous directives detailing its shortcomings vis-a-vis African Americans. Not surprisingly, many of the white leaders opposed the Black nationalism that kept the American party under the close scrutiny of the international communist movement and did whatever they could to subvert the efforts of the Black radicals until they could finally be rid of them.[3]

Black communists began to put their case to the international beginning with its second congress in 1920. The meeting was attended by Otto Huiswoud, a West Indian communist. It was there that Huiswoud met Lenin. He did his best to represent the situation of neglect of both the "Negro Question" and African Americans obtaining in the Communist Party, and his complaints were confirmed by John Reed. Huiswoud pronounced to to the congress that the "Negro Question" was "another phase of the race and colonial question to which no attention has been paid heretofore."[4]

Huiswoud's placing of the "Negro Question" in the domain of the "race and colonial question" was no accident. First, it reflected the understanding at which Black communists had already largely arrived in 1920. Second, it put the American party on notice. On Lenin's insistence, the CI had at the second congress, proclaimed that the Communist parties of the imperialist nations had a special responsibility toward oppressed nations and colonial peoples, particularly those oppressed by "their own" imperialists. Under the heading oppressed nation it had classified "the American Negroes." Huiswoud evidently believed Lenin was sending the American party a clear message.[5]

But this was a message that the American party was not at all eager to hear, and one that it did not absorb. The *Daily*

Worker, the American communist organ, had declared in 1920, "The class war knows only the working class and the capitalist class." And it reiterated in 1924, "We declare the interests of the white workers and the negro workers to be the same." The party's trade union wing declared the notion that white workers were relatively "privileged" compared to Black to be employer-inspired propaganda.[6]

Still, Black communists kept up their bitter criticisms of the American party. Finally, at the Fourth Congress in 1922, they got their wish: the Comintern set down communist policy on the "Negro Question." At the fourth congress a "Negro Commission" was established with Otto Huiswoud as chair. In addition, Claude McKay attended this congress, at which he attracted Trotsky's attention, and took part in the commission. At the urging of this commission, the fourth congress expanded its program, specifically spoke of the "the world Negro movement," and reminded its followers that it was "not simply the organization of the enslaved white workers of Europe and America, but equally the organization of the oppressed colored peoples of the world." It went on to confirm that it "regard[ed] the cooperation of our Black fellow men as essential to the Proletarian Revolution and the destruction of capitalist power" and again enumerated the duties of its constituent parties. Hence, the CI not only adopted the basic programmatic outlook of the ABB, but imparted to the American party a duty that, in theory, it could not shirk. Slowly the CP would begin to incorporate some of this understanding in its own program, saying that "The Negro workers of this country are an especially exploited class." But it would not act on this understanding, and only promised a struggle against discrimination.[7]

Black communists, however, were not satisfied with the mere passage of general resolutions. As Claude McKay declared, "The time for general resolutions about the rights of colonial people to self-determination, the equality of all people regardless of their skin color, and so on and so forth, has passed. The time for direct, practical action has arrived." Huiswoud and McKay helped set just such a course into motion. As well as writing the resolutions for adoption by the Congress, the Negro Commission issued a special report to the Comintern Presidium. It recommended, first, that a permanent "Negro bureau" be established in Moscow to ensure that Comintern decisions relating to Blacks be implemented. Second, it detailed how the communists should go about organizing Black communists and workers. Third, it handed over "draft instructions" to the various sections of the international, undoubtedly the American section in the first place, to compel them to carry out specific tasks on the "Negro Question." The Presidium took the suggestions seriously, and had already appointed one of its members to head the special bureau.[8]

After the Fourth Congress, with its signal successes, Black communists wasted little time in putting the issue before the American party. Otto Huiswoud, shortly after the fourth congress, wrote,

Comrades, it is your duty to aid [the African-American] masses in their struggles against peonage, and against economic exploitation. It is your duty to rally the Negro workers under the revolutionary banner of the Working Class Movement. Comrades, go to the Negro Masses!

But, as Black communists came to see, their white comrades were not budging.[9]

In the early 1920s, as Black communist Otto Hall later recalled, factionalism among white party leaders had rendered the position of Blacks in the party a difficult one. "They carried the factional squabble into our branch, each accusing the other of being prejudiced against Afro-Americans. . . . We felt that we were being used as a factional football." The hard work of Black communists, which had allowed their number to increase from a handful to over 75 at one point, was undercut, and their numbers in the party immediately plummeted. Hall remembered, "We ran into many instances of prejudice among some members of the Party, some of them flagrant." But he added, "[W]e stuck it out. . . . We had faith in Lenin and the Russian comrades and had heard that they sharply criticized some of our leading comrades who had gone over there, for insufficient work among the black people in this country. . . ." But Lenin became permanently incapacitated in 1923 and died in 1924, and Trotsky was pushed out of the leadership immediately thereafter, unfortunately for the cause of the ABB radicals, and the Comintern became another arena for the factional struggle that raged in the Soviet Union and reinvigorated the long-standing factional fights in the American party. Although Black communists would continue to bring the issue before both the CI and the American party, it would remain for the sixth Comintern congress in 1928 to take any sort of concrete action.[10]

The party, therefore, was free to ignore the "Negro Question." When Otto Huiswoud stood up to defend African-American workers from a racist attack by a southern delegate to the liberal-left Farmer-Labor party convention in 1925, he had to do so in defiance of the party caucus, which claimed that Huiswoud's action would "antagonize" the southern representatives. The matter, placed before the party leadership, resulted in its siding with the caucus against Huiswoud. The exact same circumstances would occur later in respect to Richard B. Moore at a Pittsburgh labor conference, with the same result.[11]

But some half-hearted steps were taken by the Communist International, itself now embroiled in factional fighting between the remnants of Trotsky's followers and the emerging Stalinist bloc. Several Black communists were brought to Soviet Russia as students, beginning in 1925. The same year the *Communist International*, the Comintern's international organ, carried an article by Lovett Fort-Whiteman, the genesis of which evidently lay in his criticisms of the American party's record at the Fifth Comintern Congress. In his article, Fort-Whiteman charged that communists had not made a serious attempt to recognize or implement the Comintern's understanding of the "Negro Question" arrived at by the Fourth Congress. He likened their attitude to that of the social democrats, a pointed swipe at their communist credentials. In an unusual "Editorial Comment" appended to the article, the *Communist International* called Fort-Whiteman's article "a testimony that our American comrades of the ruling race have not yet been able to approach the negro question in a right and proper manner, either in their agitation among white workers, or in their work among the negroes." The American party, trying desperately to uphold a "Bolshevik" image, was thus held up to ridicule before the world communist movement.[12]

The effect may have been to spur the party into action, showing that such international exposure had the desired effect for Black communists. In the fall of 1925, the long-delayed American Negro Labor Congress (ANLC) was convened by the CP in Chicago. The ANLC set as its goal "to break down . . . racial discrimination" and open trade unions to Blacks. But the ANLC did not stop with these demands. It encouraged Blacks to form independent unions where racial bars excluded them from AFL affiliates and to use them "as weapons in the fight to enter the general movement of the workers." Recognizing that the vast majority of African Americans worked outside of industry, especially as agricultural workers in the South, it called for support for their efforts at organization as well. In keeping with the program worked out by the ABB, the ANLC explicitly linked the struggles of the masses of African Americans with those of "our race brothers in Africa and the darker-skinned peoples of the colonies of world imperialism." The Congress included a call "to convene a world congress of our race" to act as "a leader and fighter in the liberation movements of all the darker-skinned peoples in the colonies of imperialism everywhere." Such an organization would, indeed, be founded, and headed by one of the young communists who cut his political teeth in the ANLC.[13]

But the efforts of the newly Stalinized Comintern on behalf of Black communists did not go much further. At the Sixth Congress in 1928, Black communist James Ford revealed that in the preceding several years the executive of the CI had issued no less than nineteen directives to the American party that it had ignored and that the Comintern had not bothered to enforce. Despite continual Black communist pressure, and the measures of the Comintern, Black communists had made little practical progress.[14]

III.

Joining the ANLC in its condemnation of AFL policies were two Black radicals affiliated with middle-class "race" organizations, W.E.B. Du Bois and Abram Harris. Both of them, however went beyond the anti-AFL position to question the viability of any alliance between white and Black workers in the U.S. The veteran scholar and activist Du Bois, who had himself been in the SP and occasionally still endorsed its candidates, used *The Crisis*, organ of the NAACP, as a forum to discuss and generally condemn organized labor. Du Bois remarked, "Many honest thinking Negroes assume . . . that we have only to embrace the working class program to have the working class embrace ours," in a polemic more applicable to the SP-affiliated Blacks than to the communist, Claude McKay, to whom it was addressed. In going only so far, Du Bois actually stood on common ground with the ABB radicals. Nor did the similarity in outlook end there.[15]

As the ABB communists had come to do, Du Bois pointed out that the white workers of the imperialist nations participated in and gained from the colonial exploitation of people of color: "White workers are today as yesterday voting armies and navies to keep China, India, Mexico and Central America in subjection and being paid high wages to do this while 'niggers' and 'dagos' and 'chinks' starve, slave and die."[16]

And Du Bois shared more than this in common with them. He found himself attracted by the Russian Revolution just as they had been earlier. Indeed, unlike most non-communist white radicals, he had not been caught up in the initial euphoria, but found his own appreciation of its achievements growing as the years passed. He visited Soviet Russia, and found himself impressed with its attempts to eradicate racism and national oppression. Nor was he put off by the liberal-democratic objections to the Soviet form of government. He remarked, "It is not a question merely of 'dictatorship.' We are all subject to this form of government."[17]

Instead, for Du Bois, "The real Russian question is: Can you make the worker and not the millionaire the center of modern power and culture. If you can, the Russian Revolution will sweep the world." Lurking behind this point, phrased as it is in class terms, is the question of race. For Du Bois, like the ABB radicals, began his thinking there and nowhere else. And although he saw the imperialist interests that racial oppression involved, he shared more in common with the race-consciousness of the early Briggs than the class-consciousness of the later ABB. Thus he commented on the events in China, "White Europe [has] brought to pass there the Great White Way of pitting the weak and oppressed and impoverished against the oppressed and impoverished and weak and letting them fight it out until they are too helpless to resist white 'Civilization' and 'Christianity.'" Du Bois, for all his insight into imperialism's machinations, would always maintain this strain of bourgeois Black nationalist thinking. It blunted the edge of his "internationalism," and also of his critique of imperialism.[18]

Du Bois, a founder and principal leader of the Pan-African Congress, shared with the leaders of the ABB their concern for the people of African descent of the world, but he differed with them fundamentally on the meaning of African liberation. The ABB's program combined a kind of Pan-Africanism with the advocacy of the unity of white and Black labor which set it apart from Du Bois's Pan-African Congress. While the ABB leaders demanded the total independence of Africa through revolution, the Du Bois-led movement confined itself to advocating that Africans be given "a voice in their own government." And where the ABB cited the systematic rape and plunder of African wealth as the necessary policy of imperialism, Du Bois's program stated, "The attitude of all the imperial powers who own Africa is fundamentally wrong," implying that their attitude toward Africa rather than their ownership of it lay at the root of its oppression. Where the ABB demanded that the imperial powers leave (that is to say, be driven by force of arms from) Africa, the Pan-African Congress politely requested that they reform their colonial policies. Neither did the Pan-African Congress address itself nor its hopes for African liberation to the working class, nor speak in class terms at all. In the words of Claude McKay, Du Bois, in organizing the Pan-African Congress, "was simply striving to effect an international union of the Negro intelligentsia with the international bourgeoisie in order to carry out certain reforms in the situation of various Negro peoples." Perhaps the shallowness of Du Bois's anti-imperialism was best brought out by his championing of Japanese imperialism in the 1930s. Where he criticized the United States and the European powers for dismembering China, he lauded the Japanese invasion as standing up to the white man.[19]

In addition, Du Bois had a penchant for compromise and a willingness to work through the established channels of power, such as the League of Nations and later the United Nations, that aroused the deep suspicion of more radical Blacks. Even before Briggs' conversion to communism, he denounced Du Bois's Pan-African Congress, saying it was "along the lines of compromise and genuflection." Despite the convergence of their politics on the surface, Briggs charged that Du Bois proved himself in his Pan-African European conference to be "the same compromiser and traitor to the Negro's legitimate aspirations [that he had been] in America during the war." Du Bois, instead of calling for self-determination for Africans, contented himself with merely asking for "'better' white government of the Black man." To this Briggs asked rhetorically, "How is a thing that is rotten to the core to be made better?" But Du Bois was incapable of consistently and steadfastly adhering to any outlook. He was a middle-class Black nationalist working within a white-dominated liberal organization. He would proclaim his allegiance to class struggle one day, and the next declare that salvation lay in some or other wild scheme of reform. And his deep-rooted eclecticism would allow him during the Depression, for example, to retreat into middle-class Black nationalism at the same time he professed more and more to be, at bottom, a believer in the class struggle and a Marxist.[20]

Du Bois would remain skeptical of the white-dominated left through the Depression. He remarked saliently, "[T]he old A.F. of L. spirit is hard to kill." His constant insistence that white workers fully overcome their racism and his unstinting criticism of the AFL as a reactionary force earned him the reputation among both socialists and communists as anti-labor and reformist, and he would remain a constant target of criticism of Black radicals throughout the Thirties. Yet Du Bois was pointing out what not only communists and socialists, but radicals like Abram Harris, would have done well to heed, for in the end Black radicals would converge around a position that amounted to almost exactly the one for which he criticized McKay in the quotation cited above. Moreover, the co-optation of white workers by imperialism of which Du Bois had warned would also prove to have a profound effect on the Black-labor alliance, which, while it lifted a segment of Black workers to the level of whites, essentially left in tact the system of oppression of Blacks. Having staked out this ground, Du Bois passed the mantle to a protege, Abram Harris, who carried it with the same inconsistency as Du Bois.[21]

Affiliated with the generally pro-business Urban League, Abram Harris, a native of the American South, during his climb through the academic and Black organizational ladder remained as aloof from the movements toward trade unionism among African Americans as did Du Bois of the NAACP. Commenting for *The Crisis,* Harris asserted, "The American Negro Labor Congress appears to me to be, fundamentally, a revolt against [the] color psychology in the labor movement; and incidentally, a protest against race prejudice in American life and the racial inequities arising out of it." To this degree, Harris himself sympathized with the Black communists. He, too, deplored the AFL's record on matters pertaining to African Americans. And Harris, like Du Bois, could well understand the embrace of radical solutions to the racial oppression African Americans faced. "Not Soviet gold," Harris retorted to those who saw the ANLC as part of a Russian conspiracy, "but social facts furnish the explanation for the convention's radicalism and its departure from the racial assumptions and logic of the older Negro social institutions."[22]

Harris could look critically upon the conservatism of the NAACP and the Urban League, and he could find common cause with the Black communists in standing against the AFL's racism, but he could not bring himself to believe in the positive program of his "communist friends." "They say that the Negro and white workers are members of the same economic class; their interests are identical, *ergo* they will unite in proletarian solidarity against capitalism. But," he asked himself, "are the interests of white and black workers identical?" He called the political logic behind such a claim "economic determinism." He concluded, "This much seems to me irrefutable: if their interests are identical there is little recognition of it on the part of [the] white and [the] black proletariat." Like Du Bois, Harris painted a gloomy picture of the prospects for Black unionization in common with whites. And if this could not be done, "[H]ow much more unlikely is it that they will unite to promote social revolution?" Even if they did, "[T]he success of economic radicalism is contingent upon the capacity of the conservative working class forces to effect a counter-reformation."[23]

In expressing this concern, Harris actually had a great deal in common with the Black communists, and stood opposed to the position of the Black socialists (the very position he would himself soon embrace). Like the Black communists, he placed the African-American worker "in a lower class within a low class." He also called attention to the feeling of superiority of "white workers from common laborers to the white-collared aristocracy" that prevented them from expressing true solidarity with African American workers. And like the communists, he was extremely critical of the "doctrinaires" who refused to admit this unpleasant fact.[24]

Evidence from Harris's own writing suggests--at the least it has been suggested--that Harris knew the pernicious effects of racism within the Communist Party firsthand: that he had joined the Communist Party upon its formation, and had been drummed out for advocating that it take up the "Negro Question" as a separate component of the "class question." In short, Harris may have begun his career as one of the small number of rank-and-file Black communists; and, in what would have been even more unusual circumstances, he did so in the South. If that is so, it is most likely that he never knew of the struggle being waged by the ABB radicals in the Northern metropolises for precisely his position. But the cause of Harris's abandonment of communism does not lie only there (although it certainly points out how correct the ABB communists were to charge the party with subverting the spread of communism among African Americans). There were other significant differences between Harris and the ABB communists.[25]

Unlike the Black communists, and unlike even his cosmopolitan mentor Du Bois, Harris conceived of the "Negro Question" in purely American terms and, therefore, he could not have arrived at the "internationalists'" solution to the "Negro Question" nor their commitment to a party so hostile to their presence (or, at least, their vocal presence). Harris expressed scepticism toward those who wanted to fashion "a highly questionable psychological and social relationship between aboriginal African and American Negro." And while Harris's rejection of such associations came in response to racist sociological theories, he was not able during this period of his life to see such connections in their true light, as had Du Bois and the ABB radicals. He denied any cultural connection between African Americans and Africans. He discounted such phenomena as Pan-Africanism, Black nationalism, "race consciousness," and the Harlem Renaissance in African-American art. And he added, "Nor can the American Negro be considered in any logical sense African." African Americans' one and only goal was and could only be "full participation in American institutions." Not only was he not an internationalist in outlook, but he was decidedly anti-nationalist in the formal sense.[26]

In addition, there was always a certain scholasticism in Harris that, as with Du Bois, caused him to stand aloof from anything that promised a mass movement of African Americans. He warned more sanguine radicals not to seek "revolution where there is only conservatism." He loved to stand aside and study the Black workers, to counsel their movements and criticize them for their follies. Harris would work for the masses but not with them.[27]

The difference between Harris and the ABB communists, whether they were erstwhile comrades or not, stands out in strongest relief in their understanding of the nature of the "Negro Question." While for the ABB radicals, the question was one of *principle*, for Harris it never seems to have been more than one of *expediency*. When conditions changed, or seemed bound to change, he stood ready to adapt himself and seek refuge in the very policy that had once driven him out of the socialist movement. In this characteristic of Harris's we gain insight into his ability to go completely over to the other side, to make common cause with the very type of white radical who had soured him on socialism and communism. But this leopard could not completely change his spots. The direct leadership of the 1930s brand of Black radicalism would still have to be left to others of a less scholarly and more political bent.

Such a figure was John P. Davis. In the 1930s, Davis would become one of Harris's close associates, later to head the radical National Negro Congress. In the Twenties, he provided a much closer prototype of the breed of intellectual who was to dominate Depression-era Black radicalism than did either Du Bois or Harris. Unlike Du Bois and Harris, Davis did not want to contribute his thought to the problems of Black workers so much as his actions. Davis attended law school at Harvard, where he joined a circle of Black graduate students that included Robert C. Weaver, Ralph Bunche, William Hastie, Rayford Logan, and Percy L. Julian, most of whom shared his quest to do something for the Black worker. Of those, Davis was closest to Weaver, whom he had known since their high school days in Washington, D.C. From there, however, Davis and his partner, Weaver, went separate directions, Davis into more radical circles and Weaver into the government. In a letter to Weaver, upon his appointment to Roosevelt's New Deal administration, Davis expressed the creed of independent radicals: "We are anxious that you do not become either the creature of a system, the rubber stamp of an advisory office, or the burden bearer of an administrator's errors in regard to race. . . . We regret further that white Americans have adopted the subtle policy of robbing us of our independence by subsidies, subventions and material aid--all of which we need." It was Davis of whom Harris would think highly enough to put him forward as his choice to replace the venerable Du Bois as editor of *The Crisis*.[28]

As with Harris, there is nothing in Davis's background to suggest that the left converted him to radicalism. At any rate,

Davis and his Harvard circle, like the "segregated scholars,"
show a long-standing interest in Black workers among Black
intellectuals for which the left could not claim responsibility.
But such an interest could not be surprising among anyone, with
whatever motives, aspiring to leadership of a people
overwhelmingly of the laboring classes. Their interest in Black
workers meant neither an interest in white workers nor one in
white labor. Indeed, Davis was never more forceful than in
condemning white labor in 1928:

> Capital has never presented as sinister and malevolent
> a front to the Negro laborers as have the white labor
> unions. . . . [C]an you give me any good reason for being
> a Socialist or joining with the "organized forces of
> labor to overthrow a despotic capitalist regime"?
> Why shouldn't Negro labor organize to defeat every
> attempt of white labor to bargain collectively with
> capital? Why shouldn't we join in the cutthroat game
> and help capital throttle white labor? This it seems
> to me is the only way to make white labor see the
> light. And so I urge all Negro laborers to adopt as
> their motto: "Hurrah for the Scab and Open Shop and
> To Hell with the Unions."

Davis has given virtually the programmatic statement of
middle-class Black nationalist radicalism in the 1920s: While
the interests of white and Black workers are irreconcilably
opposed, those of Black workers and the Black middle class are
indissolubly connected.[29]

Another of the leaders of 1930s Black radicalism, Ralph
Bunche, who followed a path very similar to Davis's, also
declared where his loyalties lay quite early in his life, in a
1927 letter to one of his idols, Dr. Du Bois: "Since I have been
sufficiently old to think rationally and to appreciate that
there was a 'race problem' in America, in which I was
necessarily involved, I have set as the goal of my ambition
service to my group." Or so these independent radicals thought
at the time. Time and experience would call into question in
whose service their labors were really expended.[30]

IV.

On the other side of the question vis-a-vis white labor and the AFL, in particular, stood the Black radicals allied with the Socialist Party, A. Philip Randolph and Frank Crosswaith most prominent among them. They shared the commitment of the ABB radicals to working with the white working class, but they differed markedly on the terms upon which the alliance should be built. While for the ABB it was a question of the forging of an alliance with the goal of liberating the African people, for the SP-oriented radicals the question amounted to organizing African Americans in common with whites for their mutual economic benefit. Seldom did the Black socialists venture beyond the question of unionization, and when they did, they went only as far as advocating that white workers join with African Americans in the fight for civil rights.[31]

The leader of Black American socialism (what in Europe went under the name of social democracy) was A. Philip Randolph. Randolph followed a contradictory path in becoming the most important Black union leader, head of the Brotherhood of Sleeping Car Porters (BSCP). Before taking over the leadership of the Brotherhood, Randolph had been editor of the left-wing *Messenger* and among the best-known Black socialists in Harlem before the split-off of the communists. In fact, Randolph and the Black radicals who coalesced around the ABB began as allies, and seemed to enjoy good relations characterized by mutual respect. Randolph was as critical of the AFL as any Black radical, calling it "a machine for the propagation of race prejudice." And, at least in labor matters, he appeared to be the most radical, giving the avowedly revolutionary IWW a ringing endorsement and proclaiming: "ON WITH INDUSTRIAL UNIONISM. ON WITH THE EMANCIPATION OF THE WORKERS OF THE WORLD."[32]

But just underneath these temporarily harmonious relations lay the seeds of the later bitter differences. Where the Black communists concentrated from the beginning on the "Negro Question," Randolph seemed to want nothing more than to avoid it. In 1919 he set down in his *Messenger* what could be called his definitive statement of the matter. The "Negro

Question" was a red-herring introduced not by Black radicals
but by the "employing class": "They have used us as wage
slaves to beat down the wages of the white wage slaves, and by
a continual talk of 'race problems,' 'negro questions,'
'segregation,' etc., make an artificial race hatred and division
by poisoning the minds of both whites and blacks in an effort to
stop any movement of labor that threatens the dividends of the
industrial kings."   Instead, Randolph held that "the Negro
workers' interests are inextricably tied up with the interests of
the white workers in America. What injures one injures the
other." Of all socialists, Randolph admired no one more than
Eugene Debs. Before long, Randolph was denouncing his former
Black radical comrades who had gone over to the communists as
"a sinister and destructive crowd which will stop at nothing in
order to realize its aim which is to wreck and ruin every
organization which is not Communistic." Black communists
countered that Randolph's politics amounted to "trailing
behind the labor aristocrats who betray the interest of the
workers."[33]

What prompted this latter charge was Randolph's about
face on the AFL. In 1925, at the behest of a small group of
Pullman porters, Randolph became the head of the most
important all-Black union movement of the period. The porters
had been impressed by Randolph's militancy, but from that
period Randolph considerably tempered his radicalism. The
AFL became the object of his highest praise. From a "machine
for the propagation of race prejudice," the AFL had suddenly
been transformed, in the *Messenger*, into the champion of the
African-American people. Randolph claimed, "To break up the
A.F. of L., . . . the object of the Communists who control the
American Negro Labor Congress, is to break down the present
strong collective bargaining power of the Negro workers in the
Federation and also outside of it."   And he added, with
astounding logic, "It must be recognized that in this connection
that the unorganized workers' conditions in America are
improved by virtue of the existence of five million men and
women organized in the A.F. of L."--despite the fact that many
AFL unions barred African Americans from membership, and
thereby from "closed shop" industries in which unions

controlled hiring. Randolph even prohibited criticism of Green in the *Messenger's* pages. The magazine was transformed, in becoming the unofficial organ of the new union, from militantly pro-worker to, in the words of Langston Hughes, "a Negro Society magazine and a plugger for Negro business."[34]

But whatever criticism Randolph may have faced for his loss of rhetorical militancy, the union he was guiding was experiencing tremendous success. By 1928 the union counted its membership in the thousands, despite almost impossible conditions for pursuing labor organizing. The union was poised for a great struggle with the company, as its membership had voted 6,053 to 17 in favor of a strike. Still, Randolph, unlike other union leaders, was against a strike from the very beginning. His actions, which included writing a conciliatory letter to the company, undermined the chances for a successful strike. Despite Randolph's opposition, the porters stood ready to strike, prepared to face severe adversity if necessary, and the chances for success looked good. Randolph, however, upon receiving a telegram from AFL president William Green advising the Brotherhood against such an action only hours before the announced deadline, called off the strike. Having lost confidence in the leadership, the porters began a mass exodus from the union, which by 1933 had shrunk to about one-tenth of the number it boasted on the eve of the strike.

Randolph did achieve one of his personal goals for the union: affiliation with the AFL. The federation had steadfastly refused to admit the Brotherhood as an international, and Randolph refused to let the union become a "Jim-Crow auxiliary." Finally, in February, 1929, Randolph's negotiations with the executive council ended with an agreement to admit the thirteen largest divisions of the Brotherhood as "federal unions." This inferior status was not the kind of treatment that any union, let alone the largest Black trade organization, deserved from the AFL. It meant little more than the right of Randolph and a few other Brotherhood leaders to attend conventions as delegates. But Randolph considered that he had gained a "beach-head" within the AFL, and later he attempted to make the best of that limited role. He became the most controversial figure within the AFL in the days before the schism over industrial unionism, waging a battle every year over his "Randolph resolution," a measure designed to compel the AFL to admit Black workers on an equal basis.   Despite Randolph's persistence, his resolution never passed.[35]

Joining Randolph in the ranks of the socialists was Frank W. Crosswaith. Crosswaith came to the U.S. from St. Croix in 1907, at the age of fifteen, and had joined the Socialist Party by 1915. Drawn toward radical intellectual circles, he soon adhered to the socialist group around Randolph's *Messenger*. In the Twenties, Crosswaith entered socialist electoral politics, several times standing for office on the SP or American Labor Party tickets. At the same time, he developed into the most ardent defender of the SP against its Black critics, primarily Du Bois and those around the CP. Paradoxically, Crosswaith managed to ignore the SP's insistence that "fraternization" (i.e., social equality) was indefensible. By the mid-Twenties, Crosswaith had joined the union movement as an organizer, first for the Elevator Operators and Starters Union, and later for the International Ladies' Garment Workers, and from 1929 until 1934, he worked as an SP organizer.[36]

Crosswaith aligned himself during the 1920s with the "center" of the Socialist Party under Morris Hilquit. In this arrangement, Crosswaith allowed himself to be used as bait in the electoral campaigns, where he was a candidate almost exclusively in Harlem, while in white areas the SP totally ignored his candidacy in a cynical ploy to woo the Black vote without losing the white. This tactic became just one of many aspects of what his biographer calls the "ambiguity" that Crosswaith faced throughout his SP career.[37]

Although Crosswaith was a leading Black unionist, he would not even go as far as his mentor, Randolph, in criticizing labor union discrimination. In fact, his biographer declares that "the greater the chance that protest over union discrimination might draw publicity, the less likely it was that Crosswaith would get involved."   Crosswaith, in anticipating Randolph's tactics of the 1960s, was willing to stifle his criticism (as well as that of others) in return for the financial support and "good-will" of the labor movement. As a result, he, wittingly or not, made himself a de facto supporter of the status quo in labor.[38]

But Crosswaith's early career was, nevertheless, marked by a consistency that Randolph's lacked: to make the Socialist Party a viable alternative to the Communist Party for Black workers. Crosswaith shared with Randolph his vehement anti-communism; if anything, Crosswaith's was more deeply-seated. He referred to communism as "the most erratic, undemocratic and impractical of all the movements of social protest extant in the world today." Like Randolph, he objected to the Black communists' elevation of the "Negro Question" to a place of importance. Crosswaith accused them of "forget[ting] CLASS while they DO remember RACE." In contrast, he maintained steadfastly that "[T]he fate of the whole working class is inextricably bound up with that of every section of the working class." Like Randolph, Crosswaith proclaimed himself completely satisfied with the approach toward Blacks of the SP, which Crosswaith called "the right attitude on the Negro question." He added, "[H]istory shows no record so persistently spotless in its stand on the Negro question."[39]

He also objected to the communists' advocacy of revolution, although he had once pronounced himself in favor of "the social revolution." In general, Crosswaith preferred to put his faith in "gradual and peaceful change through the medium of education and political democracy." The Crosswaith program for the Black worker was based upon exactly such a strategy.[40]

During the summer of 1925, while the communists were organizing the ANLC, Crosswaith and the New York socialists formed the Trade Union Committee for Organizing Negroes, with Crosswaith as its executive secretary. The organization developed out of a conference of SP-oriented leaders of the AFL and SP leaders such as Norman Thomas. According to Crosswaith, the consensus of the delegates "was that never again must organized labor lose another strike in New York City through the activities of unorganized Negro workers."[41]

The Trade Union Committee reflected the Black socialists' approach to the "Negro Question" they dreaded to raise. It proclaimed as its main goal the organization of Black workers into AFL unions. And it asked of the AFL no great alteration of its policies. Indeed, Crosswaith proudly proclaimed the A.F. of L. as the Committee's staunch ally, commenting that its representative at the conference "pledged the full support of the A.F. of L." Nevertheless, despite the alliance with the racist AFL, the Trade Union Committee did advocate labor's entrance into the struggle for civil rights. According to Crosswaith, the Committee "must not alone get Negro workers into the unions of their trades, but it must also stand by them in their fight for justice." To a large extent, the Trade Union Committee established the pattern of relations between African Americans and organized labor that the National Negro Congress would follow with the CIO. It was, in Crosswaith's vision, to "do both educational and organizing work." Not only would it unionize Black workers, but it would "aid in the education [of] both Negro and white workers toward a realization of their common economic interest."[42]

V.

For the moment, the pessimism of Du Bois and Harris seemed warranted. Even Randolph's *Messenger* found it difficult to find much in the socialist-AFL collaboration to generate enthusiasm. It commented,

Of course, even now nothing definite has been done in the interest of Negro labor by the organized labor movement. Some of its leaders are members of the Trade Union Committee for Organizing Negro Workers, but it is not apparent that this committee has anything as yet save the moral good will of some of the local unions of New York City.

And Randolph, who was actively courting the good will of AFL leader William Green in order to convince the latter to admit the upstart Brotherhood of Sleeping Car Porters which Randolph headed, even felt compelled to express some skepticism upon the matter of Green's promise to organize Black workers in common with white in an upcoming nationwide campaign. For its part, the ANLC was no more successful in turning its words into deeds, despite the enthusiasm which it generated among young Black communists.[43]

Even so, a corner had definitely been turned in the history of Black trade unionism. Randolph's union was taking off among the sleeping car porters and would gain the endorsement of the AFL, if only qualified. The ANLC and the Black communists pushed the communist union federation, the Trade Union Unity League (TUUL), to take an interest in Black workers which would bear fruit by the end of the decade. And the independent radicals led by Du Bois and Harris began to change their tune. *The Crisis* announced its intention to wage a three year campaign of advocating trade unionism among Blacks, a theme that was echoed throughout the Black press. Even the Urban League, long a foe of organized labor, lent its endorsement to the SP's Trade Union Committee for Organizing Negro Workers.[44]

The stage was quickly being set for the radical convergence, unlikely as it seemed, around something close to the socialist position of Randolph and Crosswaith. Paradoxically, Randolph was less than enthusiastic about this prospect, gibing at Du Bois for "condescend[ing] to emerge from his ivory tower and suddenly conceiv[ing] a passion for the unwashed toiler." And ironically, Randolph and Crosswaith would have the smallest of places in the movement that was to adopt their very principles. Moreover, Randolph's own efforts would help to launch the careers of the young radical usurpers. He and James Weldon Johnson secured places for young African Americans like Harris at the Brookwood Labor College in New York, and Harris himself would soon become an advocate of trade unionism and socialist Debsianism.[45]

Despite an early bit of territoriality, Randolph, in his usual fashion, managed to adapt himself before anyone else, commenting through the *Messenger*, "It is gratifying to note that there is now considerable interest manifest in the organization of Negro workers." He also correctly surmised much of the cause of this new-found enthusiasm in adding, "Doubtless the real reason is that the white unions are slowly but surely awakening to the serious necessity of unionizing the Negro worker in self-defense." Most surprising, perhaps, to the socialists and independent radicals, the CP would join with them in the campaign of white labor's "self defense." Having been challenged by the "internationalists," it responded to the threat in a most unexpected way, catching Moore, Briggs, and their adherents, completely off guard.[46]

Chapter III
The Development of Neo-Debsianism

In the years 1927 and 1928, the Russian Communist Party under Stalin began to shift leftward for political and economic reasons. As part of its program to bring the international communist movement along behind it, it issued a number of directives aimed at the various national parties that had been at the forefront of the rightward shift, or in which right-wing factions had gained control as in the United States. In the process of so doing, the Comintern took up the "Negro Question" actively for the first time since Lenin's death. But while the program that came out of it seemed to indicate a return to the Comintern internationalism of old, and to provide Briggs, Moore and the ABB communists with just the ally they needed, in reality it only equipped the American party with the means to bring about their objectives vis-a-vis Black workers without striking a significant blow for Black liberation.

The transformation of "internationalism" into neo-Debsianism began with the Sixth Congress of the Communist International in the summer of 1928. Its genesis actually had no direct connection to the events in the United States. Instead, it sprang to life as part of Stalin's struggle against the remnants of the pre-Revolution Bolshevik Party. Having veered sharply to the right in the struggle against the Trotsky-Zinoviev opposition, Stalin would now do a leftward shift to rid himself of the last of the old Bolsheviks, Bukharin. It is true, however, that, while this meant reviving some semblance of the old internationalism of the Comintern, it may have had no direct effect on the "Negro Question" had it not been for the persistent efforts of the ABB communists to bring the Comintern into the field on their behalf. Stalin and his cronies, who sought to obliterate any trace of a defeated opposition in every Communist Party, would seize upon this issue to strike at the right-wing of the American Communist Party and to maintain the strict loyalty of the victorious faction. In the process, the Comintern would make a number of clumsy alterations in its theoretical line, all done in typical Stalinist fashion: without any acknowledgment of a change. The white American communists, initially reluctant to follow the new line, would soon find within it exactly the means they needed to rid themselves of the ABB radicals.

No doubt the first impression of the Comintern's resolution on the "Negro Question" in the United States, the text of which was issued in late 1928, led all sides to the opposite conclusion. The American Communist Party came in for heavy criticism for its failure to take up the "Negro Question," with William Z. Foster's Trade Union Unity League taking it particularly hard on the chin. The resolution declared that Black laborers and farmers were not, as most white communists maintained, "reserves of reaction" but "an important part of the American working class," and "Henceforth . . . the struggle on behalf of the Negro masses" had become "one of the major tasks" of the CP. The Comintern linked the "Negro Question" in America "to the Negro questions and struggles in other parts of the world." The world over, "the Negroes are oppressed by imperialism" and had "a common tie of interest" in "the revolutionary struggle of race and national liberation from imperialist domination." The resolution even asserted that African Americans were particularly well-suited to play a leading role in that international struggle.[1]

In what has come down to us as its defining feature, the resolution further stated the following: "While continuing and intensifying the struggle under the slogan of full social and political equality for the Negroes, which must remain the central slogan of our Party for work among the masses, the Party must come out openly and unreservedly for the right of the Negroes to national self-determination in the southern states where the Negroes form a majority of the population." This was part of the two-fold task of African-American workers, who were "to assume hegemony of all Negro liberation movements." First, they would lead the struggle in their own "national movement" for "national revolution." Second, they would participate in the general revolutionary struggle together with white workers for the overthrow of American capitalism.[2]

The original Comintern directive containing the so-called "Black Belt thesis" was a hopelessly confused and contradictory document. In all likelihood, the only purpose of the resolution in its original form was to call attention to the "Negro Question" and the American CP's ignoring of it, and to phrase it in the kind of internationalist terms that Lenin had. It is doubtful that the Russian communists who drafted it knew anything of the development of ABB internationalism in the United States, nor much at all about that nation in general. It is certain that no American had a hand in drafting it. Hence, its extremely clumsy presentation reflects only the theoretical ineptitude of its authors. Their arrival at the notion of a "Black Belt" nation finds the simplest of explanations. Lenin had phrased the "Negro Question" in national terms, and the Stalinist shibboleth for every national question was national self-determination in the area of that people's majority.[3]

But having applied these simple formulas, the drafters of the "Black Belt thesis" immediately lost their way amid the complexities of the American reality. What was the basis of the nationality of African Americans and what was its relationship to "race"? This question was left unanswered. In fact, African Americans, who were to make a "national revolution" are referred to both as "the oppressed Negro race" and an "oppressed nationality." Of what was this "national revolution" to consist? What was its relation to the other revolutionary struggle? When was it to succeed? Only under socialism? Or before that, under capitalism? The drafters of the resolution seemed oblivious to these questions. Its meaning, then, could only take shape in the struggle against those who attempted to interpret it.[4]

The first to do so was John Pepper (Joseph Pogany), a refugee of the Hungarian communist revolution delegated to the U.S. by the Comintern in the early 1920s. Shortly after the Sixth Congress, and just before the first "final text" of the Comintern directive was issued, Pepper wrote an article for the *Communist*, theoretical organ of the American party, entitled "American Negro Problems," which was also published as a separate pamphlet. Coming from a prominent member of the the American party's right wing, a faction known as the "Lovestoneites" after the party's leader of those years, Jay Lovestone, and which controlled the *Communist* and most leadership positions in the party, Pepper's action had, at the least, factional overtones, especially since his article was the first concrete word American communists had of the "new line." To be sure, neither Pepper nor anyone else in that faction, nor for that matter in Foster's centrist faction, had ever shown any interest in these matters, nor was Pepper's only foray into the question consistent with the "Lovestoneite" outlook. Indeed, the remnants of the faction would completely repudiate such views after their transformation into right-wing "Christian patriots."[5]

Whatever his motivation, once Pepper took up the question, he had the task of imparting at least some meaning to the confusion that the Comintern Executive Committee had handed down. And this work, at least, Pepper took up with a certain gusto. As noted, Pepper was not actually working on the basis of the Comintern directive, which had not yet appeared, but the text of the resolution to be presented at the Sixth Congress itself. And these differed significantly in one particular. The Congress resolution states as follows:

> Negro Communists must explain to Negro workers and peasants that only their close union with the white proletariat and joint struggle with them against the American bourgeoisie can lead to their liberation from barbarous exploitation, and that only the victorious proletarian revolution will completely and permanently solve the agrarian and national question of the Southern United States in the interest of the

overwhelming majority of the Negro population of the country.

Paradoxically, in the logic of Stalinism, by basing himself upon this line, the official line of the Comintern, Pepper assured that this viewpoint would never again characterize that same Comintern's position.[6]

For the most part, in "American Negro Problems" Pepper contents himself with simply repeating what the Sixth Congress had made policy on the "Negro Question." He places it in an international context, as part of the struggle against imperialism. The vanguard of this struggle, he affirms, will be the "Negro working class." He connects their struggle to the socialist revolution in America. He argues for the necessity of the American party adopting a position for self-determination in the Black Belt.[7]

But, in addition, Pepper extrapolates, in the interests of consistency, in regard to areas which the Congress left implicit or vague. The Congress had placed the "Negro Question" discussion within the "colonial question"--Pepper draws the logical conclusion that the Black Belt South must constitute a colony. The Congress resolution emphasized that a solution to the "Negro Question" could only come with the proletarian revolution, so Pepper puts forward the slogan of the struggle for a "Negro Soviet Republic." This slogan would come under the heaviest attack, but Pepper arrives at it using compelling argumentation. The right of self-determination, closely connected to the Southern agrarian structure with its feudal base, constitutes a "bourgeois-democratic demand," but since the U.S. is already an old, established bourgeois democracy, such a program could "only be realized in the course of a proletarian revolution," since only a "proletarian revolution" is possible in the U.S. This argument should have sounded familiar to old Bolsheviks, since Lenin had used it to describe various questions arising from the the Russian revolution. Finally, unlike the Congress resolution, which had never characterized the "Negro Question," but like the Comintern Executive Committee resolution, Pepper refers to "the Negro people" as both a nationality and an "oppressed race."[8]

Pepper also repeats the strident criticisms of Black communists and the Comintern of the American party, and puts forward theses in which, for the first time, a high-ranking white communist official took up some of the ABB positions. He states that the "super-profits extracted from" African Americans constitute "one of the most important sources of the growth of American imperialism." He vilifies *"the racial prejudice of a narrow white labor aristocracy* which refuses to recognize the unskilled Negro worker as its equal." He acknowledges that the influence of "white chauvinism" extends beyond this layer of skilled workers deep into the body of the white working class. He calls for "a relentless campaign of self-criticism concerning the work among Negroes" and declares that "All signs of white chauvinism must be ruthlessly uprooted from within the ranks of the Communist Party." While these would later be common statements, they were on Pepper's part the first of their kind. And most surprisingly, in a throwback to Briggs' *Crusader* days, Pepper issues a stirring call for *"active resistance and self-defense against the lynching terror"* and other manifestations of the violent oppression of African Americans in the South. He echoes the call of Black communists for the CP to move into the South. Other aspects of Peppers' analysis, however, reveal that, notwithstanding the need for a consistent application of the self-determination line, he has not completely abandoned the "class-only Debsian" approach of old.[9]

When the "Lovestoneites," allied with the right-wing of the Comintern under Bukharin, lost the factional struggle to the centrist Fosterites, Pepper's article became not only the platform of a defeated faction, but downright anti-Comintern policy. As such, it had to be countered, and this work began almost immediately after the "resolution of factionalism" was complete. The first sally was fired in the form of an article in the *Communist* of March, 1930, by Jos. Prokopec. Once again, it came in the form of a Comintern delegate to the American party.[10]

Prokopec, in his "Negroes as an Oppressed National Minority," begins the attack on Lovestone by denying that self-determination can only be achieved by African Americans as a result of a proletarian revolution. Instead, "The ultimate task of this national revolutionary movement is bourgeois democratic revolution, and not as Pepper implies . . . [a] 'Negro Soviet Republic.'" At the root of the question, then, lies the "incomplete bourgeois-democratic revolution" in America. As such, it is wrong, Prokopec contends, to conclude that the Black proletariat must lead the movement, as Pepper did. The proletariat might be forced to begin a movement for national self-determination, but "the Negro peasantry, petty and middle bourgeoisie will be the driving force of this movement, because it is a national revolutionary movement." Indeed, for Prokopec, the Black liberation struggle is "just like all the rest of the national and colonial revolutionary movements," although African Americans are "not fully a nation" but a "national minority, distinguished by their race and color, and special oppression." Whatever their status, however, the "national revolutionary movement" of African Americans will "deal a blow to American imperialism and thereby hasten the proletarian revolution."[11]

The main problem that Prokopec does not address is just how a national revolution is to take place within an already established nation, a "bourgeois-democratic revolution" in a nation already "bourgeois-democratic." This claim is not put forward, however, on its own merits, but, rather, to contradict Pepper's justifiable assertion that only a proletarian (communist) revolution could take place in the U.S. To call for democracy, or, perhaps, a little more justifiably "more consistent democracy," in a nation already basically democratic is to call for, even if in the name of a "national revolution," a movement of reform, a *reformist* movement. Of course, such policies were already being pursued by the "old guard" NAACP, NUL and so forth. Indeed, they could be the only practical organizational forms for such a struggle, especially one to be led by the middle class (as Prokopec advocates). In this context, then, Prokopec's attempt to label this a "revolutionary" movement can only be interpreted as a desire to oppose Pepper, and to do it in the name of revolution.[12]

Prokopec gives his analysis without in the least understanding the American context, and with very little

concrete knowledge about it. Thus he makes statements like the
following:

> It is true . . . that owing to peculiar social-economic
> historical conditions (slavery, etc.) Negroes have not
> as yet a formed, organized national minority
> movement. They did not have the worship of national
> heroes of the past, and no real leaders of the present.

And, in "explaining" why African Americans have not yet
begun to struggle for political and economic rights, Prokopec,
declares, "once we convince the Negro that he is equal to other
peoples and as such has the right to self-determination, he
will feel that he is 'somebody' and will fight for his rights."
But, then, Prokopec's entry into the "Negro Question" had not
been dictated by any interest in it or knowledge about it, but
only to show the error of John Pepper's ways.[13]

Yet even after this vanquishing of the "Lovestoneite"
opponent, that is, the repudiation of Pepper's more or less
consistent rendering of the Comintern's own policy, there
remained two standpoints, both opposed to Pepper's (the former
position of the Comintern), but against one another. As against
Prokopec's embrace of almost fully consistent bourgeois Black
nationalism, there was the position still favored by the white
leaders of the American party, the old Debsian class-only
approach. And the American party, taking advantage of the
Comintern's floundering in the absence of a consistent policy,
spared no effort to put its view forward in the spring of 1930.

In so doing, it, too, hid behind the mantle of the struggle
against "Lovestoneism." But its main point was clear: there
could be no alternative for African Americans than to line up
with (or, perhaps, behind) the white workers. M. Rubinstein,
in attacking the idea, attributed to the Lovestoneites, that
industrialization of the South would "disentangle the
complicated problem of racial antagonism and relieve the
contradictions of American capitalism," explained that the
ruling class, by first invoking racial hatred, had cut off all such
avenues of change. With the large reserves of white workers in
the South, turned loose from the land by agricultural
development as much as African Americans, it had become "too
risky" for the white ruling class to employ Black workers in

large numbers. Such an attempt, Rubinstein argued, would call forth what could only be described as some sort of reactionary revolution: "The attempt to use Negroes instead of white workers on a big scale would so aggravate the racial hatred fostered by the employers as to go far beyond the objects pursued by them and would endanger not only 'public order,' but the very foundations of bourgeois class domination." Hence, by a peculiar twist of logic, the very existence of racism in the South meant that Blacks could not struggle for their own cause, but must undertake with whites "a desperate struggle against capitalism." And the same logic would also dictate that whites, as the industrial proletariat, would necessarily take the lead.[14]

This did not prevent the very argument Rubinstein "exposed" as "Lovestoneite" being used in the same issue of the *Communist* to arrive at Rubinstein's own conclusion. Myra Page explained it this way:

> Due to developments in this revolutionary epoch, Dixie workers will learn with surprising rapidity to destroy racial schisms which have formerly existed and will struggle as a united class for their objectives. Racial prejudice among wage earners has little basis in current economic life. It is largely an inheritance from past economic systems and is now perpetuated primarily by capitalist propaganda and manoeuvers. Every new factory built, every worker drawn into industry, is a blow at the caste system.

And, remarkably, such was the case despite the color bar that meant Black workers could *not* be drawn into the better jobs in industry, and in many branches, into southern industry at all. Yet Page comes to exactly the same program of joint "revolutionary struggle against capitalism." She even warns against "any opportunistic handling of this [the "Negro"] question." "Racial consciousness," she proclaims, "is to be utilized only as means for drawing the toilers of oppressed groups into revolutionary struggle against capitalism, and, in a workers' society, for furthering the development toward socialism." That is, Black workers should struggle for themselves only insofar as it aids the campaign of the (predominantly white) proletariat. If it takes the embrace of a program of self-determination to accomplish this, then so be it, so long as this self-determination does not really determine anything in and of itself. *That* (the taking seriously of self-determination as a principled goal) would be opportunism. Making use of the (evidently empty) slogan for other means is principled.[15]

Such thinking became the basis of the party's "Draft Program for Negro Farmers in the Southern States" of March, 1930, published, ironically, in the same issue of the *Communist* that carried Prokopec's article. If Prokopec had put forward a program of reformist nationalism à la Du Bois, then the "Draft Program" was pure Debsianism. With little more than a nod toward what it calls "national (racial) oppression" as part of the triple layered oppression, along with "capitalist exploitation" and "survivals of slavery," the program states upfront: "To free the rural toilers of this three-fold yoke is something that can be accomplished only through a revolution of the broad masses of Negroes *under the leadership* of the revolutionary [white?] proletariat and its Communist Party." Repeating Pepper's observation (without, however, acknowledging it), the program declares that only proletarian (communist) revolution is possible in 20th century America. As in Page's and Rubinstein's articles, the new self-determination slogan is never mentioned by name, even though it was to apply specifically to the South. Its concrete application is apparently given as follows: "We must explain to the broad masses of [Black] farmers that the only way they can save themselves from ruin is to establish an alliance with the working class and to fight under the leadership of the latter for the overthrow of the whole capitalist order. . . ."[16]

The program goes on, despite its recognition of the "super-exploitation" of African Americans "on racial grounds," to an explicit revival of Debsianism. Hence, it announces, "The Negro *agrarian proletariat* is a part of the American proletariat. Its class interests and aims are the same as those of all American workers." And in case the implications of this statement are not apparent, it makes them explicit: "The toiling masses of Negro farmers can be freed from slavery, capitalist exploitation and racial oppression only by a proletarian revolution. . . . This revolution will in its wake solve also the problems of national emancipation and will abolish the remnants of feudalism and slavery." A few pages later, as an afterthought, the program adds, "The proletarian State, and it alone, will abolish all national and racial restrictions, giving each national group the full right to self-determination and equalizing the chances of economic development for all more backward peoples and nations." And, lest any confusion should remain, the CP declares that all African Americans not a part of the proletariat or poor and middle peasantry "play an objectively counter-revolutionary role *even in the movement for racial emancipation of their own race*" (emphasis added).[17]

Hence, the anti-Lovestoneite interpreters of the Comintern Executive Council's ambiguousness lined up in two directly opposite camps. On the one hand, the Comintern's representative adopted a reformist nationalism that not only proclaimed that the interests of the Black proletariat and the Black propertied classes were identical, but that the propertied classes had, of necessity, to lead the struggle. It declared that this movement for self-determination could not wait until the proletarian revolution, but had to be won, or at least fought for, under capitalism. On the other side, the Debsians continued to maintain that, in the words of Page, it was purely and simply a question of "class against class, with racial factors entering in only as a phase of this class struggle." And if it was a question of leadership, then clearly it could not be left to the Black propertied classes, but only to the vanguard of the most advanced--and definitely not the most "backward"--section of the workers. And was this not but another way of saying the white labor aristocracy?[18]

It was up to the Comintern's Executive Committee, as supreme authority, to achieve a "synthesis" of these views. It was undoubtedly helped in this work by the fact that it still lacked any understanding of the basic issues. But at least it knew what it opposed: whatever Pepper (the "Lovestoneite") had been for. As such, its task was easy. It simply had to take the opposite approach, whatever that might mean, and

however self-contradictory the result. But neither logic nor
consistency ever stood in the way of the Stalinist Comintern's
Executive Committee (E.C.C.I.), nor, for that matter, did
principle. And so the E.C.C.I. issued one last "final text" of its
"Resolution on the Negro Question in the United States,"
published in the *Communist* of February, 1931.[19]

Since Pepper had declared that the struggle was for a
"Negro Soviet Republic" and its realization would coincide
with the proletarian revolution, the E.C.C.I. concludes that
the "Negro Question" could not "be put off until then" for
solution. Rather, the "slogan of the right of self-
determination" means in practice, "the liberation struggle of
the Negro population in the Black Belt against the yoke of
American imperialism." Indeed, the struggle is leading to "the
rapid approach of a revolutionary crisis in the Black Belt."
But this revolution will not be for a socialist society "as Pepper
demanded." It is not even necessary "that the proletariat
[have] the hegemony in the national revolutionary Negro
movement." This is to be, after all, a "national revolution,"
and more specifically, an "agrarian revolution."[20]

The E.C.C.I. then "refutes" Pepper's proposition that such
a "national revolution" means that the Black Belt must be a
colony of the North, (an idea which, the resolution declares,
"creates superfluous difficulties for the clarification of ideas").
The E.C.C.I. answers this point as follows:

> On the one hand the Black Belt is not itself, either
> economically or politically, such a united whole as to
> warrant its being called a special colony of the United
> States. But on the other hand, this zone is not, either
> economically or politically, such an integral part of
> the whole United States as any other part of the
> country.

This is stunning logic: the Black Belt was too closely integrated
into the U.S. to be a colony but not to be a separate nation.[21]

Even having "solved" this difficulty, there still remains
the question of how a sectional insurrection, which could not
even count on the support of organized armed forces, since
African Americans were virtually barred from them except
during warfare, could be successful in the absence of a revolution

affecting the entire nation. But to think that it could not was "Lovestoneism"! So the E.C.C.I. contents itself with the following statement: "Whether the rebellion of the Negroes is to be the outcome of a general revolutionary situation in the United States, whether it is to originate in the whirlpool of decisive fights for power by the working class, for proletarian dictatorship, or whether on the contrary the Negro rebellion will be the prelude of gigantic struggles for power by the American proletariat cannot be foretold now." But certainly, "it is just possible" that this feat could be achieved, although, of course, it would mean "successful revolutionary struggle against the American bourgeoisie." Besides, the Black population could count on "all [the] strength and courage" of the Communist Party in this fight--that is, "if the circumstances seem favorable." Evidently, even the E.C.C.I. found it hard to conceive of such fantastic circumstances.[22]

Moreover, these knotty questions only concerned the South, and whereas the previous "final text" had ordered the party southward, this one merely invites them to "link up" the "Negro question in the North with the liberation struggle in the South." "After all," the E.C.C.I. reasons, "in the North, as well as in the South, it is a question of the real emancipation of the American Negroes." But, in the North, this "real emancipation" is incomparably more simple: *equal rights*. "The struggle for this slogan embraces all or almost all of the important special interests of the Negroes in the North." And since the CP was almost entirely a northern party, it had little more to do than advocate equal rights, which, after a shaky early start on the question of "social equality," it had always done. And there were further encouragements for the party line of old. The resolution, oblivious for the moment to its own characterization of the "Negro Question" as "the question of an *oppressed nation*," declares that while Black intellectuals and "small capitalist business people" had undertaken "definite efforts for developing a purely national Negro culture" and even for "Negro nationalism,"

> The broad masses of the Negro population in the big industrial centers of the North are, however, making no efforts whatsoever to maintain and cultivate a

national aloofness [!]. They are, on the contrary,
working for assimilation. This effort of the Negro
masses can do much in the future to facilitate the
progressive process of amalgamating the whites and
Negroes into one nation, and it is in no circumstances
the task of the Communists to give support to bourgeois
nationalism in its fight with the progressive
assimilation tendencies of the Negro working masses.

Indeed, the communists are told to "clearly dissociate"
themselves from such tendencies and "to guarantee *the
hegemony of the Negro proletariat* in the national liberation
movement of the Negro population," notwithstanding the fact
that communists are warned that they cannot make that
"hegemony" a precondition to its support for the "national
revolutionary movement . . . (as Pepper demanded)" because
African Americans' "complete right to self-determination must
be recognized" and "defend[ed] as a free democratic right," even
if it takes a bourgeois form.[23]

Even more favorable to the prevailing view of the "Negro
Question" in the American party, the E.C.C.I. quotes the
"Colonial Theses of the Sixth World Congress" as saying that
"only a victorious proletarian revolution will *finally decide*
the agrarian question and national question in the South of the
United States." Moreover, Black communists are instructed
that

Their constant call to the Negro masses must be:
Revolutionary struggle against the ruling white
bourgeoisie through a fighting alliance with the
revolutionary white proletariat. Negro Communists
must indefatigably explain to the mass of the Negro
population that even if many white workers in
America are still infected with Negrophobia, the
American proletariat, as a class, which owing to its
struggle against the American bourgeoisie represents
the *only truly revolutionary class, will be the only real
mainstay of Negro liberation* (emphasis added).

Indeed, lest the place of the white and Black proletariat be
confused within this struggle, the E.C.C.I. makes it known, "In
the struggle for equal rights for the Negroes, . . . it is the duty of

the *white* workers to march at the head of this struggle" (emphasis in the original). And whatever the E.C.C.I. may have thought it meant by this, its interpretation was left to the American party. Combined with the Comintern's virtual equating of the struggle for equality and that for self-determination, it allowed the American party to conclude that the white workers could march at the head of both movements. The E.C.C.I. only adds,

> It is the special duty of the revolutionary Negro workers to carry on tireless activity among the Negro working masses to free them of their distrust of the white proletariat and draw them into the common front of the revolutionary class struggle against the bourgeoisie. They must emphasize with all force that the first rule of proletarian morality is that no worker who wants to be an equal member of *his class* must ever serve as a strikebreaker. . . .

In the past, the Comintern, like Black communists, had emphasized that white workers got what they deserved in Black strikebreaking for their refusal to allow Blacks into their unions. Now, Black workers must "earn" their way to equality *within the working class.*[24]

Yet, more important, ultimately, than all of this self-proclaimed "theoretical clarity," the Comintern resolution dropped its criticism of the American CP. In place of its former stinging barbs, the Comintern now became effusive in its praise. The Communist Party of the United States, it declares quite unblushingly in the first sentence of its resolution, "has *always* acted openly and energetically against Negro oppression and has thereby won increasing sympathy among the Negro population. In its own ranks, too, the Party has *relentlessly* fought the slightest evidence of white chauvinism . . ." (emphasis added). Whatever the intent behind this outright falsification, the white leadership took it as a signal that the Comintern, having accomplished its aims vis-a-vis the "opportunists," would no longer concern itself with the "Negro Question" in America; and, indeed, it did not.[25]

Henceforth, the "Negro Question" in America was solely the American party's domain, and though it was left with a patchwork political line full of holes and contradictions, the CP was free to reconcile them at its leisure. Eventually, the whole mess would be turned over to James Allen, a white communist who during all of these proceedings was being trained as the CP's expert on the "Negro Question." Immediately after the issuance of the final "final text," Allen took the first faltering steps toward his appointed task, one that would take him five years to complete.[26]

Allen first took up, in his article "Some Rural Aspects of the Struggles for the Right of Self-Determination" published in the *Communist* of March, 1931, the question of how Black Belt self-determination could be reconciled to the "main goal" of working-class unity. The great danger Allen saw in the Black liberation struggle was the potential for the proletariat to lose "hegemony over the agrarian movement" if the crisis in the countryside caused the farmers to choose "revolution before the city proletariat." Allen warned that lurking just beneath the surface was the specter of uncontrollable "race warfare." There could be only one course in the face of this threat: "Above all it is necessary to assure the hegemony of the proletariat, in order to give firm and correct leadership to the movement, combatting chauvinistic expression." The cure for "Black chauvinism," if not quite as dangerous as "white chauvinism," dangerous nevertheless, was an inter-racial movement for Black self-determination led by the Communist Party. Allen evidently did not notice that this solution did away with *self-determination*, which would no longer constitute a nuisance to the party.[27]

Allen's thinking quickly found favor at the highest levels. When in the spring of 1932 the party found itself with a minor revolt on its hands at one of its party schools, where students had divided along racial lines over the "Negro Question," party General Secretary Earl Browder stepped in wielding Allen's formula: white chauvinism was the "main enemy" but Black nationalism was not far behind. Browder explained,

> The purpose of our work on the Negro question is to establish unity of white and black proletariat in a common struggle to overthrow capitalism, and the leadership of the proletariat over the Negro masses in

the struggle for their national liberation. The purpose
of the ruling bourgeoisie is to destroy this unification,
and to establish the leadership of the bourgeoisie over
the Negro masses. The main ideological weapon of the
bourgeoisie is that of white chauvinism; secondarily,
it makes use of Negro nationalist tendencies.

Subsequently he added, "These are two roads toward the same
camp. . . . It is therefore clear that we have to struggle on two
fronts, simultaneously, against both deviations," each of which
"served American imperialism." The "internationalism" of the
ABB radicals had been turned on its head: advocacy of the
cause of peoples oppressed by imperialism now *strengthened*
imperialism. The ABB communists had been served notice to be
on their guard. The "nationalist deviation" was back.[28]

Still, Allen's work was subjected to close scrutiny as it
began to appear. An early version published in pamphlet form,
not long after Allen's article in the *Communist*, drew heavy
criticism from Black communist B.D. Amis, who aired these
criticisms in his article "For a Strict Leninist Analysis on the
Negro Question" in the *Communist* of October 1932. First of all,
he charged, Allen had reduced African Americans from a
nation to a race subject, in Allen's words, to a "special caste
system and brutal persecution based on the color line." Amis
admonished him to maintain the question in the national form
demanded by the E.C.C.I., rather than making what was
"clearly a concession to the current bourgeois racial theories."
Second, Allen had relegated "self-determination" to a mere
"part of the general struggle for Negro rights." Amis reminded
him that it was, according to the Comintern, not simply
connected to the struggle for equal rights incidentally but was
central to the "liberation struggle." Finally, Amis chastised
Allen for claiming self-determination meant African
Americans' right "to rule themselves within their own state
boundaries." This state of affairs, Amis pointed out, would be
the advocacy of a virtual Jim Crow nation, "an unreal and
reactionary caricature of the fulfillment of the right of self-
determination" which the "theoretical defenders of white
chauvinism would gladly accept." Indeed, such a formulation
Amis called "a concession . . . to white chauvinism." Obviously

self-determination meant also the right to rule the white minority in the Black Belt. The criticism of these revealing "mistakes" produced a new edition of Allen's pamphlet, with the requisite alterations.[29]

The culmination of Allen's work, which Amis had insisted take account of the economic and historical aspects of the "Negro Question," came in the form of a book entitled *The Negro Question in the United States*, published by the Communist Party's press in 1936. Here the *form* of self-determination is maintained, but entirely denuded of the content Briggs had imparted to it. For Briggs self-determination was part and parcel of the revolutionary struggle, a phase of the class struggle. For Allen, it merely takes the shape of a formal argument.[30]

The main purpose of Allen's tract is to uphold the correctness, from the theoretical point of view, of the program currently being carried out by the Communist Party, which with the Popular Front era had moved, together with the Comintern, in a reformist direction. Allen carries out this aim through a series of subterfuges, the main one being that the vast majority of the book takes the form of an historical and economic justification of the "Black Belt thesis." Those who at the time, and retrospectively, missed the significance of this doctrine, also fail to see that this argument is put in for form's sake, but the heart of Allen's argument lies elsewhere: "If so much attention is devoted to explaining the meaning of the right of self-determination it is because this aspect of the question has been so generally misinterpreted," which is to say, taken seriously. Allen goes on to explain that this right to self-determination is merely "a more ultimate program." Formally, it would be wrong to conclude that the solution of the "class question" by revolution amounts to the solution of the "Negro Question"; in other words, communists can no longer declare such a state of affairs to be the case. On the other hand, "If we have placed principal emphasis on this right [from the point of view of theory], it is not because self-determination has become an immediate problem in the sense that it appears upon the social arena for decision today or tomorrow." The logic of his argument runs as follows: Since the communists are not interested at present in the solution of the "class question," in revolution, there is no more reason for them to take any real notice of the "Negro Question" either. In theory, they are in favor of both revolution and "Negro self-determination." In practice, they have joined the alliance for the pursuance of the immediate material self-interests of the white labor aristocracy. And just as the enrichment of the most privileged section of the white workers is claimed to further the cause of revolution, so too "Every present effort to win equal rights is a step in building and extending the movement for Negro liberation." That is, no matter what the communists may do in practice, and no matter how self-serving to the white labor aristocracy, from the "theoretical" point of view it is correct.[31]

The substance of this "correct program" is nothing other than the alliance of the National Negro Congress, and all African-American organizations of whatever political bent, and "progressive unionism" in the form of the nascent CIO: The "Negro Question"

> cannot be solved in isolation, but only on the basis of an integral unity between white and Negro labor. In its resolutions on discriminatory practices in trade unions, the National Negro Congress correctly pledged support to the fight for industrial unionism, . . . for it recognized in this a progressive movement in the ranks of organized labor and an opportunity for the organization of the unorganized Negro workers in the mass production industries.

And, remarkably, the NNC did so without even the least help from the CIO, say, in the form of a resolution to organize Black workers. It is, then, apparently, perfectly acceptable from the theoretical point of view that "progressive labor" should ignore African Americans, but not for African Americans to ignore "progressive labor." And it is equally permissible for the NNC to ignore self-determination for African-Americans, but not the organization (and, hence, self-determination) of white workers. No wonder Allen was so concerned that the communist program would be misunderstood! Self-determination for African Americans meant following behind white labor.[32]

Of course, having baldly stated this fact up front, Allen had to set about the task of proving it. And since industrial unionism was almost entirely a northern phenomenon, the contradictory logic characteristic of Allen (as well as under Amis's watchful eye) leads him to direct his enquiry to the South. In looking at the existence of African Americans there, he focuses upon their concentration within plantation agriculture, which Allen calls an economic survival of slavery. Indeed, it is this "survival" that characterizes African Americans as an oppressed people, as a nation. In effect, then, Allen merely reverses history: he derives the nationality (or racial minority status) of African Americans from the plantation and slavery, whereas, as he himself notes, the plantation "semi-feudal" form of southern agriculture was built upon the racial distinction of Blacks. In fact, it is a complete contradiction to base nationality upon class. By this argument, white share-croppers, who actually outnumbered Black in absolute terms, would have been part of the same nationality. Nationality must *prima facie* precede class division. By thus "deriving" nationality from class, Allen brings back Debsianism, which had been tossed out the front door, through the rear door. According to Allen, this problem of nationality is only one of class after all! And even here Allen simply ignores the implication that goes along with this argument, that there are more privileged strata of workers, that workers are not simply workers and that their interests are not purely identical. Instead, Black workers and white are free to pursue their happily coinciding interest, their "integral unity," of industrial unionism in the North--and leave the South to the "more ultimate" solution of the hazy future.[33]

In making this incongruous argument, Allen piles up contradiction upon contradiction. For African Americans to have the right to national self-determination, they must be in the majority, and not simply a national minority. Hence, the South must be appropriately carved up to create a "Negro nation." At the same time, however, Allen denies that the South is a separate nation, since this would carry with it the conclusion that it is a northern colony. It is merely a "section," entirely dominated by northern capital. The special task of the "Negro revolution" is to uproot the slave survivals, which requires, using his terms, a "national-democratic revolution," despite the fact that the United States is, by his own admission, already a democratic nation. And all of this is to be brought about by struggles in the North for industrial unionism and equality![34]

Why does Allen (following his predecessors) resort to such convoluted argumentation? Above all he wants to avoid coming to the necessary conclusion that white workers are relatively privileged. He does admit that Black workers are "underprivileged," another way of saying the same thing; but Allen does not bother with logical niceties. His entire argument is directed against the notion of a labor aristocracy, which he claims was killed off by the Depression. Although his "national-democratic" revolution in the South could only be consistent with the argument that it constituted a colony of the North, Allen rejects this idea outright, because it would call attention to the concomitant of the labor aristocracy, imperialism. Taken out of the context of imperialism, there is no labor aristocracy, and, hence, it cannot possibly be pursuing its selfish interests. Whatever the white workers do, then, they do for all. And it can only be the duty of Black workers to follow along. This logic is the complete reversal of the internationalist position, although, to be sure, it is hardly inherent in the concept of self-determination, but only in Allen's caricature of it.[35]

Having classified African Americans as a nation for the sake of his theoretical argument, Allen then finds himself alarmed to discover that African Americans have also come to something of the same conclusion, and have even acted upon it through such organizations as Marcus Garvey's Universal Negro Improvement Association, a bourgeois Black nationalist organization which attracted millions of African-American members in the late 1910s and early 1920s. But here Allen also finds a way out, one that has the additional advantage of being flattering to white labor leaders: this nationalism is the result of the incorrect policy of white labor! Such is the strength of Allen's commitment to self-determination for African Americans that if African Americans dare to attempt to put self-determination into practice, this act is only another example of the determinative role of whites. Not only is this the negation of the internationalist position on the "Negro Question," but it shares far more in common with the imperialist outlook, which sees its own policies at the root of every development among the "colonial peoples." Ironically, such thinking represents the fruition of the internationalist warning that the white labor aristocracy might align itself behind imperialism for the joint exploitation of the Black working class.[36]

As presented by Allen, and as developed by the Stalin-led Comintern, the "Black Belt thesis" is but a theoretical makeshift, called into existence to allow the American Communist Party to pursue the interests of the white labor aristocracy while paying lip service to the "Negro Question." If the CP had to resort to such lengths, it was to gain credibility with the adherents of the internationalists. And if its caricature of their thinking was accepted, it was because the internationalists failed to call the CP and Comintern to task, but accepted this program as kindred to their own and hence acceptable. Far from absolved in this reversal of their own program, these Black internationalist communists would face the price of their acquiescence: By the end of the depression decade, even the mere formal recognition of Black self-determination would be jettisoned, and the leaders of the old position, Briggs and Moore, would be expelled. But such an overt return to Debsianism could only come about after a new generation of Black radicals came onto the scene, and brought their "solution" to the "Negro Question" with them.

II.

If Allen's work cannot be called consistent neo-Debsianism, it is only because Allen had to frame his arguments in terms taken over from the internationalists. Ralph Bunche, on the other hand, faced no such constraints, and so it would be left to him to give the programmatic rejection to Briggs, McKay, Moore and internationalism. Bunche joined Abram Harris and

John P. Davis as the intellectual leaders of the new brand of Black radicalism. These radicals had been outspoken critics of white labor in the 1920s, which made them most useful allies to the white communists. What could be better proof that the old view had been correct after all than to have its harshest critics embrace it? And this was particularly the case since Davis and Bunche joined the Communist Party or became "fellow-travellers" without demanding the programmatic changes that the ABB internationalists had in the 1920s.

Prior to the onset of the Depression, Harris, Davis, and Bunche were all connected in one way or another with middle-class African-American organizations, and all saw the "Negro Question" without reference to class. All would sharply reverse their positions in the 1930s. Harris, the first to undergo metamorphosis, became an early convert of "progressive unionism" and set himself to the task of writing a labor program for Black workers. Davis, of a more political bent, turned himself to the task of putting into effect Harris's program through the National Negro Congress, in alliance with the now reform-minded CP. Bunche had also helped to found the NNC, but he was content for the moment to leave its leadership to Davis. Instead, fond as he was of questions of an abstract nature, he took up, among other things, the task of developing a view of the "Negro Question" that complemented the theory and practice of Harris and Davis. The result was *A World View of Race*, which appeared only months after Allen's *The Negro Question*.[37]

Bunche, then professor of political science at Howard University, set out to write, in *A World View of Race*, a programmatic statement of the philosophy of race of a generation of African-American radicals. He ended up, on the contrary, writing such a document on an entirely different subject--*class*. In trying to avoid what he saw as a narrow and barren understanding of race, he succeeded only in exactly such a narrow and barren understanding of class. In seeking to clarify the class basis of racial divisions in America, he completely missed the racial basis of class divisions in America--and in the world.

That Bunche conceived of his task as anything but a temporary solution designed to meet a current crisis, as did the communists, is evident from the tone and scope of the work. Far from a political tract, Bunche roots his arguments in the latest scientific findings of anthropology, sociology, and his own specialty, political science. For Bunche, his pamphlet represents the final solution to a question that science had only just rendered answerable. As such, Bunche looked not just at African Americans, but at race in general, as a world phenomenon.

Bunche first examines the "theory of race" and finds that it has no "scientific foundation." It is, rather, "a not very consistent myth." In fact, it is no stretch of Bunche's argument to say that from the scientific point of view, race does not exist at all. And if we see in society what appear to be its results, Bunche answers: *"Group antagonisms are social, political and economic conflicts, not racial,* though they are frequently given a racial label and seek a racial justification." But if Bunche has so easily disposed of "race," he knows he cannot so simply rid himself of the necessity of dealing with its ramifications.[38]

At the root of race conflicts lie class antagonisms. If "white imperialism" enslaves people of color in the colonies, it does so to exploit them. If white workers go along with this, they do so "to console" themselves for "their impoverished economic condition." Behind racial prejudice looms the "directing motive" of "human greed." Capitalism constitutes the systemic expression of this greed, and its international expression is imperialism. Imperialism uses race as a justification, above all to the "pacified" and "subdued" peoples. These peoples, including the peoples of Africa, have no chance to free themselves. At most their revolts can be spasmodic and partial. Their ultimate liberation must await the overthrow of capitalism in its centers. "With the intensified development of monopoly capitalism in the modern world, the outlook for anything but continued and severe exploitation of the subject peoples of world does not seem bright."[39]

Turning to the United States, Bunche begins,

[Race] is one of the great factors in confusing the American populace in its efforts to understand the fundamental conflicts and issues confronting society. It has been one of the most serious obstructions in the alignment of the population along lines of natural class interest.

He especially singles out "Negro leadership" for its "stress on the element of race in the Negro problem," for its singlemindedness in wanting the "elimination of injurious discrimination against the 'race.'" Instead, he argues, they must look at class relations. In so doing, they would see that "the plight of the Negro business man or the Negro worker in this country is inevitably and inextricably tied up with the plight of the white business man or the white worker." Political equality is meaningless to Blacks "in an age when democracy with all of its fussy trappings is being universally debunked and discredited;" and as for social equality, he argues, what has it done for the poor white worker?[40]

And any other view, according to Bunche, would "lead Negroes up the dark, blind alley of black chauvinism." In other words, Bunche attacks the very foundation of the "Negro Question." To insist upon its importance is to fall into "black chauvinism," is to approach the question unscientifically, since science cannot adequately define race. Along with race, he defines the "Negro Question" right out of existence. And in the process, he resurrects the Debsian argument of old, without the "fussy trappings" of self-determination.[41]

Having dispensed with the very need for the "Negro Question," he then turns to the question of class interest. It is true, he acknowledges, that Black workers have it worse than white, but, he concludes, "race merely determines the intensity of the problem of the members of the race, not the quality." Thus, Black workers may be more exploited, but the exploitation is the same. There can be no question of white workers benefiting or of separate interests existing. It is merely a question, within a narrow range, of degree. Get rid of the capitalist system that lies behind this exploitation, and "we could look forward with optimism, and then only--to the solution of the so-called race problem." Debs himself would not have put it any differently. In fact, with Debs apparently in mind, Bunche declares, "One of the latest and soundest views of the American race problem, and for that matter, the race problem of the entire world, regards it as merely one aspect of the class struggle."[42]

The only solution, the very one Harris "developed" and Davis was busy putting into practice, follows logically from the above:

> The Negro must develop . . . a consciousness of class interest and purpose, and must strive for an alliance with the white working class for economic and political equality and justice. The Negro can make significant progress toward these objectives against the obstacles of private prejudice and public discrimination and injustice, only by uniting with the poor whites of the South and North.

Difficult though it may be, Bunche can see only "encouraging signs." In fact, so effective is this program, that Bunche advocates it for all workers of color in the world: "Their organized and direct support of the working class of the dominant populations of the world will bring an unchallengeable power to this class." Bunche has exactly reversed the internationalist position. It held that the white workers of the imperialist nations were and could only be revolutionary insofar as they took up the struggle of the most oppressed, the workers of color dominated by imperialism. Now Bunche declares that, on the contrary, the workers of color are only revolutionary insofar as they take up the struggle of the white workers of the imperialist nations. In Bunche's solution of the no-longer-necessary "Negro Question," Black radicals and white labor aristocrats could find the basis for an alliance: the interests of white labor. Bunche's concluding thought could only hearten his new allies: "Race war will then be merely a side-show to the gigantic class war which will be waged in the big tent we call the world." If, as progressive laborites saw it, the class war raging in the "big tent" meant the CIO's organizing campaigns, then indeed the part in it accorded to Black workers would constitute a mere "side-show."[43]

III.

The American party was to find that, even with the various changes and emendations insisted upon by Amis, it could accommodate itself to the new Stalinist line and still uphold its traditional orientation to the white labor aristocracy. For the new resolutions and directives, unlike the old positions of Lenin and Trotsky, now dead and defunct, did not require anything revolutionary on the part of the American communists. In fact, they left the door open to an entirely reformist approach. The sixth congress had declared: "One of the most important tasks of the Communist Party consists in the struggle for a complete and real equality of the Negroes, for the abolition of all kinds of social and political inequalities." The resolution even mentioned the "active struggle against lynching." Whether by this statement it meant open resistance by Blacks, as Briggs had long advocated, is left ambiguous. But the American communists would seize upon this to launch the "Scottsboro defense," which as a campaign organized around the legal defense of several African-American youths falsely accused of raping two white young women and sentenced to death without fair trial, had the advantages of being highly publicized, a convenient task to which to assign all Black communists, and the capability of being organized from the North. Of course, while it involved a lot of pomp and circumstance, particularly when combined with high-profile but also token party "show trials" of a few among the many whites in the party's ranks who had committed racist offences against Black party members, and emphasized legal action rather than self-emancipation of southern African Americans, it portended no revolutionary changes for the African-American masses, representing merely one case among thousands of similar miscarriages of justice that made up daily life in the South.[44]

More immediately, the CP now had an ideological basis to go after the ABB internationalists. In due time, the CP would drop its "Black Belt thesis" and take revenge on Briggs and Moore by expelling them. But, first, the ABB radicals would experience a temporary gain from the Comintern's new line and would opportunistically ignore its flawed content in order to press their case. In time, however, the Comintern would lose interest in the question and a clear field would be opened in front of the politics of "neo-Debsianism."

There is no evidence that any of the ABB radicals, the "internationalists," ever came out in writing against the Comintern's new line, though they continued putting forth their own views in the old vein, and even tried to shape the "Black Belt thesis" to suit their purposes. In part, this may have been because of the concessions to their position that it contained in its original form; in part, because, as initially drawn up, it was so ambiguously worded as to obscure its intent. And by the time its intent was made clear, the ABB communists found themselves embroiled in a practical political struggle for their survival within the communist movement.

Chapter IV
The Defeat of the Internationalists in the Communist Party

If the adherents of the internationalist view of the "Negro Question" had vanquished Debsianism in theoretical form by 1928, they were far from having obliterated its practical traces. In fact, the policies it entailed were still thriving within the American Communist Party. Ironically, the discussion begun at the Sixth Congress of the Communist International (CI) for the adoption of self-determination, although it laid the basis for neo-Debsianism, gave the ABB internationalists a forum of which they took every advantage. The CI, for a time, would listen to their charges of white chauvinism in the communist movement. And, during that period, the American Party could not afford to ignore their criticisms.

The Sixth Congress of the Comintern, held in the summer of 1928, marked a turning point, not only in Comintern policy on the "Negro Question," but also in Black communist representation to the international body. In the past, ABB communists Otto Huiswoud, Lovett Fort-Whiteman, and Claude McKay had been represented in Moscow. This time, however, the task was left mainly to Black students studying in Soviet Russia: Harry Haywood, Otto Hall, and William Patterson.

The omission of ABB communists from the CP delegation was not accidental. Richard B. Moore, who had become the leader of the American Negro Labor Congress, was accused of "anti-party activities" for raising, in Briggs' words, "the tabooed question of Negro work" at a party trade union conference and prevented from attending the Congress and putting his case before it. Both Black communists who spoke, Otto Hall and James Ford, complained of this treatment of Moore at the Congress. Briggs later commented, when given access to the party press, "[Moore] has been since subjected to a campaign of persecution and what, in the absence of formal charges and proof, appears to be nothing but the dirtiest slander."[1]

Besides the young Black communists already in Moscow, James Ford was delegated by the Red International of Labor Unions (RILU), the international communist trade union body. Although all but Patterson had passed through the ABB en route to party membership, none of them had taken part in the intellectual development of the "internationalist" position, and none felt compelled to defend it. Most were newcomers into the communist movement. But on one point they shared the passion of the ABB radicals: their steadfast opposition to the racism in the party and its inattention to African Americans.

In their articles and speeches in preparation for and during the Sixth Congress, Black communists--with the exception of Harry Haywood--spent little time on the ostensible subject matter and much time airing their long-standing grievances. They carefully documented the woeful record of the American as well as the French and British parties toward people of African descent. In the American CP, James Ford charged, the rule consisted of the "definite underestimation of Negro work in general." The party attempted no organization of Black workers, it lent no fraternal hand to Black workers expelled from the labor movement. And, in response to international pressure from the Comintern and RILU, it made only token gestures before major conferences and congresses. "During the month of April," Ford reported, "to give a small example-- there appeared in the columns of the 'Daily Worker' the amazing spectacle of 1,100 lines of written material concerning Negro workers of America." And Otto Hall added that while white communists engaged in self-criticism in Moscow, however "good for the soul [it may be], . . . we are not impressed with what is admitted here but what is carried out when these same comrades are back in the United States."[2]

To remedy this state of affairs, the Black communists in attendance repeatedly called for an intensive campaign against white chauvinism and for the promotion of qualified Black comrades to leadership positions. Ford declared, "I say that the few Negro comrades we have in the Party have been making a fight for years to bring this question before our Party, and now we bring it before a Comintern Congress."[3]

Black communists also emphasized the dire necessity of initiating work in the American South, the West Indies and in Africa. They stressed the necessity of organizing Black workers into unions, and of attracting them into the communist movement. But to do this, the communists had to approach Blacks from the standpoint of revolution rather than reform. As had ABB communists, McKay in particular, they argued for a clean break with liberal solutions to racial oppression. As Ford and Patterson put it in a discussion article, "The American Communist Party must initiate a revolutionary race policy."[4]

Finally, Black communists complained bitterly of the treatment accorded those Blacks who had spoken up in the past. As James Ford informed the congress, "Negro comrades who are continually bringing this question before the Party are persecuted and driven out of the Party." In one case he recounted, a Black comrade (apparently Moore) had even been "accused of being a spy of the reactionary forces of America" because he had raised the question of "Negro work" at a communist-led trade union conference.[5]

The association of militant Blacks with reactionary forces did not result from chance. Rather, as Black communists repeatedly brought out, a view had permeated the American party that African-Americans constituted a "reserve of capitalist reaction" that steadfastly opposed progress. For this majority of the leading white communists, African Americans not only did not represent an ally, but even provided the shock troops of the class enemy.[6]

Not surprisingly, the CP had attracted few African Americans. Ford put the figure at less than fifty. Seizing the moment, Ford and William Patterson questioned the revolutionary integrity of the white American communists: "An American Communist Party without Negroes is only a parody of a Bolshevik party."[7]

Yet the sixth congress served as more than the opportunity to settle scores. Black communists put forward their own program for the "Negro Question." All of them spoke of, to use the words of Otto Hall, "the world significance of the Negro question." Although they all emphatically rejected the "class only" approach of Debsianism, they argued that in their vast majority, the "Negro people" formed part of the working classes, and particularly part of that section under the direct domination of imperialism. As such, the "Negro people of the world" were a vast reserve of revolutionary forces. Therefore, they concluded, not without reason, more than new slogans the communists needed to take action. Particularly urgent was the task of organizing trade unions among African Americans, West Indians, and Africans.[8]

The organization of the ANLC provided another target of their criticism. The existence of this paper organization satisfied white communist leaders that their duty for "Negro work" had been fulfilled. As Huiswoud commented with sarcastic double entendre, "Most white comrades [have] conceived of Negro work as the work of the Negro comrades." It was not enough to have the ANLC as a "propaganda sect," publishing a newspaper but doing little else. Huiswoud insisted, "Our main aim must be to build a mass movement based on the industrial workers, particularly the organized workers," and especially aimed at southern African Americans. Ford and Patterson added that the ANLC as it then existed constituted a "Negro Communist Party," rather than an organization in which the African-American workers could overcome their justified suspicion of whites and enter the revolutionary movement. He pointed out that the ANLC was too closely identified with the CP and too sectarian.[9]

Following the conclusion of the sixth congress, Black communists began to get results. The American party established both a top-level "Negro Department" and "Negro Commission" and began electing and appointing Blacks to the leadership bodies. A campaign to eradicate white chauvinism slowly got under way, pushed all the while by leading Blacks. The pages of the *Communist*, theoretical organ of the CP, were opened to criticisms of manifestations of white chauvinism in the party.[10]

Cyril Briggs undertook this work with particular zeal. He presented white communist leaders with the "frank admission that the task of winning the Negro masses to our program was seriously and sincerely taken up only since the Sixth World Congress." Before that, "Negro work" had been of "a sporadic nature intended in the main as a gesture for the benefit of the Comintern." White chauvinism in the party, he charged, had rendered "progress in Negro work well-nigh impossible." And, in what was even more painful to party leaders at a time when the factional struggle was reaching a head, Briggs insisted that white chauvinism was not simply a matter of the past, and that both factions were responsible. Black communists, he reported, were systematically ignored in the drawing up of policy on "Negro work." Black communists new to the party, he insisted, encountered so much racism that they "merely [came] to the conclusion that the Communist Party, instead of being a Party of internationalism and working-class solidarity, is 'just like the republican, democratic and socialist parties' in the reaction of its members to the race question." This state of affairs, he warned, would have to change.[11]

With Black communists brandishing the new resolutions passed by the Comintern as a sword in their struggle against party intransigence, their attacks could no longer be ignored. For example, when the words "the Negro Question in the South" in an article in the *Communist* by Cyril Briggs were changed to "Our Negro Problem in the South" (a change which was also made in the page headings), Briggs did not waste the opportunity to issue a broadside:

> It should be crystal clear to any Communist who gives the question the serious consideration it deserves that the Communist Party can have no Negro *problem*, South or North. Our problem is rather a problem of white chauvinism among the working class and in the very ranks of the Communist Party itself.

The editor, no doubt reflexively, and certainly rather lamely, noted, "The change[s] to which Comrade Briggs refers . . . were both due to typographical and technical reasons." Still, he quickly added, "But of course Comrade Briggs' remarks are fully justified." The old excuses were no longer sufficient. At a time when Briggs was calling white chauvinists to task *by name* in the pages of the *Communist,* even the editor could no longer afford to ignore his message, however inconsequential he may have considered his "mistake."[12]

Black communists made clear that Black workers were fully justified in their suspicion toward the party and that the burden of winning their trust rested on the party itself. Briggs wrote in the *Communist,* "It is the task of the Communist Party of the U.S.A. to prove effectively to the Negro masses that the Communist Party is the party of *all* the workers, of black and white alike." To do so, the party had to undertake the concrete task of transforming its words into deeds.[13]

In particular, Black communists argued for a genuine assault on the racism that dominated the American labor movement, including its left wing. Black communists argued that until the party could show the way by eliminating racism from its ranks and in its unions, no progress would be made in the larger union movement. Transforming the latter formed one of their most ambitious goals. Otto Huiswoud declared, "We must forever break with the attitude and concept of the labor bureaucracy whose argument is, first organize the white workers, then take care of the Negroes."[14]

First, Black communists had to be sure that the unions organized by the Communist Party adhered to such a policy. And experience quickly told them that this would not occur without a sharp struggle. The first test came in the Gastonia textile strike of 1929, a strike involving both Black and white workers in the South led by a communist union, and which became nationally known for the ruthlessness of the violence used to suppress it. Despite the zeal with which African-American workers greeted the unionizing campaign, the white communists in charge of the campaign allowed them to languish and their enthusiasm to expire while they worked first upon the white workers. The authority of the Black communists sent in by the party was ignored. Meetings organized by the union featured segregated seating. Black communists maintained a steadfast insistence, however, that full equality be carried out in practice in both the North *and* the South.[15]

Writing in the *Communist*, Briggs excoriated the "shameful capitulation before white chauvinism" and the manifestation of "imperialist ideology." He railed against the attitude that the party must have "one program for the North and another for the South." He insisted that the party stick to its principles. Among the three party members he reprimanded by name in the party press, he singled out party member Jack Johnstone, a white communist member of the secretariat in charge in Gastonia, for responsibility. Giving full publicity to his public accusations against Johnstone, he blamed Johnstone for proclaiming that the party's program applied only to the North and for setting up "Jim Crow locals in the left wing unions" on his own initiative. Briggs charged him with failure to adhere to the party line, which he merely reported to the southern communists accompanied by the announcement that he had opposed it at the meeting where it was adopted. Briggs further exposed Johnstone's argument that adopting a position of full equality in the South meant "an abandonment of the white workers."[16]

Events in Gastonia soon belied Johnstone's position and backed up Briggs' that workers could be organized along non-racial lines even in the heart of Dixie. When the Gastonia authorities and mill bosses attempted to whip up a lynch mob against Otto Hall, the African-American organizer sent in by the party, the white workers, acting without the knowledge or assistance of the party union leaders, who were temporarily absent, sprang to Hall's defense. Hall was returning from a nearby town when the lynchers gathered to work their terror shortly after the infamous tent city massacre. Having previously provided him with a body guard, the white textile workers now burst through a police blockade and forewarned Hall of the fate that awaited him upon return. They put him on a train, the cost of which they bore out of their own pockets. As Briggs commented upon hearing of the incident, "It seems that we had less trouble in convincing the Southern white strikers of the correctness of our policy than with some of our own comrades in the strike area!"[17]

Moreover, Briggs revealed that even in the North the party unions effectively ignored African Americans. Briggs called the attitude of the party needle trades union "criminal" for its attention to the thousands of African-American workers in the industry only in times of strikes, when it needed them. He reported, "While this union has scores of functionaries, with departments for Greek, Italian, Jewish, etc., workers, it has not a single Negro functionary and no department concerned even remotely with the organization of Negro workers." He insisted that Black organizers were needed to organize Black workers, a principle that the National Negro Congress later showed to be true.[18]

Nor did Black communists, as has been implied, limit themselves to making opportunistic use of the overzealousness of the international communist movement. Having established their case against the American party, they began to launch criticisms of the international communist movement as well. Sticking to their contention that the pressing need remained the organization of the Black masses of Africa, the West Indies, Latin America and the U.S. into trade unions, they began to work on the Red International of Labor Unions (RILU), or Profintern, as well as its American affiliate, the Trade Union Unity League (TUUL). In 1928, the RILU, perhaps aware that change was imminent, formed the International Trade Union Committee of Negro Workers (ITUC-NW), at least partly at the urging of Black delegates to the conference. For several years, the ITUC-NW and its organ, the *Negro Worker*, fulfilled the role as the world revolutionary organization of the "Negro people" that the ANLC had called for. The organization was headed and its journal edited first by James Ford and later by George Padmore (a West Indian).[19]

At the fifth congress of the RILU in 1930, James Ford lashed out at the trade union wing of the Comintern, whose leader, A. Losovsky, had been instrumental in the adoption of the Comintern's position on self-determination and its criticism of white chauvinism in the American party. Despite the establishment of the ITUC-NW, little progress had been made with Black workers. In following Briggs, who had previously taken particular aim at the TUUL's "disgraceful retreat before white chauvinism" in its Southern campaigns, Ford charged, "A general laxity [has] been determined in this period because of white chauvinism that exists in the ranks of the white working class affecting even the revolutionary sections." Losovsky replied, "I must state that, most unfortunately, comrade Ford is perfectly right." He admitted that the Black workers of the world were "entitled to look with suspicion upon the revolutionary trade union organizations, when it came to the racial problem." In turn, Losovsky criticized the TUUL for having done too little to "stigmatize white chauvinists." The ITUC-NW aired these criticisms openly in its journal, as had become the custom since 1928. Gradually, the American communist unionists, led by William Z. Foster, had the idea seared into their political consciousness that any form of discrimination or of segregation, of which they had been guilty countless times, violated revolutionary principles. To whatever degree communists later carried that conviction with them to the CIO, as it is generally held, the campaign to eradicate white chauvinism in the communist movement and its trade union sections by Black communists played the decisive role.[20]

Neither the *Negro Worker* nor Black communists let the matter rest. Once again in early 1932, in giving his report to the RILU for the ITUC-NW, Otto Huiswoud complained bitterly that despite the resolutions from the fifth congress, RILU sections "have simply resolved to do nothing." Their intransigence, he charged, had rendered the Committee ineffective in any area other than political propaganda. He pointed to the increasing resistance to the colonizing powers in Africa and admonished, "The growing revolts . . . must get the immediate attention of the R.I.L.U. sections. . . . We must make the African colonies the center of gravity of our work." Once again the American, British, and French sections came under attack. Of the TUUL, he remarked, "One must say that the work of the T.U.U.L. among the Negro masses in the United States is too abstract, too general and not one real serious

attempt is made to begin the actual organizational work in a
number of [basic] industries . . . [with] large numbers of Negro
workers." Nor was the situation different in the other sections
from imperialist powers: "Practically no work has been done on
the part of the sections of the R.I.L.U. [to organize Black
workers], not even in the metropolitan countries." As had
become the custom among Black communists, in particular those
connected with the *Negro Worker*, the question of the
organization of the Black workers was presented as an
international question, with the "Negro people" being divided
between the colonies and the metropolitan countries, but facing
essentially the same conditions, and waging essentially the
same struggle.[21]

II.

Although the barrage of criticism continued, the basis for
it, the left turn of the Comintern, came to an end in the early
thirties, and even earlier in the American CP, leaving only
left-sounding sectarian rhetoric. There followed in quick
succession a number of changes in the American party that,
although nominally of a purely tactical nature, served to
undercut the position of Black communist critics of the party,
and particularly those whose view of the "Negro Question"
traced back to the ABB. When the Comintern moved
decisively in a rightward direction, the American party
became free to follow its own policy, which first subordinated
and later denied the international aspect of the "Negro
Question," cordoned it off from the question of the struggle
against imperialism, and hence removed the "revolutionary
duty" which had provided Black communists with their
sharpest weapon. Henceforth, the party raised only the banner
of reform, which applied only to American Blacks, and then
only to those in the North. Always careful not to renounce in
theory what it had abandoned in practice, the party managed
to retain at least the organizational allegiance of the Black
communists of ABB background, even as it systematically
demoted them, and moved to get rid of them once and for all for

adhering to a "nationalist deviation." At the same time, divisions appeared among Black communists. A number of younger, mainly American-born middle-class intellectuals grouped around James Ford, and loyal to the party and its doctrinal adherence to neo-Debsianism and reformism, joined forces with the white party leadership against the ABB communists and their allies. In light of these events, the CP's "advanced" position on the "Negro Question"--as it appeared in a society in which even liberals, and many on the left, could not bring themselves to acknowledge the humanity, let alone advocate the political and especially the social equality, of African Americans--became but a token, albeit still very much a remnant of past struggles, which masked its total renunciation of the position of the ABB and its allies. Hence, when it began to advocate "racial egalitarianism," it was not so much as the negation of racism as it was the repudiation of its own "revolutionary duty" to advance the cause of the "Negro people," not only in industries in the North, but in its liberation struggle on a world scale. The CP was once again free to pursue the interests of the American white working class, or at least a section thereof.

Because the ITUC-NW was subordinated only to the RILU (and by implication, the CI) while the ANLC was under the American party, the transition toward reformism appears first in the latter. In June, 1930, the *Liberator*, the official organ of the ANLC, suspended publication without notice. This was nothing unusual for that journal, or any of its kind. But when it resumed publication in September a definite change had come over it. From its former focus on the anti-imperialist struggle of the "Negro people of the world," particularly of the West Indies, it had suddenly shifted to being almost exclusively an anti-lynching journal. Its headline upon resumption read, "The Liberator Rejoins the Fight Against Lynching."[22]

Moreover, the *Liberator* announced impending changes for the ANLC. In and of itself, this development represented nothing surprising. All sides had long been dissatisfied with that organization. But the question remained in which direction, and to whose advantage, would the changes be. That contest would be settled against the ABB communists. Before its suspension of publication the Liberator had editorialized, "With the growing crisis and unemployment, more than ever must be emphasized [*sic*] the absolute necessity of militant organization of the Negro workers, who constitute the most oppressed section of the American working-class." It stressed that the ANLC was "the expression of the new industrial Negro proletariat" and that leadership of the "Negro liberation struggle" must pass into its hands, since "it alone offer[ed] the Negro masses a program and perspective for struggle against the imperialist oppressors of the Negro workers and agricultural laborers of the United States, Africa, the West Indies, etc." Upon resumption of publication in 1930, it declared that the upcoming "historic convention," in contrast, "must lay the basis for a wide struggle against the oppression of the Negro race *as a minority group* and as workers, and win the masses, Negro and white, to the support of the demand for full political, economic and social equality . . ." (emphasis added). Somewhat incongruously, it still supported the right of this "minority group," where it "form[ed] the majority," to self-determination.[23]

With the convening of the long-awaited congress in 1931, the ANLC passed out of existence and was replaced by the League of Struggle for Negro Rights (LSNR), in a harbinger of things to come. Almost point by point it was the complete antithesis of what Black communists had spoken for. First, rather than a way station on the road to the revolutionary movement for the Black masses, rather than a mass organization at all, the LSNR was to be "a group of followers of the *Liberator*. The aim is not to build a mass organization, but to build *The Liberator* into a mass organ as the agitator and organizer of the Negro liberation movement." Beyond that, the LSNR provided no justification for its own existence, other than to support the CP and TUUL. Indeed, far from separating it clearly from the CP, the party attached it more closely than ever. During elections, the *Liberator* became little more than an election leaflet for party candidates. Moreover, the paper gave up all claims to joining the struggle of northern and southern African Americans, first concentrating on the North, and then, in April 1933, changing its name to the *Harlem*

Liberator and becoming a purely local paper. From the time the "Scottsboro boys" campaign got under way, the *Liberator* for all practical purposes became its official organ. Its masthead called only for "fighting against all persecution of the Negro masses and for unconditional political and social equality." True, an occasional editorial proclaimed the old internationalism, it did carry a few articles on the West Indies and especially South Africa, and its "campaign" against lynching as well as the Scottsboro campaign did point out the extreme violence in the South. Still, the change remained unmistakable. Behind it lay the party's change of heart. "Negro work," it declared, "must . . . be conceived of primarily as the development of mass struggles for Negro rights." The party program had become one of reform measures with a bow to the Comintern's as yet unrenounced "Black Belt Thesis."[24]

In 1932, the shift toward reformism continued. The LSNR became an affiliate of the International Labor Defense (ILD), which formed the legal arm of the Communist International, and of which William Patterson had just become head. The annual election campaign, which began in June, trumpeted "The Communist Party of Absolute Equality." And, for the first time, it carried a feature on a Black communist, James Ford, who had been nominated the communists' vice-presidential candidate and was its leading Black figure, having held a host of posts in the party, RILU, and TUUL. The next year, the publicity campaign for rising stars in the party continued, with the article "Young Ben Davis--New Type of Negro Intellectual." The *Harlem Liberator* informed its readers,

> Young Ben Davis typifies the new Negro intellectual of the South. Ten years ago he might have joined the N.A.A.C.P. Today young Ben Davis is fighting with the I.L.D. Today he stands side by side with the Negro workers, binding his Amherst education and his Harvard law school training to the heroic job of shaking off the wolves who attack both Negro and white workers alike.

The party, which once hoped to attract Black workers, now took enormous pride in siphoning off at least part of the layer of the Black intelligentsia that had once gravitated to the NAACP.[25]

The year 1933 would prove to be pivotal in the removal of the last vestiges of the ABB program. Early in the year, George Padmore, editor of the *Negro Worker* and head of the ITUC-NW, gave a speech critical of the international communist movement for its policy toward Blacks. It was to be the last accorded prominence in communist literature, if more were given at all. Speaking before the World Congress of the ILD, Padmore defiantly challenged American, French, and British imperialism to class war on behalf of the "black masses." Warming to his task, he admonished his comrades to pay attention to the "vicious policy of imperialism" in the colonies. He reminded them, "The American comrades have a moral obligation and a revolutionary duty to perform." He called for "concrete deeds" in place of "phrases." Invoking the names of Marx and Engels, he announced, "Only by demonstrations calling for the greatest possible sacrifices will [we] be able to build a steel bridge of international solidarity between the toilers in the metropolis and those of the colonies and oppressed nations." The *Negro Worker* carried the speech given by its editor of three years in February. The *Harlem Liberator*, long edited by Cyril Briggs, printed it in May, with an "editor's note" commenting on how Padmore had "brilliantly analyzed world conditions in their relation particularly to the Negro people."[26]

By the end of that summer both Padmore and Briggs had been replaced. In August, Padmore wrote an editorial explaining that he would no longer be the editor of the *Negro Worker*, but wishing the new editor well. At some subsequent point amid events which remain shrouded in mystery, Padmore, whose drift toward Du Bois's brand of Black nationalism made him a soft target, was accused of "petty bourgeois nationalism," relieved of all his positions, expelled, and vilified. Significantly, the *Negro Worker* ceased publication for a period of ten months after Padmore's farewell edition without explanation, until May of 1934, just before the controversy between Padmore and the CP erupted in the Black press, at which time the journal abruptly started up again under Huiswoud's editorship. In September, Briggs, the founder of the ABB, a strong proponent of "Negro nationalism," and one of the most effective critics of white chauvinism in the party, announced that a "reorganization" of the editorial board of the *Harlem Liberator* would also be taking place. A short time later, Maude White, an African-American woman in her early twenties who had just returned from studies in the Soviet Union, took up the post of editor. In 1934, the *Harlem Liberator* became the *Negro Liberator* under the editorship of "young" Ben Davis.[27]

Not only did Briggs have his paper taken away from him, but the party assured that his influence in its ranks would wane by replacing him and his long-time comrade Richard B. Moore as the leading figures in the Harlem section of the party. Sent in to take their place was James Ford, who arrived in August with, as a recent commentator, Mark Naison, puts it, "a mandate to remold the political life of the Harlem section." Among his tasks, Naison reports, were "to strengthen party discipline [and] restore the authority of the Central Committee," as well as to "wage a struggle *within* the Harlem Party against nationalist tendencies." Naison maintains that Ford had the "full backing of the Central Committee and the benefit of his own personal friendship with Party secretary Earl Browder." Although Naison has nothing better, apparently, than the memory of a couple of party "oldtimers" to go on, all of his conclusions seem likely enough.[28]

Indeed, it was only a year earlier that Browder and the Central Committee had acted to put down a rebellion by young Blacks against neo-Debsianism at a party school which showed that Briggs' "nationalism," that is to say, the internationalist position on the "Negro Question," was finding adherents among a new generation of Black communists. Browder had then sounded the tocsin against the "nationalist deviation" (as it would come to be called) and the struggle against it would intensify as the decade progressed. The promotion of Ford, who had begun his party work under the direction of Briggs and Moore in the ANLC, to leadership over them was greeted by them as the beginning of their fight for survival in the party. Both disliked Ford intensely, believing him to be an opportunist out for this own good and a stooge of the white party leadership.[29]

But it would be wrong to say, as has been suggested, that Briggs and Moore headed up a "left opposition" within the Harlem party. No such cohesive group ever formed among Black communists as had formed in the 1920s and spawned Trotskyism. Instead, Black communists, even those of ABB descent, put loyalty to the party and to the Communist International above principle and silently watched on as one after another of them was singled out for expulsion. Strangely, these valiant fighters of old failed to put up a struggle.[30]

Acting to mitigate such an uncompromising stand against the developing anti-internationalist crusade (which even Naison admits replaced anti-white chauvinism as the central theme in the party's "Negro work") was the tremendous devotion Black communists felt, if not to the American party and its leadership, than at least to the communist movement which had made the Russian revolution. Quite literally, most of their adult lives had been devoted to it. Moore had been a full-time political activist for the party (from which he derived his living) since 1926 (Briggs probably for even longer). Moore's unrelenting zeal for communist work led to the breakup of his family. As he declared during the most famous of the "show trials" of white chauvinists in party ranks, "We must remember that a verdict of expulsion in disgrace from the Communist Party is considered by a class-conscious worker as worse than death at the hands of the bourgeois oppressors. As for myself, I would rather have my head severed from my body by the capitalist lynchers than to be expelled from the Communist International."[31]

When Padmore, incensed at his expulsion, put his case before the people of Harlem via the *New York Amsterdam News*, the party's reply was given by Cyril Briggs, the former employee of that paper, and himself recently removed from an editorship. Briggs took the opportunity to excoriate Padmore's alleged advocacy of schemes to secure Liberian independence. Briggs accused Padmore of abandoning the internationalist position in ignoring the "growing revolutionary struggles of the Liberian masses." But if Briggs was correct in perceiving that

Padmore had begun to abandon the principles that Briggs and the ABB communists had fought to have adopted, he seemed to miss the larger significance of Padmore's expulsion, and its connection to his own demotion in the U.S. party. Neither did he apparently pay any heed to Padmore's charges that the Comintern was prepared to sell out the peoples of Africa and of African descent to court favor with the British, the French, and, to a lesser extent, the American imperialists. But events lent credence to Padmore's claims, and forced at least some of Briggs' allies to begin to question Comintern policy.[32]

Padmore's accusations seemed substantiated within a period of two to three years as the Comintern, as part of its "Popular Front" strategy, dropped its opposition to British, French, and American colonial possessions in Africa and elsewhere in order to pursue an "anti-fascist policy." Where once the rallying cry of the *Negro Worker* had been "Liberation of the oppressed nations from Imperialism," under the "Popular Front" it became "No Colonies to Hitler," an attitude that tacitly accepted the colonial empires in Africa of the British and French. At its worst, the *Negro Worker* became an outright champion of French imperial interests when the Stalinists, in alliance with the socialists, came to power in France. The formerly anti-imperialist journal now advised Africans to be happy they were under the "emancipating" control of the French rather than the "uncivilized" Germans. Padmore's "petty-bourgeois nationalism" paled in comparison to this overtly imperialist stance. What had become of Briggs's biting satire of the "holier-than-thou attitude which this race of robbers [the British imperialists], murderers and self-elected rulers has steadily pursued throughout its foul and bloody history"?[33]

In truth, these divisions in the Black communist camp had deep roots. Briggs had already made clear his belief that the party was deliberately putting forward "the least militant" Black communists into leadership roles. And Briggs had not only failed to defend Padmore, whatever his sins, against what Briggs could only have viewed as the greater sins of the party, but he had manifested this tendency with respect to Black communists before. In 1928, during the events in Gastonia, he had accepted the word of the very southern party organizers whose racism he attacked that Otto Hall had embraced the idea of segregated locals. Hall was thus forced to defend himself against Briggs at the very time he was under attack from the white southern party functionaries. This divisiveness was to prove costly.[34]

Moore, while apparently less scathing of such people as Padmore, nevertheless defended the party in its growing assertions of faultlessly correct policy on all matters. He declared, for example, even while Padmore was still challenging the party to take action, "It was the Communist Party and the Communist Party alone which dared to bring forward the revolutionary program of struggle against the national and social oppression of the Negro people." For his part, Otto Huiswoud, Briggs' and Moore's comrade from the ABB days, was appointed to replace Padmore as editor of the *Negro Worker* and head of the ITUC-NW, and wrote editorials in defense of the very "Allied" imperialism he had grown up under in Dutch Guiana and passionately hated. If it now took such statements to maintain the trust of the party leadership, in the face of all the battles that had been waged, including the persecution Moore had undergone to bring the party to even recognize the "Negro Question," then the days of the ABB radicals within the party were numbered.[35]

For its part, the party was too shrewd to persecute Briggs, Moore, and their allies all at once, and thus to weld them into a united opposition. Shortly after the apparent demotion of Briggs, Moore was named head of the LSNR. And after he gave up that job, purportedly for health reasons (the favorite Stalinist excuse for demotion), it was assumed by Harry Haywood, the most determined advocate of the so-called Black Belt thesis. Black communists allied with Briggs and Moore allowed themselves to be divided against themselves and played one against the other. Both sides, Briggs' and Moore's as well as Fords', avoided an open rupture. Ford used them, not to boost their influence, but to exploit it for a time. As Naison explains:

> When he first arrived in Harlem, Ford shrewdly avoided an open break with the people he

superseded. . . . He . . . tried to keep opponents in
positions of leadership even when he undercut their
political base. . . . So long as they were willing to obey
Party discipline, Ford was willing to give his internal
opposition a large share of the Party's public
agitation.

Briggs and Moore fell into this trap like political neophytes.
While Briggs suffered demotion, Moore accepted the
appointment as head of the League of Struggle for Negro
Rights, only to be promptly removed in favor of Harry
Haywood.[36]

Like Moore, Haywood, who himself espoused something
close to the internationalist position to the "Negro Question"
and also opposed the growing liberalism in the party in this
area, agreed to take over without the least defense of his
demoted comrade. He evidently believed that his selection
meant an endorsement of his well-known positions. His
acceptance speech, as it were, announced that Depression
conditions had made it "urgently necessary to more boldly and
determinedly put forward the program of the LSNR for a
revolutionary way out."

In 1934, Haywood gave the main report on "Negro work" to
the party's convention, and seemed oblivious to the reformist
turn the party was taking. He continued to declare that only
revolutionary change could bring about a fundamental
transformation in the living conditions of the Black masses. He
also insisted on the party's adherence to the self-determination
of the Black Belt. He emphasized the urgent necessity of
organizing Blacks into trade unions, warning that "Negro
reformists" were entering the field, spurred by the "Leftward
drift" of the masses. He saved his fiercest attack for John P.
Davis, head of the Joint Committee on National Recovery, an
organization founded to lobby the New Deal government on
behalf of Black workers, even though Davis was very close to
the party, if not already in it. Through the JCNR's legalistic
maneuvering, he declared, using the revolutionary-sounding
verbiage of the day,

The fight of the Negro toilers is made to appear not a
fight against the fascist New Deal policy, but merely

> a fight for fairness in the application of this policy.
> Thus, the Joint Committee on National Recovery, a
> united front of Negro reformist organizations, . . . act[s]
> in an unofficial advisory capacity [to] the New Deal
> administration.   Of course, all this activity of the
> Negro reformist leaders around the New Deal has for
> its purpose the disorganizing and confusing of the
> Negro masses. . . .

Years later, after his own expulsion, Haywood would continue
to maintain that the party only took its turn toward reformism
in the *late* Thirties, no doubt in part because it continued to
allow him to expound the self-determination doctrine even as it
had converted it to a dead letter.[38]

Most likely, Haywood's words did not bother the party
leadership. For one thing, Haywood would allow himself to be
used to spearhead the campaign against the "petty-bourgeois
nationalist deviation", which meant, in practice, against
Briggs and Moore; it was only poetic justice that Haywood, who
shared more in common with them than with Ford whom he
praised in his report, received the same treatment in due course.
Moreover, even if these words were read in party gatherings, no
longer were the pages of its journals to serve as forums for its
Black critics or reminders of the revolutionary duty of
communists. Indeed, the organs of the LSNR and ITUC-NW
were not to last long at all.[39]

III.

With a new leadership in place in the American center of
Black radicalism, Harlem, with the ABB communists and their
allies divided and in retreat, the party went to work uprooting
the internationalists' positions in party work. In late 1933 and
early 1934, the LSNR moved once again toward projecting itself
as a mass organization. It served notice, however, that this
was not to be confused with the organization of the masses
Black communists had called for. Instead, this was to be a
"broad mass organization capable of unifying and leading the
struggle against Negro oppression." An idea of what LSNR

leaders had in mind came in its announcement of its new president, poet Langston Hughes, and in its ecstatic reaction at the greetings, not of a committee of workers, but of another figure from the middle-class Harlem Renaissance, Countee Cullen. A conference it sponsored unanimously elected well-known middle-class reformer Mary Church Terrell chairperson. Its organ, once a record of the liberation struggles of not only African Americans, but West Indians and Africans, now featured most prominently articles on a wide range of subjects, political and otherwise, by Ford, Patterson, Hughes, and Ben Davis, as well as emphasizing the advocacy movement within the NRA that Haywood had so recently denounced. No longer did it advocate building a revolutionary movement of the "Negro people of the world," instead carrying editorials like the following, "Let a movement be built that spreads the idea of liberation far and wide, that fights for the economic security of the Negro toilers,"--under capitalism. All the while the *Harlem* (and later *Negro*) *Liberator* continued to denounce the "reformists," although it failed to specify what set it apart from them. The paper even described the LSNR as a "mass organization of a non-political character"![40]

In the meantime, the party finished off the ABB communists. Having settled scores with Briggs, it now focused on Moore's advocacy of the "Don't Buy Where You Can't Work" campaigns, in which African Americans boycotted shops and businesses that refused to hire African Americans. In particular, it argued that Black workers could not displace white workers in their struggle for better conditions. This new line prompted Moore to comment, "Why all this talk about antagonizing white workers? Are not these white workers in Negro neighborhoods living on the back of the Negro masses?" As Naison remarks, "In Moore's view, the position Ford outlined placed the burden for maintaining working-class unity on the black workers rather than on the white."[41]

The party made it official policy that campaigns to eliminate discrimination in hiring would be dependent upon the party trade unions affiliated with the TUUL. In practice, their support was only partial; with the party in retreat from its short-lived attention to genuine interracial solidarity, the

TUUL unions once again refused to throw themselves wholeheartedly into the struggle for Black liberation. As Black communist Abner Berry later recalled, "The Party had already decided that we fight for the right of Negroes for jobs, but would guarantee that white workers would not be fired." Once again the party had fallen back to advocating Black rights so long as they did not infringe upon white privilege. ABB internationalism was dead; it remained only to remove the corpses. In the late Thirties and early Forties, Briggs, Moore and their supporters were expelled for "extreme nationalist tendencies." Earlier, Haywood had been removed for his nationalist views.[42]

Although the white leadership of the Communist Party stood solidly against them, the ABB radicals cannot be absolved of their share of the blame in their own demise. They were too easily set one against the other, too willing to accept any charges as long as they were against someone else, too reluctant to throw down the gauntlet against the return to the policies of the 1920s they had fought so hard to eradicate. Despite all their work, the ABB communists never achieved full theoretical or practical clarity on the "Negro Question." They had left themselves vulnerable to such "championing" of African Americans as the Comintern had adapted as policy beginning in 1928. Most of all, they proved too willing to take advantage of the apparent move in their direction by the post-Lenin Comintern to initiate a practical struggle built on a false foundation. They failed to heed their own earlier advice about caution toward white radicals who refused to take up wholeheartedly the cause of the most oppressed workers in America. In return for the promise of immediate gains, they put aside their principled concern for the long-term interests of African-American workers.

W.A. Domingo had long ago warned that the communists must offer something more to Black workers than the liberals. They had now embraced exactly the liberal position, even if in the most consistent form to be found in America. The CP was well on the way to an open embrace of reformism that would culminate with its launching of the National Negro Congress under John Davis's leadership.[43]

Chapter V
The Black Radical Consensus Program for Black Labor, Part I

In the first years of the 1930s, the Great Depression descended upon the world, but it hit African Americans and sections of the working class even earlier, as unemployment soared in the late 1920s, bringing with it destitution and discontent. These developments had a two-fold effect on the "Negro Question." First, they brought about changes in the structure of the working class that would cause the labor aristocracy to seek a temporary alliance of convenience with the Black working class, at least its northern industrial component. Second, in its wake a number of young, middle-class African-American intellectuals abruptly shifted from advocating purely racial policies that were antipathetic to white labor to thorough-going champions of the organized white labor movement as the savior of the Black masses.

In the Thirties, amid the radicalization of American intellectuals, with the casual talk of the need to rid society of the menace of capitalism, the turn toward socialism seemed natural. To a degree that made for fits of discomfort, subsequently, when the anti-communist witch hunters in the Congress and Senator McCarthy began their work, American intellectuals became arm-chair socialists. Even internationally known novelist F. Scott Fitzgerald, who spent the Twenties chasing wealth, fame, and the aristocratic Zelda, began studying Marx and wrote, in the early 1930s, "To bring on the revolution, it may be necessary to work inside the

Communist party." The intellectuals' manifesto supporting
William Z. Foster, communist candidate for president, in 1932,
read like a who's who of American literary life. By that year,
the American economy was in shambles. Production had fallen
to half its 1928 level. Industrial employment fell by 34%, and
total unemployment, as estimated by the AFL, reached a
staggering 30%. This was more than a repetition of the business
cycle.[1]

The radicalizing effects of the Great Depression, making
radicals of those who had been liberal or even conservative and
pushing former radicals even further left, have been described
by white radical A.J. Muste. He said that, with the
depression, intellectuals and labor leaders could no longer offer
workers the growth of capitalism as the vehicle for improving
their lives.

> Nor could one point out to the unemployed and
> unorganized, the starving and persecuted, the stodgy,
> unimaginative, and passive labor movement of that
> era. A new labor movement with a different
> philosophy seemed clearly indicated. Under the
> circumstances, a philosophy emphasizing economic
> determinism, the decisive role of class struggles in
> human history, the enervating and corrupting influence
> of religion, the need of revolutionary action toward a
> revolutionary goal, the role of a vanguard party of
> dedicated revolutionaries, had an immense attraction
> for us.

Among young African-American intellectuals, the prevailing
mood was summed up by Ben Davis, son of a prominent Georgia
Republican, early in the depression decade:

> We young intellectuals are fed up with the cowardice
> and the suave treachery of such organizations as the
> N.A.A.C.P. and the Interracial Commission. We know
> that they betray the Negro workers. We know that
> they can always be counted on to echo the language and
> actions of our oppressors.... And so we young Negroes
> take our stand. You'll find hundreds of us where I am
> standing; beside the sharecroppers of Tallapoosa, the
> steel workers of Birmingham, and the masses of

Negroes and whites who have taken up the battle of the Scottsboro boys.

This combination of the quest for a "new labor movement with a different philosophy" among white radicals and a new approach to racial politics among young Black radical intellectuals who were "taking their stand" produced a Black radical consensus of the 1930s around a program for African-American workers.[2]

The "new labor movement" Muste spoke of meant the replacement of the traditional AFL craft unions with those of the industrial variety, that is, those which organized workers of an entire industry rather than splitting the workers in trade unions according to occupation. The idea itself was far from new even in America. The Knights of Labor and, more recently, the Industrial Workers of the World (IWW) had organized themselves along such lines. And the United Mine Workers (UMW), the largest and most powerful AFL union, continued to do so. Moreover, as these three examples, representing, as it were, three stages in the American labor movement, reveal, the mere form of organization could correspond to far different purposes. The Knights of Labor, the earliest important national federation, appeared long before American class relations had cemented, when the workers could, to a large degree, realistically expect to escape their condition; when demand for labor exceeded supply, wages were relatively high, and the chances for successful strikes good. The Knights, therefore, naturally did not take to a policy of "class struggle." At most, they brought the newly emerging working class together, and proclaimed to the nation its ability to act independently. The IWW, on the other hand, reached its height at the very time when American capitalism was at its most "ruthless," when the shameful exploitation of women, children, the aged, and so forth, was most glaring. The syndicalist Wobblies, seeking to overthrow capitalist exploitation through control of the factories, constituted the most revolutionary trade union movement in American history.[3]

But, among them, the closest model for the "new union" movement would be the UMW, or at least its sister organizations in the needle trades, the International Ladies

Garment Workers Union (ILGWU) and the Amalgamated
Clothing Workers of America (ACWA). Where the Knights
had pursued class solidarity and the IWW class conflict, the
UMW and the needle trades unions practiced class compromise:
in return for the agreement by their industry to recognize them
as the sole and "legitimate" bargaining agent of the workers
and for collective bargaining, or the working out of wage
agreements on an industry-wide basis, these unions would, in
turn, accept the industrial despotism of capital. This formula
had been most successfully implemented by the UMW. Its
bywords were high wages and the "closed shop"--union control
of hiring. Although the bureaucrats at the head of these unions
felt personally at home in the AFL's climate of power-
brokering and boss politics, relations between the "new unions"
and the old remained strained and would, in 1935, break out
into open warfare.[4]

The UMW, through the person of its leader John L. Lewis,
would be the motive force behind the formation of the CIO, but
the task of preparing the ground in union and left-wing circles
Lewis, never of a particularly ideological bent, left to others,
primarily those associated with the needle trades. It was
natural that it should be they. The UMW's existence,
tentative as it may have been, was secure by labor standards,
its union officials, compared to those in the needle trades,
formed, according to one contemporary commentator, a "labor
aristocracy." In contrast, if the trade union representatives of
any industry could have an interest in the kind of state
unionism produced by the Depression-decade New Deal and
CIO, it was those in the needle trades, which faced a plethora
of small operators bent on nothing so much as lowering wages
and destroying unions. From the start, those unions were
hotbeds of radicalism, and the socialists stood in the foremost
place within them. It was these same socialists, or at least
those with their outlook, who spearheaded the movement for
what they called "progressive unionism."[5]

At the forefront of this battle stood A.J. Muste, radical
Christian pacifist for the rest of his life, and Trotskyist for the
Depression-decade, and Louis F. Budenz, a socialist-turned-
Trotskyist-turned-Stalinist-turned-Catholic-government

informer. While Budenz edited the progressive unionists' journal, *Labor Age*, Muste operated its ideological headquarters, the Brookwood Labor College, both founded in 1921. From the labor college, forty zealots a year were turned loose into labor circles to spread the new union gospel. More important, the converted had a center from which to broadcast their message and organize their plan of attack.[6]

Eventually, and inevitably, Muste and Brookwood succeeded in raising the ire of the AFL (some said it was the ostentatious and ideologically revealing display on May Day of pictures of Lenin, Marx, Debs, and deceased AFL president Gompers, all adorned with red ribbons). The AFL began a campaign to isolate the school in 1928. Muste and Budenz began a campaign--the Conference on Progressive Labor Action (CPLA)--to replace the AFL. If the CIO could not have been formed without Lewis's punch, literally and figuratively, then it could not have found the left-wing crusaders that made its organizing possible without the CPLA. Not coincidentally, that organization appeared on the scene on the very eve of the "Great Crash" and the Depression that followed.[7]

The CPLA, under Muste and Budenz, fulfilled its purpose admirably, as no other organization could have: it brought the entire left into the "progressive unionist" fold. Their socialist credentials provided them the means to preach to the converted as well as to those straying from the flock. When the CPLA developed into the "revolutionary" (Muste's quotation marks) Workers Party, and then merged with the Trotskyists in 1935, the support of the latter was secured. And, although the communists did not particularly like Muste, they preferred him to the socialists proper. At a time when their program had converged with the socialists, but their rhetoric continued to denounce the group they had split off from (they could, of course, never accept the Trotskyists, who had split off from them), the communists would share the stage with Muste in a "Trade Union Conference for United Action" as early as 1933.[8]

What made the CPLA most useful, however, was its ability to attract young Black radicals. For a group of radicals with a long track record which included nothing in the way of interest in the "Negro Question" until 1927, the Musteites were surprisingly successful at attracting Black support. Indeed, through its association with Abram Harris, the CPLA can be credited with (if only inadvertently) launching the Black radical consensus of the 1930s.

The contours of the debate over the "Negro Question" had already been established by the ABB and SP approaches to the alliance between white and Black workers. The period from the late 1920s to the mid-1930s would witness the metamorphosis of the two sides into neo-Debsianism, which paved the way for the eventual convergence toward a radical consensus. Ironically, the socialist position would gain its fullest expression in the thinking of its former critic, Abram Harris, who by virtue of not being directly associated with the SP would also attract adherents among like-minded communists. As this development coincided with the overthrow of the strongest supporters of the ABB position and the emergence of a new generation of reform-minded intellectuals as Black party leaders, the basis was laid for the "popular front" consensus with the socialists on a program for Black labor.

II.

In the late 1920s and early 1930s, adherents of the old socialist position split into two camps, which can loosely be called the "intellectual" and the "practical." Those in the intellectual camp, with the newly-converted Harris as leader and Du Bois as prototype, focused on the role of the intellectual, whose "guidance" and powers of reasoned persuasion were deemed crucial to the formation of a labor program and its execution. Following in the footsteps of Du Bois, they received advanced degrees from the elite universities of the East. For the most part, they parlayed them into academic or professional careers. Several, including Harris and Ralph Bunche, obtained positions on the faculty of Howard University, a predominantly Black university in the nation's capital. Others, most notably John P. Davis and Robert Weaver, became lobbyist-advocates for Black labor to the New

Deal government of President Franklin D. Roosevelt. Whatever their particular career or field, however, they all had in common with each other that they were not of the working class, although most of them came from poor backgrounds. Their academic or professional status and training was a direct contrast to the cadre of Black radicals who came of age in the twenties--Randolph, Crosswaith, Briggs, Huiswoud, and so forth--which sought its home either in the labor or the socialist movements. With the emergence of Harris, Ben Davis, John Davis, Bunche, and others, the training ground of Black radicals shifted from the political arena to the university. More important, perhaps, the radical intellectuals shifted the center of the ideological struggle from the political parties and movements to academic forums at which the university-trained radicals were likely to feel more at home. Research by "experts" and articles in academic journals came to replace direct political experience and polemics in radical organs. On the other side, the Black radicals of the Twenties of socialist persuasion, led by Randolph and Crosswaith, formed the nucleus of the "practical" grouping. They insisted that only practical measures needed to be taken, since the solutions to the problems of Black workers were evident to all who took part in the trade union movement.

The conflicting perspectives on the way to effect a solution to the "Negro Question" led the adherents of the two groups along different paths. Randolph and Crosswaith had, throughout most of the Twenties, clung to the hope that white labor would simply change its policy through the practical experience of continually losing strikes in which Blacks served as strikebreakers. By the end of the Twenties, however, they gave up their vain hope and began agitation in the AFL and the SP, respectively, for a simple campaign to enlist Blacks. Harris, on the other hand, offered himself and other Black intellectuals as the solution. Reasoned arguments aimed at educated labor progressives would accomplish the aim. Harris, Davis, Bunche, and others, presented research memoranda, case studies, detailed programs and proposals to responsible officials of labor, African-American political organizations, and federal government agencies.

Randolph did not argue his case in the journals, but took to the floor of the AFL convention to run a high-profile campaign on what he considered a matter of basic justice. Randolph, as head of the BSCP, which gained admittance into the AFL in 1928 as a block of federal locals, that is, locals affiliated directly to the AFL, used his "beach-head" in the main body of organized labor to push what came to be known as the "Randolph Resolution," which called on the AFL to employ Black organizers and extend "the aggressive and constructive organization campaign now being conducted" to Black workers. Year after year Randolph presented his resolution, and year after year the AFL leadership blocked its adoption. Still, Randolph's battle focused attention on the AFL's racist policies.[9]

While Randolph kept AFL leaders on the defensive in their own conventions, Crosswaith worked on the SP. With Randolph having abandoned active work in the party to pursue his duties with the BSCP, Crosswaith assumed the mantle of the leading African-American socialist. In 1928, at about the same time Randolph set the stage for his AFL campaign and Black communists began intensive agitation in the CP and Comintern, Crosswaith became fed up with the SP's traditional "Debsian view" of race, which amounted to benign neglect. He launched the United Colored Socialists of America, which, without the endorsement of the party, set out both to attract Blacks to the SP and the SP to the cause of Blacks. Crosswaith attempted to get the SP to abandon its age-old policy of subsuming racial questions purely under those of class.[10]

All of Crosswaith's efforts would have receded into the background had it not been for the Depression. In a historical irony, just as the Communist Party was undergoing a rightward shift of its program toward the reformist thrust of the "Popular Front," the Socialist Party, or at least the largest section of it, began to move to the left toward an espousal, at least in rhetoric, of revolutionary means of change. Suddenly the "Negro Question" took on new meaning. The new "radical" socialists decided to take up the "Negro Question" anew, portending a possible abandonment of pure Debsianism. Such a change could have meant a great deal to the SP's fortunes vis-a-vis Blacks. The SP had steadily lost Black membership following the formation of the communist parties until, by the thirties, it included only a handful. Moreover, the AFL had refrained from using its still considerable influence in organized labor to lobby for the Randolph Resolution, and had tolerated racism in its ranks.[11]

In the context of this stirring of radicalism in the party, Crosswaith's campaign began to show some effect. In the early thirties, at least some SP locals in Virginia and North Carolina dropped their color bar and began to recruit Blacks. By 1935, this policy would reach even the Deep South. At the least, Virginia and North Carolina Blacks proved receptive. Then came the SP's best historical claim to a contribution to Black liberation, the Southern Tenant Farmer's Union, an organization of the semi-enslaved tenant farmers of the South. After its founding by Arkansas socialists in 1934, it grew to 10,000 members within a year, and to 25,000 at its apex in 1936 as its influence spread to surrounding states. Still, despite the reputation it has gained for interracialism, problems abounded from the start. For the most part, it would remain silent on segregation, and itself would be segregated, and it never raised the issue of social equality. By 1937, despite being 80 percent Black, the leadership remained white-dominated, drawing pointed criticism from Black members. It also paid its white organizers more than their Black counterparts. The union's decline came at the end of the Thirties, when it also became affiliated with the CIO, amidst a general exodus of its Black leaders.[12]

The STFU was to be the high-water mark of the SP's aborted metamorphosis on the "Negro Question." Despite a well-publicized decision in 1936 to form a national subcommittee on Blacks, the party's first organizational acknowledgment of their presence, the SP maintained its traditional Debsian philosophy. The SP brought Randolph back to head the committee, but, as usual with Randolph, this arrangement denoted his name and someone else's work--in this case Crosswaith's. Nothing came of this committee, or any of

the SP's measures. Finally, other Black socialist leaders lost
patience and split off in a dispute over the SP program--or,
rather the lack of one--for African Americans, and Crosswaith
returned to the trade union movement.[13]

Despite his efforts, Blacks, for the most part, remained as
aloof from the SP as it did from racial questions. Crosswaith
did remain a loyal socialist throughout the Thirties,
appearing several times on its New York ticket. But this was
mainly because the socialists, while virtually gone from the
political scene, retained their traditional influence in the labor
movement, or at least in certain key unions. In 1934 Crosswaith
returned to the labor movement as an organizer with the
ILGWU, as that union sought to organize the Blacks then
flocking into the industry. He proclaimed to African Americans
that trade unionism was "our only hope":

> As for Negroes we cannot hope for victory in our fight
> for civil rights and social justice until we lift our labor
> power out of the swamps of unorganized, under-paid,
> abused and unprotected workers. The weapon with
> which to achieve our liberation from these evils is
> organization both on the industrial and political
> fields. The sooner Negro leaders and others learn this
> sound and wholesome lesson, the sooner we will come
> out of the valley of oppression to walk upon the
> highlands of equality with all God's children.

He declared that all Black leaders and workers had to
recognize the truth of these words "At this time when the
responsible leaders of American labor are learning that labor
cannot hope to maintain the gains already made, nor to extend
them, so long as Negro labor remains outside the ranks of the
organized labor movement." This outlook fit well into the
developing Black radical consensus, although Crosswaith
would only play the smallest of roles within it. His position as
an ILGWU organizer required, or at least he thought it
required, unquestioning loyalty and uncritical support that was
too much even for radicals of Harris's and Davis's bent.[14]

Nonetheless, back in his old environs, and with an even
better base, Crosswaith used his new position as a springboard
to launch the Harlem Labor Committee. The new group evolved

into the larger Negro Labor Committee, won the endorsement of Walter White of the NAACP and Norman Thomas of the SP, and fought off an attempt by the Popular Front era CP to join forces with it. Crosswaith had attained a status in the labor movement second only, perhaps, to Randolph. He could not be ignored, but neither could he, in the view of the more "mainstream" Black radicals, be trusted. They would pursue the same strategy with regard to Crosswaith as with Randolph: make use of his name without giving him any more personal power.[15]

Du Bois and Harris could not have been surprised at the lack of success encountered by Randolph and Crosswaith. According to them, it would be neither the agitator nor the political organizer, let alone the masses, who would bring about change. Rather, it would be the intellectual. Having neither the communists' faith in the revolutionary potential of the masses, nor Randolph's in the ability of the AFL to throw off its traditional racial exclusivism, Du Bois and Harris searched for an intellectual solution to the problems of the Black masses. Du Bois maintained his skepticism about the efficacy of a labor-Black alliance and would never join the radical consensus. Instead, he embraced a program of "Negro cooperatives," which only earned him the reputation of being a "segregationist" as well as a conservative. Both labels missed the target, although they, unfortunately, left him isolated from Black radicals at a time when Du Bois stood almost alone in recognizing the limitations of the "pure class" approach at which Black radicals had arrived. In truth, Du Bois was moving steadily to the left and apparently began to find the conservatism of the middle-class NAACP, which he eventually came to acknowledge and denounce, embarrassing. In the April 1930 *Crisis*, he went as far as to claim that the NAACP's program was in "essential agreement" with that of the ANLC, a proposition that Cyril Briggs rightly ridiculed. But Du Bois actually did agree with the communists on many issues, and he was on the verge of decisively breaking with the liberal-dominated NAACP. For its part, the NAACP leadership put little stock in the young radicals' charges that Du Bois was an old-guard conservative, and moved toward expelling him. But while Du Bois might arrive negatively at the program of the Black communists of ABB lineage, he could not bring himself to embrace their positive program, leaving him in a half-way station that earned him the scorn of all, or rather, almost all.[16]

As Du Bois quickly became the favorite target of both right and left, including the new generation of Black radicals that Abram Harris was to assume leadership over, he retained the loyalty of Harris. Harris wrote to him, "You ought to be sure by now of how much I feel myself a part of you, that in spite of fundamental disagreement there is hardly a single living man for whom I have greater affection and genuine admiration." Nor was the "fundamental disagreement" where it might be expected. Harris had, it seems, arrived at a point of view very similar to Du Bois's. He advocated a kind of "cartel socialism" which he said complemented Du Bois's cooperative idea. Moreover, he readily accepted Du Bois's notorious "Talented Tenth" thesis: "I contend . . . that no program of economic welfare that is planned for the Negro is going to succeed until his socalled intelligentsia is emancipated so that it can furnish guidance." He even touted Du Bois as the only figure suited to lead the "new movement" for such an objective. They differed only in Harris's contention that such a movement was practical, that there existed the requisite talent. In Du Bois's view, the Depression had "strangled to death" the necessary "independent mind[s]" and "scholarship." He lamented, "There is no more tremendous proof of the Marxian dogma than the fact that our fundamental economic situation today is making science, art and literature among us almost impossible." In Du Bois's view, therefore, before all else, a practical program for alleviating the crisis had to be followed. For Harris, the possibility for change was not so remote:

> I know that I am criticized for constantly demanding that the Negro intellectual think of the race problem in terms of general economic and social changes. But the more I study the economic life of the country the more I am convinced that if the Negro intellectual does not begin to think in this fashion he will effect no

permanent change in the conditions of the Negro masses.

In other words, change depended above all upon the intellectual.[17]

By the mid-thirties, Harris had become the acknowledged leader of the newly-emerged group of Black radical intellectuals by both talent and experience. Having received his Ph.D.--in economics--a few years before most of the others, and having previously worked with the Urban League specializing in Black labor affairs, he had already established his reputation in radical circles by the time the others arrived on the scene. Hence, he represented a valuable contact and equally a natural figure to rally around. Moreover, Harris had already worked out a coherent platform that attracted others to his cause. To be sure, from any objective standpoint Harris had achieved nothing new. His program for labor was little more than what Randolph, Crosswaith, and before them, Eugene Debs had said. But Harris shaped it in such a way that he made it apparent who he believed had to formulate organized labor's program for African-American workers and their program for labor, which he took to be the same. As early as 1927, in an article for *The Crisis* on Brookwood Labor College's "Symposium on Negro Labor," at which he had given one of the papers, Harris commented, "[Organized] labor, particularly in America, or [sic] when confronted with matters of race, needs intellectual guidance, despite its reliance on pragmatic, business unionism and its traditional steering clear of theories of social development." Harris, like the young radical intellectuals who would follow him, had become interested in Marx's theories, which, however, did not in the least cause him to stand out in leftist circles. Still, Harris left the clear implication that in the hands of the other participants at the forum, which included Randolph, Crosswaith, SP leader Norman Thomas, Urban League official Charles S. Johnson, and sociologist E. Franklin Frazier, the history of Black workers had not been adequately understood or taken into account. By then, Harris was already in the formative stages of his own "definitive" work on that subject, *The Black Worker.*[18]

By 1930, the same year he completed his book-length
study, Harris had already formulated his program for
organized labor and the Black worker. The title, "The Negro
Worker: A Problem of Progressive Labor Action," coupled with
its form as a report to Muste's Conference on Progressive Labor
Action, indicate Harris's approach. From the outset, Harris
made the objective clear: "The task of progressive labor action
is the organization of those workers who have been neglected
by traditional trade unionism." Beyond that Harris argued
that organized labor had to convert to the industrial form of
unionism and that the political independence of labor from the
two-party system was also a necessity. Of course, Harris
blamed organized labor, meaning the AFL in the first place, for
its policy toward Blacks, but he argued that more than its lack
of action in organizing Blacks, it had to be "censured" for its
"refusal to make some attempt toward a realistic understanding
of the problem and issues involved." Consequently, the first
task facing "progressives" was to understand the "problem."
Harris advised labor progressives that African-American
workers, "of recent industrial experience," had to be
systematically educated and warned of the "opportunistic and
petty-bourgeois" character of "Negro economic and political
leadership." Falling back on the position advanced by the
socialists in the Twenties, Harris claimed that "effective
action cannot ignore the position of Negro labor if for no other
reason than that white labor is fully protected only when
Negro and white workers are equally organized." Flowing
logically from that, the goal became the acceptance by white
workers of "Negroes into working-class fellowship."
Ironically, Harris could, at nearly the same time,
hypocritically criticize Debs's position as "an escape from the
reality of the relations between the white and Negro workers
rather than an assault upon race antipathy."[19]
    In truth, Harris was the first of the "neo-Debsians," and
his writings in the late 1920s anticipated in spirit Bunche's
later "definitive statement" of this outlook. If Debs and the
early American socialists had come to such a view negatively,
by *not* thinking about the "Negro Question," Harris and his
associates came to it positively, through their "research" on

the question. Harris, did not, as Bunche would, completely deny *race* as a scientific category, but he denied its applicability to America. African Americans were a subject "race" and, as "is not infrequent . . . the economic and social subjugation of one race or class by another has led the subordinated group to adopt the culture of the dominant." Therefore, Harris asserted, neither racial differences nor cultural lay at the root of the problem. Not "race prejudice," but "racial antipathy" afflicted African Americans. And economic oppression was responsible, specifically slavery. "Racial antipathy" simply reflected a policy of *"divide et impera."* It remained, then, for workers Black and white to unite and revolt.[20]

Harris, then, who had been such a firm critic of organized labor and the kind of "idealism" characteristic of Blacks on the left, had now himself come to exactly their position, or, if anything, only to a "purer" class approach. And although Harris had changed his view of the expediency and possibility of organizing white workers in common with Black, on one point he stuck to his old standpoint: he continued to place practically no faith in the ability of the Black masses to effect change on their own behalf. Once again he charged Black communists with "see[ing] revolution where there is only conservatism." Furthermore, Harris demanded no more of organized labor's leadership than that it understand the problem, when even Randolph insisted that some concrete action be taken. Whether following from an excessively intellectual approach or some other reason, such a minimal program opened the door for the acceptance of the CIO as "racially egalitarian" before it had ever established a record toward Black labor, simply on the basis of the promising outlook to which its leaders seemed to adhere. Moreover, Harris did not, even as Crosswaith's socialist Trade Union Committee of the Twenties, raise the question of organized labor's entrance into the struggle of African Americans for fundamental democratic rights. Hence, his program represented a step backward from that program. If Harris's thinking provided an attraction to the young group of rising intellectuals who were turning their attention to Black labor with the coming of the depression, it may have been the continued insistence that only research and study could reveal the solution to the "problem," although so far it had revealed nothing new to Harris.[21]

Moreover, Harris, for all his intellectual work, had come no closer to a solution of the problem that vexed Randolph, Crosswaith, and other Black trade unionists and socialists: how to get the trade union movement to take action with respect to Blacks. Harris stuck to the traditional position that white labor could not be secure until Black workers were incorporated in its ranks. Yet white labor had apparently been willing to live with that insecurity for more than five decades. What made that situation likely to change now? History seemed to be against Harris, especially considering the record of the AFL with respect to its exclusion, not only of African Americans, but also women, immigrants, and the unskilled. Both the "practical" and "intellectual" adherents to the "pure class" approach would find this obstacle formidable. Harris, however, would not, as Randolph and Crosswaith, limit himself to working within the predominantly white trade union and left-wing movements. That legacy, at least, remained from his days of independent Black radicalism. Indeed, Harris, almost alone among the young Black radicals of the 1930s, would not tie himself organizationally to any of the traditional left-wing parties or to organized labor, although he was the only one to take, briefly, a post within the government bureaucracy.[22]

Joining Harris as a convert to the CPLA was Ernest Rice McKinney. While Harris came to it from the thin ranks of the independent Black radicals, McKinney was lured away from the communist milieu. In 1929, McKinney became the newest, and the most loyal, of Muste's followers among the young Black radicals, moving with him from the CPLA to the Trotskyist party in the mid-Thirties. Like Harris and his fellow radicals, McKinney had been a Black nationalist of the Du Bois type earlier in the Twenties, and had embraced Black capitalism as the answer. He now wholly rejected that solution. Even under the employ of African-American owners, African-American workers "would be exploited just as they are exploited today." McKinney, like Harris but unlike the ABB communists, saw no essential difference in the exploitation of white and Black workers. Moreover, there could be no "compromise" with Black nationalism of Du Bois's type, however temporary and for whatever purpose. "This means," he wrote, "that Negro workers must give up any foolish notions about race consciousness and race solidarity and begin to acquire a far more fundamental and basic class consciousness and class solidarity transcending the bounds of race." But he did add a caveat that Harris did not: that white workers reciprocate. Indeed, McKinney, almost alone among the new generation of Black radicals, was prepared to declare that "White Workers Are Guilty"--of complicity in the oppression and degradation of their Black class brothers and sisters.[23]

But if McKinney recognized that white workers could "help" the capitalists in that field at least, he drew no further conclusion from this alliance. He stuck to his insistence on pure class-consciousness, although "historical and psychological factors" in the South might very well dictate the necessity of "separate organizations for Negroes." Liberation would come through the organization of workers into unions, which, in the syndicalist outlook of "progressive unionist" ideology, would somehow bring about the "ultimate aim" of capitalism's overthrow. No intermediary steps before that point, and evidently no further measures after, were needed. McKinney rebuked Black leaders for their concern "with some vapory thing called the Negro's rights." Pursuing a political course, as had Black leaders since Du Bois's triumph over Washington, was wrong, as "political power follows from and grows out of economic power." McKinney touted the CPLA's program of progressive unionism as the solution in its entirety. As for the place of the Black worker within it, McKinney enthusiastically cited the case of a white worker who "had seen the light and was ready to take the Negro into the labor movement, not as a Negro but as a worker." This statement, although McKinney was oblivious to the parallels, recalled abolitionist Wendell Phillips' comment that an emancipation without a revolution in southern property and social relations "frees the slave and ignores the Negro." At McKinney's hands,

those of 1930s Black radicals, the labor movement, and the
left-wing parties, African American "wage-slaves" of the 1930s
were now to receive that same treatment.[24]

III.

Just as Abram Harris traversed an intellectual course from
labor critic to advocate of a "progressive" labor alliance, so did
other young Black radical intellectuals somewhat later. But
their paths were not the same. Some, such as John P. Davis,
had adhered to a distinctly non-political outlook that
Langston Hughes vaguely described as "burn[ing] up a lot of the
old, dead conventional Negro-white ideas of the past." At
that time, during the height of the cultural movement among
African Americans known as the Harlem Renaissance, Davis
had been far more concerned with the plight of young Black
intellectuals and artists in their struggle to overcome the
domination of the older generation in town. In the summer of
1926, Davis joined writers Langston Hughes and Zora Neal
Hurston in the publication of a short-lived journal of the
Harlem Renaissance, *Fire*. Davis handled the business end. In
the fall, he returned to his studies at Harvard Law School.
There he rejoined a circle of Black graduate students in the
New England area in the early Thirties, featuring such young
Black intellectuals as Robert Weaver and Ralph Bunche, both
of whom were graduate students at Harvard. Through his
association with the artistic and academic world, Davis was
connected to both groups of Black intellectuals who would
converge around the Harris program.[25]

In late 1928, while Harris was already applying himself
to working out a program for Black labor, John P. Davis had
asked, "Why shouldn't Negro labor organize to defeat every
attempt of white labor to bargain collectively with capital?
Why shouldn't we join in the cutthroat game and help capital
throttle white labor?" Davis soon received an unexpected
answer to his rhetorical questions in the form of the Great
Depression, which exposed the illusions of some Black

intellectuals that white capitalists were the Black workers' ally.[26]

Now, with world capitalism sinking, or seeming to sink, all the world's laboring classes, and at least a good section of its non-laboring classes, into hopeless and indiscriminate misery, young Black radicals like Davis began to see the problem in the capitalist system. "The depression did not visit us by accident," Davis declared. "Economic laws caused it." Capitalism, driven by the irresistible urge for profit, ground more work out of its slaves, mechanized to a fever pitch, and kept a lid on wages: "In a word [it sought to] squeeze out of the working class progressively larger amounts of the wealth, they *and they alone* produce." The young Black radicals, like their white radical comrades, became dedicated "underconsumptionists." The "Nature of the Solution," Davis declared, was to be found in the "increased buying power" of the masses.[27]

Davis's colleagues at Harvard came to substantially the same conclusion. Ralph Bunche, who once looked to Du Bois and his NAACP for guidance, now sought his solutions elsewhere. He proclaimed that "the collapse of the capitalist structures under the world-wide depression brought out, in bold relief, the sharp class antagonisms which the developing capitalistic economies had nurtured." This reflected the "basic dilemma of capitalism":

> Either capitalism must surrender itself to intelligent planning and scientific social planning, (and this it cannot do, for such planning involves a single ownership of the means of production for use rather than for profit), or else it must blunder on, repeating the same errors and perpetuating the rigidities which inevitably lead a poorly planned industrial society into periodic depression.

Bunche and Davis, as Harris before them, came to believe that capitalism had to be scrapped.[28]

Davis in these circumstances, as Bunche and his fellow Black radicals, concluded that, at root, the "Negro Question" was "an ECONOMIC not RACIAL problem." Yet the young Black radicals, casting aside Du Bois's skepticism as symptomatic of his essential conservatism, fell back on such arguments as, in Davis words, "There could be no such thing as *White Prosperity and Black Poverty.*" Naively, they assumed that any structural changes would, virtually automatically, include African Americans. They forgot for the moment, in their enthusiasm, how many times, as recently as World War I, the promised changes had not disturbed America's long-standing "peculiarity." Ernest Rice McKinney expressed the common conviction of the young Black radicals when he declared, "It never dawned on the white toilers in the capitalist vineyard that the Black wage slaves were part and parcel of them. I believe though that three years of unemployment will create a new outlook." In their minds, if not in practice, three years had been enough to undo the work of three hundred.[29]

Before the convergence around Harris's labor program could be complete, however, the young radicals had first to convince themselves that nothing could be gained from attempting to work through and in the New Deal administration, which seemed to hold the promise of faster results. The idea generally existed among the African-American graduate students at Harvard that Blacks needed to organize to get fair treatment under the New Deal's recovery apparatus. Together with fellow Harvard graduate Robert Weaver, Davis stepped forward with a proposal to take definite measures. Upon their graduation, in the summer of 1933, the two founded the Negro Industrial League, which sought "to insure the protection of the interests of the race in such measures as are taken" by the Roosevelt Administration. At the time they believed that this task meant participating in the National Recovery Administration code hearings.[30]

The object of the most concern for Black political leaders and intellectuals like Davis was the National Industrial Recovery Act, the legislation that advertised itself as a plan to protect workers while getting the nation's productive sector back into shape, and what is known today under such names as "Reconstruction Programs." Black leaders viewed it as promising only the perpetuation of their suffering. As the Urban League's T. Arnold Hill wrote, "In leaving agricultural and industrial employees out of the [NRA] code formula, the bulk of the Negro workers . . . will continue to live under a system which is little better than slavery."[31]

The provisions of the Act established the National Recovery Administration to set minimum wage and maximum hour standards for the industries under its jurisdiction. At hearings held by the NRA, the fate of hundreds of thousands of Black workers was being debated by New Deal officials and representatives of industry. Unfortunate for the overwhelmingly unorganized Black workers, reasoned Davis, no one represented their interests at these code hearings. Neither the National Association for the Advancement of Colored People nor Hill's own Urban League had attended a single session.[32]

The Negro Industrial League took up an issue that no other African-American group would, but that did not make the paper organization any stronger than Weaver's research and Davis's legal briefs. After a few months with the League, Davis decided that organizational unity among Black groups presented the only chance for effectiveness and sought a coalition. In July, shortly after the League had set itself up in Washington, Davis had already contacted both of the traditional "race" organizations, the NAACP and the Urban League, for a "pooling of interests." Davis believed he needed to attract the backing of the NAACP because of its prestige in the fight for the advancement of African Americans. But he also wanted to involve church and fraternal groups, which had contact with the greatest number of African Americans.[33]

Davis envisioned a "powerful Negro lobby" that would be able to "speak with authority for the major organized forces among Negroes, that [could] speak quickly and intelligently." Davis was specifically interested in getting Black representation on New Deal commissions, in ensuring active attendance at all NRA code hearings, in establishing working relationships with some influential officers within the various New Deal agencies, and in achieving equal treatment for Blacks under the agencies' programs.[34]

The Urban League declined Davis's invitation, but the NAACP, amid complicated circumstances, tentatively accepted. Under Walter White's leadership, the NAACP was conducting a campaign to dissociate itself from its founder W.E.B. Du Bois, editor of *The Crisis*. At the time Davis approached the NAACP with the idea of a coalition, the struggle between Du Bois and White had come to a head. Du Bois had realized the devastating effects of the Depression on Black people and insisted that the Association had to address their economic condition. Du Bois sounded a stern warning to White and his associates that the NAACP faced "a time of crisis and change, without a program, without effective organization, without executive officers who have the ability or disposition to guide the [NAACP] in the right direction." Adam Clayton Powell, Jr., the influential pastor of the Abyssinian Baptist Church in Harlem, succinctly summed up his feelings, "Our own NAACP has sold us out." With the resulting pressure on White to salvage the NAACP's revered position in the Black community, Davis's proposal offered an opportunity to show interest in an area for which the NAACP had developed no program. White agreed to "cooperate in this joint effort only for the period necessary for examination of the various codes being submitted to the NRA. . . . At the present time we do not anticipate that this period need be longer than the estimated six months set forth in the tentative budget dating from August 1, 1933."[35]

Davis's agreement with the NAACP meant the birth of the Joint Committee on National Recovery. Officially launched September 15, 1933, the JCNR continued its lobbying until the founding of the National Negro Congress in February, 1936. From the beginning, Davis served as the executive secretary and only full-time officer of the Joint Committee, which numbered twenty-one national organizations, mostly church and fraternal groups, in late 1933 and grew to a maximum of twenty-four by early 1935. The coalition did not represent an attempt to integrate the activities of the constituent groups in areas other than research and lobbying. There was no attempt at leading a mass movement on the issues it treated. Its responsibilities included only gathering information on the economic and social conditions in which Blacks lived, presenting the information to the appropriate

New Deal agencies and commissions, and arousing public opinion to push for "remedial action" by the government.[36]

To Davis, the threat to give federal approval to lower wage minima for Blacks in certain, mainly Southern, industries under NRA codes posed the most immediate danger to Black interests and represented the most urgent matter for the Joint Committee to address. The immense pressures being exerted by industries for lower wage standards specifically for Blacks portended calamitous results, Black radicals declared. Hill warned that such circumstances could lead to "actual warfare at a time when it takes little to foment either racial or industrial discord." Robert C. Weaver, who had moved on to a post in the Interior Department, showed the direction in which the thinking of young Black radicals had moved, in proclaiming: "It would . . . destroy the possibility of *a real labor movement* in this country."[37]

Davis's stiff opposition to the plan helped bring about its defeat. In late 1933 the NRA gathered together a group of twenty prominent Black leaders at Howard University in order to gain their sanction for the proposed differential. Thirty employees of the NRA attempted to persuade the Black representatives to agree to their terms by implying that a refusal would be tantamount to accepting the responsibility for mass displacement of Black workers. Davis had just arrived in Washington from an intensive month-long fact-finding tour of the South to attend the meeting, to which he had not been invited. He presented a thorough case against the wage-differential proposal, citing the sub-poverty conditions under which Blacks in the South already toiled. In the end no African American present agreed to go on record supporting the NRA officials' position. Subsequently, the affair was kept out of all but the Black press. Raymond Wolters, in assessing Davis's achievement as advocate of Black workers in government conference rooms, writes, "Largely as a result of [the Joint Committee's] agitation, the NRA decided that it would not be advisable to give the sanction of federal approval to lower wage and hour standards for Black workers. In every case the requests of Southern businessmen were denied."[38]

But even this greatest "moral" victory claimed by the Joint
Committee in its two and a half years was only partial. When
denied the direct course, resort was made to covert means of
achieving the same end. Lower wage minima were set for the
South, where three-fourths of Blacks lived. In addition, Davis
pointed out that jobs performed solely or mainly by Black
workers were also singled out for lower wage scales. On these
backhanded manners of keeping the wages of Black workers
lower than those of whites, the government would not relent.
Although Davis attended over one hundred code hearings, he
achieved only the most meager of practical results, by his own
standards, from these lobbying efforts.[39]

Nor did the efforts of Black radicals within the
government achieve any more. Davis's idea, apparently, had
been to push the government into action on behalf of Blacks, not
to push his way into the government. But Davis had been
particularly interested in the appointment of African
Americans to the NRA. Abram Harris became the only Black
so named in the history of that agency. The appointment of the
Howard University Economics professor to the Consumer
Advisory Board followed negotiations with the Joint
Committee, and according to Davis, came only "after repeated
refusals of General Johnson to appoint any Negro to the Labor
Advisory Board." Harris, however, soon resigned his post to
demonstrate his lack of faith in its administration. Davis
reported that when Harris "resigned in disgust," he declared,
"The only solution involves a change in class relationships, . . .
government by the workers and farmers." Davis evidently
came to the same conclusion during this period and joined the
Communist Party.[40]

Davis found himself in agreement with Harris, despite the
latter's distrust of the communists, on other points as well.
Believing all other options exhausted, Davis also pinned all
his hopes on labor. Davis observed that "more flagrant are
violations of laws affecting the Negro's economic life in the
South than are those affecting his civil rights." Pointing out,
in discussing the NRA's textile code, that white workers also
suffered, he developed wherein the difference lay: "For [white
workers] there was also the twofold opportunity of escape into

a better paid occupation, and improvement of conditions through collective bargaining." On another occasion Davis noted that one of the reasons behind the poor living conditions of the Negro was that "Negro workers are not organized." Davis did not, however, quite abandon the notion that the fight had to be waged on a racial basis as well. He insisted, "Superimposed upon the heavy burdens we must bear because we are workers, is another burden we must bear because we are Negroes." Hence, he would believe a little more strongly than Harris in the necessity of separate Black organizations.[41]

During the time Davis spent intensively researching the situation of the Black worker, through his many travels across the nation to look into their conditions, his experiences had driven home for him the necessity of Black membership in trade unions. His many endeavors on behalf of the Black worker in the meeting rooms, code hearings and offices of government would ultimately lead him to the conclusion that the interests of Black workers could only be secured by ending the economic injustices they faced. Davis studied the experiences of Black workers with organized labor and wrote a monograph entitled "The Negro in Labor Struggles Since the New Deal." He compiled the results of strikes in many industries where Blacks worked in significant numbers. He concluded on the basis of highly selective evidence gathered mainly from newspaper reports that "Negro workers [have] given definite statements of the falsehood of the allegation that Negro workers are scabs, that they will not organize. . . . [T]he record of the Negro union man . . . is one worthy of the highest praise."[42]

His developing left-wing views and radical connections caught the immediate attention of those in the NAACP. In October, 1934, NAACP treasurer Mary White Ovington wrote to Walter White, Davis "has seen the absurdity of the Social Welfare present method of relieving labor and he knows there must be something drastic [done to change it]." Charles Houston of the NAACP warned, "The only way the [NAACP] is going to keep [Davis] from running off with the show--unless he breaks his neck in the meantime, which is always possible with John-- is for the [NAACP] to put on a bigger and better performance of its own." With his adept maneuvering, Davis had established himself as the political leader of the young Black radicals, just as Harris was their intellectual leader.[43]

Davis understood that the Black masses wanted and needed results. Davis counselled his fellow radicals, "Today we must show them that we will not fail. Tomorrow they may not listen to us." Harris sensed the same thing. Harris, therefore, all the while had been stirring the ground in the NAACP. At a time when Du Bois was forced out for excessive radicalism, Harris sought to convert the Association to his program. The NAACP, in the throes of a crisis of legitimacy, was searching for a means to convince its followers and the Black community at large of its commitment to practical action in the face of the crisis. The committee it formed to draw up a proposal for a new program became just the vehicle Harris needed to publicize his cause in the Black radical community. To cement the connection, he proposed Davis be brought in to edit *The Crisis* in the wake of Du Bois's resignation. His strategy worked perfectly, as Black radicals soon rallied around the "Harris Report." This report, as concerned Black labor, was but a slightly modified version of the one Harris had presented to the CPLA. Once again Harris stressed education of white and Black workers to promote unity of labor. This time, however, Harris included a nod toward the specific concerns of African Americans, including the prevention of lynching and the elimination of "public discrimination and Jim Crowism" among the "immediate problems" that required reform legislation. Although the NAACP proved lukewarm at best, it seemed of minor importance as Harris's plan for encouraging labor organization found a ready audience among his Howard University colleagues, and Howard became the center of, first, the Howard Conference on the Economic Crisis and the Negro, and then the subsequent founding of the NNC. The radicals believed that they were on their way to something "bigger and better."[44]

Chapter VI
The Black Radical Consensus Program for Black Labor, Part II

The emergence of the young radical convergence around the Harris program, with its neo-Debsian approach to the "Negro Question," at the same time that the ABB internationalists were pushed out of the communist movement, set the stage for a new organizational form around the emergent radical consensus program for Black labor. The young radicals, for their part, had failed in their bid to take over the NAACP and so lacked a vehicle to put their program into practice. Whatever potential may have existed in Du Bois's NAACP, which had traditional ties to the Socialist Party, it was no longer Du Bois's, and no longer open to them. The National Urban League, though home or former home to several of the radicals, including Harris, was too closely associated with business interests to be converted into a base of operations for labor organizing. And John P. Davis's Joint Committee on National Recovery, as a lobby entirely dependent on the good will of the NAACP, which was now virtually precluded, was also no longer an option. Besides, with the NRA having been struck down by the Supreme Court, it had become virtually defunct, its sole justification having disappeared.

On its side, the Communist Party also lacked the organizational means to attract African Americans. The internal struggles had, to all intents and purposes, destroyed the League of Struggle for Negro Rights. Moreover, the Stalinist Comintern was in the formative period of its "Popular

Front" line, by which member parties were instructed to band together with all "democratic" forces in the struggle against fascism. This line declared the need for the communists to rally "broad forces" around the "anti-fascist" crusade, which the American party could not hope to do in its own name. New organizational forms would be required.

In a complete turnaround from its former policy in regard to African Americans, therefore, the CP opted for an organizational expression of the "Popular Front" among African Americans with a program bearing as little resemblance as possible to the party's own. James Ford went on record advocating a National Negro Congress, and that party's press regularly pushed the idea throughout the spring of 1935. But beyond thus bequeathing the name, and the all-important funding and connections it could provide, the CP, never greatly interested in what it called "Negro work," was more than willing to leave the organization to others. And since it took little interest in the Congress' program, it was left to the young radicals to make the NNC what they wanted it to be: the organizational expression of their Black labor program.[1]

The formation of the NNC was put, therefore, entirely in Davis's hands, and he brought the combined forces of the young Black radical trend to bear on the task. First of all, Davis wrung one last act out of his dying Joint Committee. He had the NAACP and other backers agree, before they withdrew, to fund a final project, a national conference to look into the conditions of Black workers and bring to light all the relevant facts. Howard University, home to a number of Davis's radical comrades, was to be the site, and its Social Science Department, headed by Ralph Bunche, its co-sponsor. Invitations were dispersed widely, with Davis and Bunche intimating a larger purpose in declaring that "the conference is definitely not interested in research for research's sake. Our purpose is to find out the present social and economic conditions of the Negro in America, to determine their effect on our whole national economy and to act on the basis of this data."[2]

A month before the May 1935 conference, Davis made public his intention to use the Howard Conference to launch the National Negro Congress. He ended an article for the

NAACP's *Crisis* by sounding the call for such a Congress, and mailed advance copies to two hundred or so prominent African-American figures. The article was also widely reprinted in the Black press.[3]

The appeal the idea of a national congress held for African Americans evidently surprised even Davis, who was used to behind-the-scenes negotiations on behalf of the masses, rather than appeals to those masses. He reported before the Conference took place that his call was "surprisingly well received." Endorsements came in from, among others, the Rev. Adam Clayton Powell, Senior, the influential pastor of the Abyssinian Baptist Church in Harlem; A. Philip Randolph, president of the Brotherhood of Sleeping Car Porters; and Elmer A. Carter, editor of the Urban League's organ, *Opportunity*.[4]

Some of the letters sent to Davis suggested a growing militant mood among Black workers and laborers and those who sought to represent them. Elbert W. Moore, Minister of the Second Baptist Church in Columbus, Ohio, stressed that the Congress, if it would succeed, had to address the "forgotten man," the Black worker, and focus on action-oriented political discussion. He joined his voice to the increasingly radical sentiments emanating from church groups, explaining that "the Negro church is dependent upon wage earners for support, therefore [the worker's] minister should be your best supporter financially and otherwise." A minister, he continued, had to back a National Negro Congress "if he believes what he preaches." In expressing another common sentiment, he said that he did not "consider any Negro in the employ of the present administration competent to advise me what to do," but that he had confidence in Davis' leadership abilities. Joel M. Miles, Secretary-Treasurer of the Association of Rock Island Dining Car Employees of Chicago, declared that the new generation of Black youth would not follow the old "corrupt leadership." In order to gain broad support, Miles, in also signalling a growing grass-roots militancy, suggested that a new organization must have "revolutionary" leadership. Miles predicted that the success of the NNC would be foretold by the Howard Conference. It probably would have pleased Miles to

know that the centerpiece of the conference would be Harris's
program for Black labor.[5]

II.

Under the direction of Davis and Ralph Bunche, the three-
day Conference took on such a radical tinge that even the U.S.
Congress became concerned.[6] Left-wing rhetoric echoed through
the conference halls packed by the nearly two hundred fifty
participants, and representatives of the Communist, Socialist,
and Workers parties shared the stage with academics and New
Deal bureaucrats.[7]

Davis signalled the left slant within his opening address:
"I believe the conclusion will be inescapable that there must be
an immediate change in emphasis from protection of private
property to protection of human beings from misery and
poverty." He then quoted an indictment of the capitalist
system from a report by the New York East Methodist
Episcopal Church saying the attempt "to reform the system has
only proved that it is beyond reform. The conviction grows,
therefore, that capitalism must be discarded." The report
further decried "the tenderness with which the sacred cow of
private profits has been protected while suffering has been
indescribably inhuman."[8]

After Davis sounded the tocsin against the capitalist mode
of production, Bunche read its epitaph. The New Deal, he
proclaimed, with its "illogical, inconsistent, vague, and
confused" basis, was but the attempt to save capitalism,
necessitated by "the collapse of the economic structures" of old
along with the sharpening of class struggle. Insofar as it took
measures to save the capitalists, it ran into conflict with the
workers. When it tried to take the laborers' side, it acted
against the capitalists' needs.

The dilemma of the New Deal, then, merely
reflects the dilemma of capitalism. Either capitalism
must surrender itself to intelligent and scientific social
planning, (and this it cannot do for such planning
involves a single ownership of the means of production

for use rather than profit), or else it must blunder on, repeating the old errors and perpetuating the rigidities which inevitably lead a poorly planned industrial society into periodic depression.

Hence, Bunche told the Howard audience, state planning without class conflict--socialism, as the less theoretically-inclined termed it--or the constant repetition of disaster. He left no doubt, despite his use of the "neutral" terminology habitual to the academic, which side he, and anyone with any sense, should bet on.[9]

But the young radicals had more in mind than denouncing capitalism and predicting its quick demise. They wanted, above all, to set down the way forward--the Harris program. While Harris attended the conference and provided commentary, it was left to his Howard University colleague, Emmett Dorsey, to present the radicals' program to the assemblage. Dorsey announced his agreement with Davis and Bunche that capitalism was irredeemable. He continued, "The only tenable economic program for Negroes at this moment is one that is pointed in the direction of a transformation of our economic system and the de-segregation of the Negro population." Such a course meant "united action by white and black workers" toward the ultimate goal of "political power." He finished his presentation by reading the entire Harris program, which he described as the best "program of economic planning for the Negro." The central thrust of the Harris program, to educate white and Black workers that their only salvation was joint action and the only place to work it out was in the "progressive unions," became the theme at the Howard Conference, which set the agenda of the National Negro Congress.[10]

The Harris program's call for organizing African-American workers into unions together with white workers received support from almost every speaker for its potential for improving the plight of Black workers. Even those expressing reservations, such as Du Bois, questioned only the potential for its implementation, rather than the soundness of the idea. Proponents, on the other hand, agreed with Dorsey that the only path out of the current crisis was for the Black masses to identify their interests with those of the white workers through labor organization. Unionization was heralded as a solution for all Black workers, including those in agriculture and domestic service. Speakers pointed out the recent efforts and limited successes in organizing both agricultural and domestic workers.[11]

When A. Philip Randolph, as the most famous African-American trade union official, called for the organization of Black workers in his presentation, it came as no surprise; but when formerly anti-union Black leaders did so, it represented a harbinger of things to come. Thus, for example, T. Arnold Hill of the National Urban League proclaimed the organization of Black workers "the only way out." This high-ranking official of the traditionally conservative and pro-business Urban League exemplified the deep roots that the 1930s brand of Black radicalism had struck among young Black intellectuals since the Depression had descended, in declaring:

> We have talked of organization in the past; we have made half-hearted attempts toward it. Our mistake has been that we have sought to organize Negroes on the basis of race and race alone. This can never be successfully done, for interests of Negroes within the race are as divergent as are the interests of all white workers and Americans in general. It is futile for the Negro workers to wait for Negro intellectuals, college professors, businessmen, artists, and poets to realize the essential solidarity of their economic interests. . . . If workers are to have organization to protect their special interests, they must organize as workers.

Calling attention to the "progressive unionism" movement on the verge of triumph, Hill declared, "Within the ranks of organized labor, philosophies and techniques are being set up which presage a new and dominant labor movement. Such a movement will need the Negro's labor strength." And, while Hill did not share the prevalent view on the imminent demise of capitalism, he could agree that "Negroes must secure the organized cooperation of white workers with black workers in the interest of all labor."[12]

One exchange served to underscore the level of commitment to the Harris program's vision of the efficacy of a strong interracial union movement. Although he spoke in favor of Black participation in organized labor, Howard A. Myers, executive director of the labor advisory board of the NRA, was attacked for blaming the lack of organized Black workers on white workers, rather than on employers or racist and reactionary labor leaders. When asked, following his speech, what he considered to be the cause of the discrimination by white workers against Blacks, Myers answered that, being an economist and not a psychologist, he did not know. Lester Granger of the Urban League ridiculed that answer, admonishing Myers to "stop joking your audience." Granger advised him that economic causes were at the root of the "cut-throat competition": the lack of jobs and income. Granger put the blame squarely on the "employers and the system behind the employers." A Black worker added that "the only good thing the National Run Around has done has been to draw Negro and white workers together." Nor did dominant radicals accept Myers' view that white labor leaders within the AFL were "tireless in their efforts" to organize Black workers.[13]

Representatives of the Socialist, Communist and Workers parties expressed the pointedly pro-labor viewpoints of the organized left. Their presence emphasized Davis' point that the radicals would not limit their inquiry "to the scope of any present system of national economy." While their messages varied, what was more striking, in view of the past differences between social democrats, Stalinists, and Trotskyists, was how similar their programs had become, and how much they resembled that of the young radicals.[14]

James Ford, representing the Communist Party, gave the most extensive analysis of the three, grounding the current problem in the same historical context of economic oppression given by other speakers. In fact, the major difference setting off Ford's talk was the ultimate, and attention-getting, solution of revolution, which the Black press immediately picked up on. In the main however, his presentation conformed to the prevalent views at the conference: organizational unity of

African-Americans with the working class, Black-white unity, and the urgent need for the organization into unions of Black industrial workers, agriculturalists, domestics and the unemployed. He pointed to the encouraging movement within the AFL, which would within a few months result in the formation of the CIO, as a call to arms for Black workers and all African Americans. He ended by repeating Davis's call for a National Negro Congress, the only other speaker to do so. Ford's speech confirmed that the CP fully endorsed the Black radical consensus program for Black workers and the organizational direction it was taking.[15]

Speaking for the Trotskyist Workers Party, Ernest Rice McKinney, who like Ford would become a figure in the movement to build the NNC, put the struggle in the context of the impending doom of capitalism. He argued that not only could the Black workers not follow the direction of other sections of the African American community, but they had to cut all ties with the "the Negro ruling class." Like Ford, McKinney spoke in general terms of revolution. On the other hand, McKinney distinguished himself from all but Du Bois, and also from his pre-Trotskyist Musteite CPLA thinking, in stating, "The Workers Party rejects . . . the spurious doctrine that the Negro worker has no special problems and can be treated *en masse* just as a worker." What conclusion did McKinney draw from this? Rather illogically, McKinney repeated the old socialist position he had just criticized by name: "The Negro worker must realize his class position as a worker and not attempt to maintain a race position as a Negro first, last, and always." To eliminate any doubt about his neo-Debsian credentials, McKinney explicitly rejected nationalism or any form of African-American self-determination. McKinney signalled that he, the leading Black Trotskyist, remained in the camp of the young radicals ideologically and stood ready to join in their organizational enterprises.[16]

In contrast, Norman Thomas's speech on behalf of the Socialist Party, read in his absence, generated little enthusiasm for the topic. Naturally Thomas repeated the age-old position of American socialism on the Negro Question, "The Negro in overwhelming mass is a worker, and his salvation is bound up with the triumph of the working class." The only new twist to this declaration was that, in an ironic sign of the times, James Ford cited Thomas's words as a step in the right direction by the socialists. Thomas held out the possibility of nothing more concrete than the success of some organization "far mightier than the present Socialist Party," and, if only by omission, eloquently expressed the SP's lack of interest in the young radicals' cause. Thomas's position, in its authority as the SP "line," helps to explain, perhaps, the distance loyal Black socialists A. Philip Randolph and Frank Crosswaith would maintain to the young radicals and NNC, at the very time the younger group had come around to very nearly the socialist position.[17]

In contrast to the favorable reception of the left-wing parties, existing Black political organizations came in for pointed criticism for the inadequacy of their response to the Depression conditions. In his address, Du Bois blamed the NAACP's failure to work out an economic program to aid Blacks on the Association's dependence upon white liberals. In explaining the organization's inability to lead Blacks, he argued that "agitation and legal defense must be kept up so far as possible but that possibility at present has its limitations." Emmett Dorsey agreed that the Black masses "have lost their faith in the NAACP." He charged that its "one-time militancy is rapidly evaporating and its ideology is becoming increasingly tenuous." He argued that the NAACP had adopted the attitude of a "priestly caste" among Blacks and had abandoned the Black workers to pursue middle class goals, in common with the Urban League, the Garvey Movement, the churches, and the lodges.[18]

By far the least popular were those who had the misfortune to be associated with the Roosevelt administration. The *Afro-American* reported, "Although government officials spoke on New Deal policies, practically all discussion and many of the other papers denounced the administration setup." A comment by a government representative under intense questioning revealed the pointedness of the attacks: "It is my job to meet the people and make excuses for what we don't do. . . . I wish that I could tell you that there will be no more

discrimination, but I can't. I am up against a stone wall."
Bunche concluded that the New Deal would only "crystallize
those abuses and oppressions which the exploited Negro
citizenry of America have long suffered under laissez-faire
capitalism." He would not accept the idea that the problems
Blacks faced under the New Deal had to be weighed against
the general good, saying that such logic amounted to telling
Blacks to "stay in our own BLACK yards." He believed that
the conference "discredited" New Deal defenders.[19]

The other favorite target for abuse was W.E.B. Du Bois,
whose program was, in the words of the Baltimore *Afro-
American*, "ripped . . . to pieces" by Professors Harris and
Dorsey, with Dorsey inflicting a "severe tongue-lashing" for
good measure. What had Du Bois said to occasion such abuse?
He had done nothing less heretical, in the eyes of the vocal
majority, than question the efficacy of a white-Black labor
alliance, which constituted the unanimous theme among the
young radicals at the conference, and was heartily defended by,
among others, Harris, Dorsey, Davis, Bunche, Lester Granger,
T. Arnold Hill, Ernest Rice McKinney, and James Ford. Du Bois
made no attempt to mend fences. He began by launching
straight into the then organizational base of the young
radicals, Davis's JCNR, co-organizer of the conference in its
last meaningful act. With his usual perspicacity on matters of
these kind, where they did not involve his own efforts, for
example, with the League of Nations and African colonies, he
charged:

> Of the fact of discrimination [under the NRA], the
> Joint Committee has unearthed ample proof, but as to
> what we are going to do about it, the Joint Committee,
> quite naturally, has nothing to say and nothing to
> think. Indeed, everything that has happened in the
> NRA and the New Deal might easily have been
> foretold before the NRA was established.

Here Du Bois had undoubtedly put his finger on the divergence
of program and action that lay at the core of the radical
consensus. How could this fight for justice under the New Deal
possibly win when, according to the radicals' own claims, the
New Deal was designed to uphold the prevailing system,

which was undoubtedly founded on the oppression of African Americans? But Du Bois did not stop with the pointing out of the folly of their recent political efforts. He went on to attack their plans for action. They could talk about the need for African Americans to forge an alliance with labor. "This, however, is not nearly as easy as it might seem." He pointed out, "the farmers and servants who compose the mass of the workers among colored people are not organized" even among whites. Obviously, African Americans were excluded from the majority of unions. And if the focus were to be on those that "recognize something of the real solidarity of labor interests," to call such a small percentage of Black and white workers "a labor alliance, is seriously to overstate the case." With this trenchant criticism Du Bois no doubt touched a raw nerve. It was well and good to talk, but which unions were initiating drives to organize Black workers? Even after the CIO was formed a few months later, when did they mention a word about any such concrete campaign? But Du Bois offered no alternative to African American workers. While he professed to be "convinced of the essential truth of the Marxian philosophy," he believed all revolutionary or meaningful avenues of change to be cut off.[20]

In his own way, Du Bois was merely raising the question that the ABB had long ago posed: what were to be the terms of the Black-labor alliance? And here he and all others who mentioned, not the biological, but the social, the actual significance of race, uncovered the shallowness of the Harris program and the understanding that undergirded it. Adherents of Harris's program all started from the same premise, the *complete, inseparable, identity* of the "interests" of Black and white workers (or at least the white workers represented by the so-called "progressives").

Taken to its logical end, it amounted to a denial of the social significance of race almost altogether. When African-American sociologist George Haynes suggested that the different "folkways" of African Americans had to be taken into account, he elicited the following categorical statement from Harris: "When you adopt that point of view, you will have to approach our people differently from the method of approaching the whites. We know that leads us up a blind alley." Emmett Dorsey put it this way, "The economic plight of the American Negro is that of the American working class." The "Harris Report" stated essentially the same idea: "[T]he special grievances [of African Americans are] . . . a natural part of the larger issues of American labor as a whole." This view of the young Black radicals accorded very well with the developing position within the CP. The complete negation of the ABB position had been reached, not only by white leaders in the CP, but by Black radicals: It was not the duty of the white workers to lend every possible aid to the liberation struggle of the Black workers (of the world); rather, it was the duty of the Black workers to rally behind (a section of) the white workers' fight for their (the white workers') own immediate economic interests, that is, for a program of mild reform. Couched in radical phrases though it might be, it still came down to that reality in the end. As Du Bois had pointed out, and as Black communists had argued for some time in the Twenties and early Thirties, to strike a blow for Black liberation meant to do it in the South, among the agricultural workers. To bring about the organization of the industrial workers of the North without touching the conditions of the Black masses of the South was to complete the formation of a two-tiered working class: one with at least some interest in the continued growth of the prevailing state of affairs; the other completely against it. And despite its expressions of concern for the southern Black proletariat, this was precisely what the NNC was to sanction, however inadvertently, in practice.[21]

At a meeting hosted by Ralph Bunche following the final session of the conference, a group of the most prominent figures began to plan the Congress. Davis was named temporary secretary and was joined on the initiating committee by, among others, Charles H. Houston, an executive officer of the NAACP; William H. Hastie, a member of the NAACP's National Legal Committee; Dean Kelly Miller of Howard; Ralph Bunche and Alain Locke of Howard, Reginald Johnson of the Urban League; and Nina Roberts of the YWCA. The purpose of the committee was to draft a proposal for the Congress to serve as the basis for a nation-wide discussion to seek "a common agreement as to what steps shall be taken." Only then would the call be issued.[22]

Those who had looked to the Howard Conference for seemingly radical solutions were not disappointed. Kelly Miller, frequently subjected to attacks for his conservative views and finding himself very much alone on the radical-dominated NNC committee, lamented after the conference, "Surely, we are moving to the left." The young radicals had, through the Howard Conference, succeeded in putting their Harris program at the top of the agenda of the National Negro Congress. Fortuitously, the events that unfolded within organized labor between the establishment of the initiating committee and the convening of the Congress put the radicals' goal of an alliance with organized labor within their immediate reach.[23]

III.

The movement to build the National Negro Congress coincided with heightened efforts to end discrimination in the American Federation of Labor. After its early racially liberal policy in the last two decades of the nineteenth century, the AFL had assumed a posture hostile to the efforts of Blacks to join unions on an equal basis with whites. As many as eight affiliates of the AFL excluded Blacks from membership by constitutional bars. Still others found more indirect but just as effective means to exclude them. The AFL leadership, under Gompers' successor, William Green, an ostensible liberal hailing from the United Mine Workers, did nothing to change the situation, claiming it had no authority to meddle in the affairs of the member internationals. When, in the Twenties, delegations representing Black organizations met with the AFL executive council, the Black leaders were told that the low level of Black unionization was the fault of Blacks themselves for adopting anti-union positions. Green and his colleagues did little to dissociate themselves from the charges frequently made at AFL conventions that Blacks were natural strikebreakers and refused to join unions. The AFL's policies had so alienated leading Blacks that many feared that by allowing it to win exclusive bargaining rights without compelling it to admit Blacks the NRA was putting the government's sanction to its Jim-Crow policies. W.E.B. Du Bois registered his contention in *The Crisis* in late 1933 that "the most sinister power that the N.R.A. has reinforced is the American Federation of Labor." About the same time, the Joint Committee turned its attention to what Davis referred to in his monthly report to the executive committee as "the worst offender against Negro workers." Davis contacted Green in order to initiate "a definite rapprochement of all labor, regardless of race," but nothing came of his effort.[24]

During the AFL convention of 1934 the critics outside labor joined with a floor movement spearheaded by A. Philip Randolph. Randolph had been seeking to reform the AFL's policy toward Blacks from the inside at conventions for several years as head of the delegation of the Brotherhood of Sleeping Car Porters. At the 1934 annual meeting in San Francisco, he would have many allies. Black unionists were in a militant mood, following a protracted strike among longshoremen of the city in which African Americans had played an active role and shared in the benefits of the victory. Similar scenarios of Black-white worker unity, often despite the presence of Jim-Crow unions, had been enacted in Seattle, and Camden and Seabrook, New Jersey. The African Americans were joined by a small but vocal left-wing rank-and-file movement demanding to know why African Americans played key roles in labor struggles but were not granted equal, or any, status in the unions. In addition, the NAACP, just then feeling the pressure of Harris's campaign to radicalize it, cooperated with other local Black leaders and some of the Black longshoreman to picket the convention hall.[25]

Adding to the already charged atmosphere, a committee of workers submitted a resolution calling for complete equality for Black unionists, which the convention unceremoniously voted down. Randolph then added a stirring indictment of the racial attitudes within the AFL and proposed a less sweeping resolution of his own. The Randolph Resolution called for the convention to announce itself in favor of "the elimination of the color clause and pledge from the constitutions and rituals of all trade and industrial unions." In addition, it demanded the expulsion of all unions which had such color bars inasmuch as they violated the federation's constitution. Finally, Randolph proposed that a commission be formed "to investigate the question of the status of Negro workers in [AFL] unions, and the general policy of the American Federation of Labor on the matter of organizing Negro workers, and report to the next convention its findings with recommendations to future policy in relation to Negro workers." Only the final measure was approved by the convention.[26]

The commission formed to study the matters finally convened in July, 1935, after much stalling by Green. Significantly, the Howard Conference had met two months before and the movement to build the National Negro Congress was underway. Moreover, presenting the case for Black labor were some of the same African-American leaders who had come together to call for the Congress, further pushing the Congress toward a key role in labor struggles. In addition to Randolph, speakers at the AFL hearing included Reginald Johnson of the Urban League, Charles Houston of the NAACP, and Davis, each of whom had participated in the initiation of the sponsoring committee. Their presentations emphasized that the AFL's policy and past record toward Blacks was insupportable and that changes were urgently needed. A prepared statement by the National Urban League placed the blame for the lack of organized Black workers on the leadership of AFL locals, rather than on rank-and-file whites or Blacks themselves, and excoriated the federation's leadership for sabotaging efforts at effecting change initiated by the NAACP and the Urban League. Houston, signalling the nearness at this time of this ideologically important NAACP officer to the position of his radical associates in the NNC, called upon the AFL to initiate an educational campaign to convince white workers to join forces with Black to organize all workers. He also endorsed, as did Randolph, a plan presented to the craft federation by Davis.[27]

The Davis proposal to which they lent their support included the provisions of the Randolph Resolution which

would have required the end to constitutional and de facto bans
against Black membership in any AFL affiliate, as well as the
hiring of Black organizers and the launching of an education
campaign among Black workers. In addition, Davis demanded
the integration of Black workers into the federation on a full
and equitable basis, calling for the end of Jim Crow locals and
the limited federal status given to such unions as the
Brotherhood of Sleeping Car Porters. He also proposed that
Black representation be assured on the AFL executive council,
and that the office staff of the headquarters be integrated.
Davis pointedly warned AFL leaders of the meaning of their
failure to act: "We may be forced to join with progressive forces
in the labor movement to oust any leader who persists in
discriminating against Negroes."[28]

Following the hearing, Green and the AFL leadership
moved swiftly to bury the commission's findings. Green
unilaterally blocked the holding of additional hearings
throughout the nation to collect more data. That suggestion
had been put forward by Houston and had gained the approval
of the Committee of Five, the name given to the Commission.
Instead, Green called for the commission to issue a final report.
That document did not include all the provisions of Davis'
plan, and what it did contain favorable to African Americans
was largely the work of the committee's secretary, John Brophy
of the United Mine Workers. But Brophy's efforts came to
naught. The executive council would not even abide by the
provisions of the resolution passed at the 1934 convention
which required the committee to present its findings to the 1935
convention. Green and the Executive Council suppressed the
document and offered in its place one drafted by George
Harrison of the "lily-white" Railway Clerks. Harrison
recommended only "education," and nowhere even mentioned
the Committee of Five. Incensed by this turn of events,
Randolph put up a fight. He read from the pronouncements of
the Committee of Five and insisted that it be put to a vote. But
the presiding officers rejected the report as not representing the
"spirit of this convention" and ended debate on the question.[29]

The controversy surrounding the Committee of Five came on
the last day and followed the pivotal showdown between craft

and industrial unionism. That conflict centered on whether workers should be organized into unions based on their occupation or the industry in which they worked. The federation leadership had traditionally recognized the jurisdiction of unions to all workers performing the particular craft, regardless of which industry employed them. That setup was favorable to those who truly performed a craft, such as carpenters. But those engaged in industry found it difficult to gain concessions from large corporations when the workers were divided into several unions, each under separate national leadership, and unskilled workers generally found themselves unrepresented. When the convention voted in favor of a resolution that effectively guaranteed craft unions continued control of any worker over whom they claimed jurisdiction, several of the largest industrial unions laid the foundations for what would become the Congress of Industrial Organizations.[30]

The new union movement potentially held great significance for Black workers. Most Black workers in industry were unskilled. Furthermore, the unions, most notably the United Mine Workers and the International Ladies' Garment Workers Union, that had already organized large numbers of Blacks led the industrial movement. The UMW, under John L. Lewis and John Brophy, were the real power behind the emergent AFL rival, and they had perhaps the most liberal attitude toward Blacks. Lewis openly favored the organization of Black workers. For the time being the formation would remain the Committee for Industrial Organization and would operate within the AFL. Its mere existence, however, outraged the craft-dominated federation, and within a year efforts began to expel the dissidents.[31]

Black leaders now at least had a choice of allegiance in pursuing their objective of encouraging the unionization of Black workers, and most were fed up with the AFL. Two years earlier Du Bois had predicted that if the AFL did not initiate a more enlightened policy toward Black workers, Blacks would join forces with "the mass of exploited laborers for an organization which represents their injuries and their wishes . . . [which would] sweep the A.F. of L. off the face of the earth." The answers that *The Crisis* published to its April,

1935 essay contest, "The Negro and Union Labor," revealed a refusal to accept the leadership of the AFL in light of its racial policies. First prize was awarded to a writer who, in opposing the position of the AFL, declared: "If union labor is to succeed in this country, it will have to organize Negroes on equal terms with whites. Otherwise, it invites its own destruction as well as that of the Negro." NAACP head Walter White's reaction to the events in Atlantic City underscored the far-reaching consequences within Black political organizations of the AFL's refusal to drop the color bar. In a letter to Lewis, the generally circumspect White announced, "The recent hypocritical attitude of the American Federation of Labor in suppressing the report of the Committee [of Five] . . . has destroyed the last vestige of confidence which Negro workers ever had in the AF of L."[32]

Yet, if the CIO would be the beneficiary of the contempt among African Americans for the AFL, the past record of CIO unions toward Blacks did not promote unreserved adulation. Several of the original eight affiliates did not share the liberal reputation of the United Mine Workers in matters of race. Moreover, the CIO's original statement of principles included no mention of African Americans. And even with their advanced position relative to other internationals, the UMW was not beyond reproach. Davis summarized the philosophy of the UMW officers as amounting to extreme opportunism: "'We will organize Negro workers to protect the interest of white workers, guaranteeing to them economic privileges. But we will not permit the trade unions to foster any change in the status quo of the Negro people.'" Moreover, Randolph, as head of the largest independent Black union, elected to keep his organization in the AFL, despite a personal invitation from Lewis to join the departing "progressive unionists." Still, the CIO represented to radicals, Black and white, the long-awaited culmination of the "progressive unionism" movement.[33]

IV.

The progressives in the AFL had done their part toward working class emancipation, now the radicals were determined to do theirs. Throughout the summer and fall of 1935, the National Negro Congress movement picked up strength. Endorsements came in from women's, civic, and professional organizations, church and fraternal groups, the Workers Councils of the National Urban League, and labor unions, including some AFL locals. The notable exception was the NAACP, which, despite the presence of some of its officers on the initiating committee, declined the invitation to participate in a coalition including the Left. But that did not stop various local chapters from supporting the Congress. In addition, such Black literary figures as Langston Hughes and Arna Bontemps offered their cooperation. Black newspapers and journals also aided the cause.[34]

The developments within organized labor, coming concurrently with the building of the National Negro Congress, solidified the position of the radicals' labor program at the top of the Congress' agenda. The point came out strongly in Davis's pamphlet, *Let Us Build a National Negro Congress*, which was published by the national sponsoring committee in October, 1935, and of which 50,000 copies were distributed. The thirty-one-page pamphlet was essentially a summary of the findings of the Howard Conference but reflected the feelings aroused by Green's handling of the Committee of Five hearing. Although written before the outcome of the AFL convention that month, it included direct references to the opportunity presented to Black workers and to the NNC by the developments in labor during the period leading up to it. Davis devoted one section to a discussion of the segregation practiced by the AFL unions, which often resulted in contracts specifically barring Blacks from particular jobs and industries. But despite the past record of organized labor, he emphasized that the Congress would throw its weight behind organizing Black workers, offsetting the effects of "misguided leaders [who] have drawn Negroes away from the labor movement." Blacks, he claimed, had to realize that "the only way out for Negroes is through widespread labor organization." He emphatically placed the matter at the forefront of the movement: "This is the central issue on which all Negroes must agree: *To fight Jim-Crowism in trade unions*" (italics in original).[35]

The selection of best-known Black trade unionist and socialist, A. Philip Randolph, to the post of president further indicated both the Congress' emphasis on labor and its radical orientation. Randolph preserved the Left tone of the Howard Conference from the ambitious opening sentence of his introduction to Davis's *Let Us Build a National Negro Congress*:

> In this deepening crisis of monopoly capitalism, of which the existing industrial depression, with its myriad and varied concomitant social disabilities and degradations, is an acute manifestation, the Negro in politics, industry, education, and his entire social life, is faced with a decisive and imperative challenge, to develop and fashion a new and powerful instrumentality with which, not only to arouse and fire the broad masses to action in their own defense, but to attack the forces of reaction that seek to throttle Black America with increasing Jim-Crowism, segregation and discrimination.

With his name attached to the Randolph Resolution, the BSCP leader personified the struggle for Black equality within organized labor. Randolph also gave the Congress movement access to other trade unionists with whom he had some contact. For example, Randolph was used to solicit the cooperation of the progressive-dominated leadership of the Chicago Federation of Labor. In addition, Davis asked Randolph to write to the United Mine Workers requesting that they endorse the NNC, a suggestion that had arisen out of a meeting between Davis and John L. Lewis. Davis, without hesitation in using Randolph's name, but perhaps not so confident of his adherence to radical orthodoxy, sent Randolph specific instructions on what to write.[36]

As the movement to build the NNC progressed, labor came to occupy an ever more prominent place within it. Letters were addressed to all AFL affiliates in Chicago to urge them to send delegates. Labor Committees were set up in various cities to organize union representation. At one point, as close as three weeks before the Congress was to convene, the idea was seriously proposed within the sponsoring committee of postponing the Congress to allow more time to encourage union participation. By this time it was too late to make such a change, but the stage had already been set for what would be a large union turnout.[37]

The recent events within the AFL had their effects on how much support the Congress expected or even wanted from the main actors within the federation. Davis actively sought the CIO's cooperation as one of the main resources for building a broad base of Black workers, as well as to establish definite contact with the "new unionists." The UMW, as well as some of the other industrial unions, had organized large numbers of Blacks and their cooperation was essential for ensuring the representation of African Americans with union experience. In contrast, Davis asked little of AFL unions outside the CIO. Still, even as it made its loyalties obvious in other respects, the NNC would, in name, remain neutral in the dispute. Randolph was asked to take the presidency after he had refused to leave the AFL, and he indicated no disapproval of Davis' contacts with the CIO. He participated in Davis' efforts to secure from Lewis a speaker to represent the UMW and the CIO in addressing the Congress on the topic of "The Negro and Industrial Unionism."[38]

Davis, at least in his official capacity, had not publicly announced himself unequivocally for the CIO. But he privately indicated to Lewis's associate in the CIO, John Brophy, that he was "positive [the] more than [a] thousand delegates [would] be solid behind" the CIO. It is true, Davis did tell another labor leader that "at the very heart of the program of the Congress is the plan for a nation-wide campaign to organize the hundreds of thousands of unorganized workers into unions affiliated with the A.F. of L." But here Davis was being coy: he knew very well that this campaign was planned by the CIO; he was simply taking advantage of as yet unsevered relations between the industrials and the crafts.[39]

V.

In all, 817 delegates from 585 organizations, with combined memberships of over 1,200,000 people, attended the first National Negro Congress in Chicago, February 14 to 16, 1936, to work out a joint program. In addition, untold numbers of organizations wanted to send representatives, but could not afford the expense of travel during the Depression. The effects of the worst winter in fifty years also played a part in keeping some away. Yet the numbers surpassed the expectations of the planning committee. The founding Congress had on its agenda: the right of Blacks to have jobs at a living wage and to join trade unions as full and equal members; adequate and non-discriminatory relief and social security; aid to Black farmers and the insurance of their right to organize; full civil rights and the end of lynching and racial violence; complete equality of Black women and youth; and opposition to war and fascism, including the defense of Ethiopia from the Italian fascists.[40]

Of all the sessions, the one on labor attracted the most interest and lively debate. Representatives from eighty-three unions discussed their problems with delegates from all kinds of groups. So widespread was the interest that the labor session included one third of all official participants, leaving others with small groups. Given the absence of the ailing Randolph, the numbers were even more surprising.[41]

The main issues at the labor session included discrimination within the AFL and the struggle to bring about its end sparked by the Randolph Resolution, industrial unionism, the need to organize Black workers, and a political agenda for labor. Much of the attention, as reflected in the resolutions, focused on the controversy between industrial and craft unions. Despite the decision by several large internationals in basic industries not to send delegates, the idea of industrial unionism gained support. The resolution on industrial unionism read: "The National Negro Congress endorses in principle the movement of industrial unionism and seeks to secure definite cooperation of the Committee on Industrial Organization in the organization of Negro workers in mass production in industrial unions." Another resolution, however, called for a similar working relationship with the

AFL.   Still, while the craft unions were blamed for deliberately excluding Blacks, industrial unions were hailed as offering an environment less conducive to segregationist policies.   The delegates voted to endorse the Randolph Resolution and to oppose the holding of AFL conventions in Jim Crow states.   The Congress also called for the selection of the laundry, domestic and tobacco industries for special emphasis in labor activities and for the formation of Negro Labor Councils to promote union membership among Blacks.[42]

The mood of the convention left the implementation of labor policies as the primary task facing the newly elected leaders, but it had charted an ambiguous course.   Congress officials were instructed to seek relations with both major federations, despite their contrasting attitudes toward the unionization of Blacks.   Although expressing support for both may have been advisable for achieving Congress unity, it remained at the very least an impractical policy.   In appearance, the ambivalence ran through the very heart of the Congress, dividing its president from its national secretary. Randolph, although an outspoken critic of AFL policies, had committed himself to leading a battle for justice within the ranks of labor's most powerful body.   Davis, on the other hand, had already begun cultivating relations with the leaders of what he hoped would emerge as its replacement.   In reality, Randolph was a figure-head, Davis the driving force.   The NNC would take its place behind the industrials.[43]

VI.

The National Negro Congress marked the fulfillment of the consensus Black radical program of the mid-thirties, just as the founding of the CIO did for the "progressive unionism" campaign. The convergence of the two events seemed to the young Black radicals to indicate the dawning of a new day, just a short step from liberation itself. If progressive unionism was to be the new liberating ideology of labor, then neo-Debsianism was to be its counterpart for African-American workers. Ralph Bunche, an NNC co-founder, captured the spirit in an article for

Race. He wrote, "[T]he incontrovertible truth [is] that the salvation of the American Negro and the solution to his vital problems is to be found in working-class unity. . . ." As such, the National Negro Congress held out great promise:

> In no other general Negro gathering has the note of labor been so popularly received. The ideology of organized labor was dominant. . . . And if the Congress does its work well it should be paving the way for its own eventual dissolution. Its fundamental purpose should be to make Negroes socially conscious, to give them a realistic understanding of their mass positions as workers in society, to promote labor orientation and to stimulate the enrollment of the Negro masses in the ranks of organized labor.

Bunche not only provided an account of the future of the NNC, but he indicated the fate of the "Negro Question" in the new radical consensus: it was to be returned whence it had come in radical circles, to subsumption under questions of class. Bunche said as much for the NNC. Having done its work, it would only properly give way to the labor movement itself, which would be allowed to take care of the "Negro Question" in terms of such issues as might occasionally arise. Indeed, if Bunche found fault with the Congress as executed under Davis's (and not his own) leadership, it was only that "Certainly a great opportunity was missed in failing to adopt as the central theme . . . industrial unionism." In other words, the Congress had made itself too independent of the great crusade of the progressives, had not made it clear enough (or so Bunche thought) where its loyalties lay.[44]

Abram Harris, who played the instrumental intellectual role in building this consensus, continued to seek the intellectual road to the fulfillment of the program for which the NNC formed the political vanguard. In alliance with a group of like-minded intellectuals, he founded The Conference on Social and Economic Aspects of the Race Problem, publisher of *Race*. This journal was virtually the organ of the radical consensus grouping, with its editorial board and most frequent contributors including Ernest Rice McKinney, Ralph Bunche, Lester Granger, the Black socialist George Streator, and

Harris's collaborator on his book *The Black Worker*, the white socialist Sterling Spero. Judging by the number of the Popular Front contributors, the CP also approved of the project. The journal proclaimed its purpose as follows:

> There is no "solution" of the "race problem" short of an organized, uncompromising struggle based on the mass organization of black and white workers and poor farmers and other sections of the population most interested--an uncompromising struggle for complete equality, economic, political, and social, of Negroes and whites and the end of all discrimination, legal or social, based upon "race," "color," "national origin," or "blood."

The quotation marks which enclosed the list of terms given at the end of the statement showed how close these radicals had come to denying any place to race or even nationality. Perhaps that the publication lived through only two numbers gives an added indication of the importance they attached to *Race*, and the strength of their conviction that their understanding of the "Negro Question," their work to implement the Harris program, and the triumph of the progressive unionists in the form of the CIO, had combined to ensure the speedy "liberation" of African Americans.[45]

If some radicals only stepped up to the line, only indicated the direction they believed matters of race and nationality were headed, others crossed the threshold. In the first number of Race, Lester Granger provided his view of racial matters in labor. Reporting on the 1935 AFL convention, at which the basis for the CIO was laid, he put it this way:

> On the Negro question, on the issue of industrial unionism, as on that of a Labor Party, the Atlantic City Convention resolved itself into a struggle between an entrenched Old Guard of politicians and a newly-arising progressive faction. . . . It should not be difficult for Negroes to decide on which side they will line up.

Hence, the "Negro Question," like industrial unionism and a labor party, depended only on the victory of the progressives. According to Granger, Blacks had a virtual "duty" to sign up with the "progressive" revolution. The progressives' cause, their issues, were now those of all African Americans. On the world scale, where the ABB had placed it, it was just as easy to resolve the question into the great struggle against fascism. Langston Hughes pronounced, in 1937, the epitaph on an era of Black radicalism. As the title of his article for *The Crisis* put it, there had been "Too Much of Race." Soon there would be none: "And the fascists know that when there is no more race, there will be no more capitalism, and no more war, and no more money for the munition workers, because the workers of the world will have triumphed."[46]

The eloquence and poetic quality of Hughes's writing almost gives life to the words, almost makes them convincing. Yet Hughes merged all political questions into that of working-class power, jumped from the concrete circumstances facing Black radicals in the Thirties to some distant and attractive point. No such transition would, or could, occur. To declare the end of race and nationality on theoretical grounds could do nothing to end racism, national oppression, colonialism, and the other various forms of the oppression of Blacks. But Hughes thought he saw reason to prophesy:

> [I]n America, where race prejudice is so strong, already we have learned what the lies of race mean--continued oppression and poverty and fear--and now Negroes and white sharecroppers in the cotton fields of the South are beginning to get together; and Negro and white workers in the great industrial cities of the North under John L. Lewis and the C.I.O. that refuses to recognize the color line.

In reality, however, industrial unionism would not perform the miracles attributed to it. Indeed, it would not even take upon itself its much-ballyhooed, but actually exceedingly modest, role in the civil rights movement without a determined struggle on the part of Davis and the National Negro Congress.[47]

Chapter VII
The Congresses Join Forces:
The Formation of the Black-Labor Alliance

The dissolution of every movement founded on a single-minded adherence to an *a priori* principle begins with the achievement of its most cherished goal. It would be no different with either the "progressive laborites" or 1930s Black radicalism. The former landed right back in the "business unionism" of the AFL, the latter was led like a magnet to the "narrow racial politics" so recently buried in the "reactionary" past. Nowhere was the rapid degeneration of the leftwing orthodoxy of the 1930s shown more clearly than in the alliance struck between its main exponents, the alliance that seemed to flow naturally from the nature of their two movements. The effortless combination of their goals, which were to be obtained by the application of the same simple principle, "progressive unionism" and its "labor unity," was to cost far more effort to Black radicals than they had bargained for.

As the newly constituted National Negro Congress, under its only full-time officer, John P. Davis, moved to put the radicals' labor program into effect, the organization faced the realization that its pursuance of the CIO's goals was one thing, and its securing of the CIO's cooperation quite another. Indeed, the intransigence of the CIO would cause the more faint-hearted of the young Black radicals to lose courage and hope. But Davis, never as firm a neo-Debsian believer in the promised immediate labor solidarity, was of a more practical and pragmatic bent and more experienced and adept at behind-the-scenes political maneuvering. In the face of CIO inertia, he began to calculate just which arguments, and when necessary, which kinds of forces and coercive measures could be brought to bear on the CIO to get it to move. The time of the ideological young radical had passed. The hour of his political brother had struck.[1]

Perhaps Davis was a hypocrite. Perhaps he never meant a word he said in all his talk about "discarding capitalism" and the new socialist dispensation. Perhaps he was the most cynical and least genuine of the young radicals. And then again, perhaps he was merely the least naive, the most politically astute, and the only one with the slightest sympathy for the Black worker. For whatever reason, as head of the NNC Davis discarded the radical rhetoric about the end of racial politics, about the unbounded future of the united labor movement, about placing class before all else. In its stead, Davis set out to gain all he believed could be obtained for African Americans from the situation at hand, and to prove, perhaps, that, even if the dawning of the new era of "progressive labor" was no revolution, in any case revolutionary changes do not require revolutions, or even revolutionary movements.

Above all, Davis understood that for all the arguments of his radical associates, and for all his own verbiage, organized labor, even in its most "progressive" form, had as yet worked only for the organization of Black workers into unions and completely ignored the source of their racial oppression in American society. As noted in Chapter 6, he ascribed to the most liberal CIO union, the United Mine Workers, the most opportunistic of policies vis-a-vis African Americans. He complained that even unions with a substantial Black membership, including locals where they constituted the majority, were not "permitted to express progressive opinions upon such basic issues as the right of Negroes to vote and serve on juries, support of anti-lynching legislation, [and] defense of the Scottsboro boys. . . ." Davis had, thus, already brought the radical labor program down from the lofty goal of revolution to the mundane objectives of reform.[2]

Nevertheless, Davis was ready to base all avenues to change on the promise of this "reactionary" union policy of taking an interest in Blacks only as union members, since, he asserted, it was "greatly superior" to that of other unions. For Davis, then, the implementation of the radicals' labor program pointed in one direction only, the fulfillment of this promise, however slim. The union Davis thought most exemplified the attitude he described was the United Mine Workers, which represented the motive force of the Committee for Industrial Organization. To Davis, then, the radical program meant cooperation with the CIO in the organization of Black workers. If, stripped of the radical rhetoric in which it was encased, 1930s Black radicalism no longer sounded quite so radical, it was just one of the many ironies that emerged from the consummation of the cause. For, in addition, the Black-labor alliance was not to be the end of racial politics, but its rebirth, the chance for it to score some meager victories.[3]

Davis continued to mouth the central tenet of the radical consensus program: "The only hope of the Negro to effect any meaningful improvement of his social and economic status is through his alignment with progressive forces of organized labor." But he also made clear that Black support for any union movement, no matter how "progressive," would be conditional: "[The] labor leadership should financially support the Congress in its campaign to organize Negro workers and in its struggle for civil liberties for Negroes." Thus Davis saw the role of the NNC as incorporating progressive labor fully into the equality struggle together with Blacks. Only such an alliance would achieve genuine solidarity of labor. To forge that unity, Davis believed that white unionists had to stand behind a program that included support for the Randolph Resolution, full rights for Black workers, the National Negro Congress, civil and voting rights for Blacks, the defense of the Scottsboro boys and imprisoned Black communist Angelo Herndon, and federal anti-lynching legislation.[4]

But if labor solidarity entailed such ramifications, however modest the reforms at which they aimed, then the Black radical program faced a dilemma. For the CIO had, at most, signalled its willingness to organize Blacks into its unions. More than this it had never promised, or even intimated. And it was hard for the Black radicals to find the means within even their own ideology to compel the "progressive unionists" to do more, for they had declared the end to all but the general good of labor. And the progressives maintained steadfastly that all that they undertook was for the general good of labor. Having abandoned the "revolutionary duty" position of internationalism, Black radicals now faced the age-old question of all earlier Black radicalism of how to compel white labor to move. Davis was to find the answer in the moderation of the demands placed before white labor.

If Davis intended to fight to wring what he could out of the CIO, he still placed a great deal of faith in what the CIO could provide: the organized pressure of millions of workers-- the labor lobbyist's dream. Davis was an old hand at lobbying and behind-the-scenes politicking, and he took right up with the NNC where he had left off with the JCNR. But this time, Davis hoped to use organized labor as the wedge he had lacked in the coalition of African-American organizations without effective clout in the offices and meeting rooms of Washington. Thus Davis viewed cooperative relations between the National Negro Congress and organized labor on legislative and social issues as an important milestone. First, it presented an opportunity to rally Blacks around the progressive union cause and spur organizing among Black workers. Second, the alliance could improve the chances of the U.S. Congress passing bills Davis believed to be of importance to African Americans.[5]

Davis did not, however, project such cooperation as the final answer to the struggle for Black equality, as he might have in his earlier JCNR days. Davis told the Convention of Social Workers in May, 1936, that only the mass struggles of Blacks to overcome their economic oppression would ultimately alter the tragic condition facing the Black masses. He stressed that the NNC would pursue such a course, but he continued,

> We are under no illusion that these attempts will be instantly successful. There must come many changes before success. We will hasten these changes by taking part in and guiding other forms of struggle: for civil

liberties, for federal legislation to curb lynching,..for genuine social and unemployment insurance, for federal relief standards sufficiently high to provide a decent standard of living.

Davis, then, to that extent at least, had ceased to think as a quasi-syndicalist progressive laborite and had begun to map out a strategy for the interim goals Black radicals had to a large extent eschewed, at least in their most high-flown theory. In other words, he returned to the old "discredited program" of the NAACP. Ironically, having failed to convince the NAACP to direct its program to the organization of Black workers, the radicals now set out to use the organization of Black workers to bring about the NAACP's program. Davis, as practical radical, only differed from the NAACP leadership, evidently, in operating on the premise that securing these transitional changes required the assistance of the trade union movement.[6]

Davis's program called for establishing a relationship with labor on two fronts of mutual interest: bringing unorganized Blacks into unions and working toward reform legislation. He saw the relationship with the CIO as unfolding in stages, and he counselled that the NNC had to proceed patiently but resolutely. His program involved, first, the Congress cooperating in the CIO's massive organizing campaigns. Second, the NNC would join the CIO in its struggles for progressive, pro-labor legislation, in working with Labor's Non-Partisan League, the legislative branch of the CIO and some sections of the AFL. Finally, organized labor would be drawn into legislative issues Davis deemed of greatest importance to Blacks through its relationship with the NNC. These stages correspond to the three periods that characterized the first two-and-half years of the Congress' existence.[7]

The initial step in carrying out Davis's program entailed rallying the Congress leadership and active membership around involvement with organized labor. Davis encouraged the establishment of labor committees in the local councils of the NNC in industrial centers to blaze a trail of accomplishments to stimulate interest in other areas and to attract the attention of organized labor.[8]

Meanwhile, Davis pressed toward developing a
relationship with the CIO. Davis held discussions with John
L. Lewis and John Brophy of the CIO, and Philip Murray,
chairman of its newly formed Steel Workers Organizing
Committee (SWOC), charged with the task of bringing unions
to the industry most hostile to their presence.[9]

Negotiations centered on the involvement of the NNC in
the pending organizing campaign in steel. That industry, with
its eighty-five thousand Black employees, offered a good
opportunity for the NNC to win its labor spurs. Davis
advertised the steel campaign as the most important that could
be undertaken "for large numbers of Negro workers, [the most]
solidly beneficial to Negroes everywhere."[10]

The issues discussed by Davis and the CIO leaders became
the key points of contention throughout the relationship
between the two organizations. Davis thought that white
workers should tangibly demonstrate their fraternal feelings
for their fellow workers. As such, Davis sought a three-part
agreement from the CIO. Most important, Black organizers had
to be employed in reaching Black workers. In addition, Davis
indicated the need for special literature designed for Blacks in
the industry and, finally, to line up the Black community
behind unions. The NNC was to provide qualified and
experienced Black organizers, most of whom were activists in
the labor committees. The Congress would also commit to
undertaking a certain amount of the financial burden of the
campaigns among Black workers, as well as making Davis
available for various functions, including trips to the target
areas and producing literature, free of charge. The organizers,
and the whole campaign, would be under the auspices of the
SWOC.[11]

At its first meeting since its election by the Congress, the
executive council approved the direction Davis charted toward
cooperation with the CIO organizing drives. The NNC
leadership unanimously adopted the national secretary's
report, which read in part, "In every council we must develop a
program for aiding trade unions in their campaign for Negro
membership." To carry out that function more effectively, the
council established a committee, with socialist Frank

Crosswaith as chairman, composed of the leading Black trade unionists connected with the NNC. In its major decision, the executive council voted to support the CIO and resolved that "the National Council elect a committee to negotiate with the CIO on its policy of industrial unionism, and that [it] ask for Negro organizers in specific localities and industries where large numbers of Negroes are employed."[12]

II.

The decision to join the CIO's efforts gave the NNC's program the official consistency Ralph Bunche had believed it to have lacked. The Cleveland meeting marked the beginning of the NNC's outspoken advocacy of the CIO's cause, which Davis quickly put into print in *The Crisis*, calling the CIO the "new, progressive and vigorous force" in American labor. And in 1936 and 1937, the most vigorous of contests the CIO would ever wage took place in the steel industry, one of the last bastions of the open shop. The campaign to organize the steel industry, the terrain of some of the most memorable and bitter battles in American labor history, would take most of the CIO's early attention and money, and Davis was determined that the NNC would be where the action was.[13]

Young Black radicals who had not lost their ardor once their idealistic words were being turned into practical deeds waxed eloquent on the historical significance of the steel campaign. Edward Strong, the youth director of the NNC, declared,

Toward changing [the oppression of African Americans] the drive to organize steel . . . unions [has] greater possibilities and wider implications for Negro youth in industry and agriculture than any single incident affecting our people since the Civil War.

And Davis added,

Not for themselves alone, but for all Black America, will Negro steel workers strike a telling blow for economic freedom by organization. . . . 85,000 Negro steel workers with union cards will signal the

beginning of the organization of all Negro workers.
They will mark a start toward the liberation of
hundreds of thousands of Negro sharecroppers, of
hundreds of thousands of Negro women sweating away
their lives as domestics.

The steel campaign, Davis concluded, reaching an apogee of
anticipation that the CIO leaders in steel were hard-pressed to
match, would be a "drive to write a Magna Charta for black
labor."[14]

Davis's use of hyperbole did not end there. He promised,
"We will make powerful friends for the Randolph Resolution,
for the National Negro Congress. . . . [W]e can expect to have a
broad trade union base of unions of the CIO, and ample funds
[from the CIO] for almost any program in advancement of
Negroes of which we can conceive." But, in an indication of
things to come, all of these benefits were reserved for the hazy
future. The practical present was a different matter. For now,
it was a question of the SWOC's desire for "action from us and
not promises." The contrast was revealing: the all-important
work of the CIO could not wait. African Americans could. The
wait would be a long one.[15]

Probably through Davis's contacts with the CIO, he gained
the ear of the top leaders of the SWOC, including its chairman,
Philip Murray, who like Lewis and Brophy, was from the
United Mine Workers. Davis reported to NNC leaders that he
was granted entry into closed meetings of both the CIO and
SWOC. But he did not need such access to learn the view of
Murray toward Black workers even after the NNC entered into
the campaign. Murray publicly proclaimed: "It is our
conviction . . . that the organization of the negro steel workers
will follow, rather than precede, the organization of the white
mill workers." In short, the SWOC retained the very
"attitude" that Otto Huiswoud had noted years before to be
that of the "labor bureaucracy" of the old AFL.[16]

The "progressive" alliance of the NNC and CIO thus
entailed that the task of proving that Black workers could be
organized devolved upon the NNC. NNC leaders fought to
convince the SWOC to put forth the resources into organizing
Black workers, for they feared that if Black workers did not

get in on the ground floor of the union, they could face inferior treatment for some time to come. Preventing such an outcome depended, Davis declared, on the NNC's "strain[ing] itself in order to meet the needs of the steel workers."[17]

With the SWOC, the NNC's success would be no more than fair. The former employed only a small, entirely inadequate force of Black organizers, leaving the NNC to make up the difference at its own expense. But the SWOC did eventually agree to co-sponsor a modest conference for Black workers and sponsored a speaking tour by Davis in the areas of the steel drive. And that conference did go on record advocating civil rights for African Americans, at least tacitly in the name of the SWOC.[18]

With Black steel workers, their accomplishment was more impressive. With the organizers of the SWOC and NNC plus a contingent of NNC volunteers in the field, by 1937, the NNC's campaign had brought tangible and much-needed aid to the SWOC's efforts to organize steel workers. The attitudes of Blacks to unions, of which they were suspicious from years of neglect and mistreatment, had undergone a significant transformation, and NNC representatives in the field reported a favorable response to their efforts. Sociologists Horace R. Cayton and George S. Mitchell, who studied the steel drive contemporaneously, considered the SWOC "fortunate" to have the NNC as an ally. They wrote, "The Pittsburgh conference was of extreme importance in that it brought together Negro steel workers from many parts of the country to discuss face-to-face the problems which had been bothering them not only as workers but as Negroes." They also agreed with the NNC's position that Black organizers were essential not only to recruiting but to keeping Blacks in the union. They believed that the significance of the Black organizers the NNC had fought for so resolutely "in winning Negro union members for the S.W.O.C. can hardly be overestimated." They praised the NNC as well for effectively counteracting anti-union sentiment in the Black community, resultant upon the companies' policy of attempting to buy off the Black ministers and leaders. Perhaps the greatest testimony to the success of the Congress' efforts was that despite the SWOC's predictions, "Negroes joined the

union in most places in about the same proportions as did the
white steel workers . . . [and] in some cases . . . in even greater
proportion." This would not prove, as Davis and the radicals
had hoped, enough to convince the CIO to change its attitude
toward Black workers, but, then, that attitude had nothing to
do with facts.[19]

III.

During its second year, the Congress pushed forward its
developing relationship with the CIO. Having demonstrated
its usefulness in the steel campaign, it now began to establish
ties with the CIO unions in other industries. It began to
cooperate with Labor's Non-Partisan League in seeking a
"progressive" legislation, that is, it supported the latter's
agenda. To Davis, the NNC had thus entered a new phase in
fulfilling his program for recruiting Blacks into unions and
bringing labor into the fight for civil liberties.

The experiences of the steel campaign served as the basis
for the NNC to extend its union activities. Following the
model worked out in steel, the NNC encouraged other
affiliates of the CIO to hire Black organizers in order to attract
Black workers. The Textile Workers Organizing Committee,
although it had relatively few Blacks under its jurisdiction,
promised attention to the concerns of Black workers and to
entertain NNC suggestions for organizers. The NNC aided the
Maritime Federation of the Pacific Coast during its strike, and
the leader of the local Congress affiliate in the San Francisco
area was one of the union's leading African Americans. The
NNC reached an agreement with the International Ladies
Garment Workers Union to organize Black workers in Chicago.
After a strike among hotel workers in Washington, D.C., the
vice-president of the union commented, "The credit for these
victories belongs to the National Negro Congress." The NNC
also joined a strike among cleaning and dyeing workers and
lobbied to bring them into the CIO.[20]

But in entering into two more organizing campaigns that
affected thousands of African American workers, the NNC

would encounter new problems that brought it into conflict with both a major international and the CIO itself. In the automobile industry, the United Automobile Workers of America resisted the Congress' offers of cooperation. In tobacco, an industry dominated by Black workers and in which there was no CIO affiliate, a disagreement arose between Davis and CIO officials over the emphasis to be given to NNC-led efforts to organize the employees. At the least, the complications cast doubt upon the cooperative relations in steel extending to other industries. At worst, they threatened an end to the NNC's potential influence within organized labor, jeopardizing Davis's plans to bring the CIO into the civil rights struggle.

Most factors in the automobile industry indicated a situation so similar to steel as seemingly to assure the UAW's interest in a joint undertaking with the NNC. As in steel, the number of Blacks employed in auto made their cooperation crucial to the outcome of the union's quest. The auto makers had also taken pains to co-opt Black workers, and with much more success than in any other industry. Because of the favorable impression within the Black community of magnate Henry Ford, whose plants employed the majority of the Black laborers in the industry, selling the union would be especially difficult. Ford, no friend to Afro-Americans in reality, had posed as a supporter of Black employment in industry as a safeguard against union encroachment. He literally bought the support of the Black community in Detroit, including the ministers of the largest churches. Within this context, the NNC would find it difficult to so much as organize a local chapter.[21]

More than these strikingly familiar problems, the tension with the UAW posed limitations on the potential for the NNC to play a role in the second of the great industrial campaigns of the CIO. The union, and in particular president Homer Martin, eschewed the importance of gaining the cooperation of African Americans, taking the age-old view of white labor that Black workers constituted what they traditionally called "reserves of reaction." With local NAACP and Urban League officials owing their allegiance to Ford, their benefactor, the NNC represented the only organization willing to support the UAW.

But the support was all on one side. While Davis praised the
cooperativeness of the other CIO internationals, he complained
to both NNC members and the national CIO about a complete
lack of attention from the UAW.[22]

The auto union seemed to want to do more to hurt its image
among Blacks than to help. For the first several months of
1937, the recruitment of Blacks was retarded by rumors and
press reports of UAW practices unfavorable to Blacks. Charges
against the international included that at one Ford plant
Blacks were forced to join segregated locals, that at another
plant Blacks were being denied seniority rights, and that in a
third case a union official openly discouraged Blacks from
joining his local. The frequent allegations prompted
condemnation of the union by the NAACP.[23]

Yet in the face of what most Blacks perceived to be a
hostile attitude toward them on the part of the union, the
NNC maintained a commitment to the organizing drive. Davis
did his best to counteract the negative publicity the NAACP
had created. He involved the CIO leadership in bringing
pressure to bear on Martin, and a statement was released
denying the NAACP's characterization of the UAW as selling
out Black workers. Davis spoke to Roy Wilkins, editor of *The
Crisis*, arguing that, despite the union's spotty record, Blacks
should not so thoroughly denounce it. Whether these efforts
had any effect on the NAACP's later retraction, the NNC had
successfully cultivated a public image of complete loyalty to
the union.[24]

Davis adhered to a policy of airing his criticisms
privately to avoid damaging the potential for relations with
the UAW while he worked behind the scenes to develop a
political relationship. He believed that public actions
remotely critical of the union's policies were out of the question.
Although neither Davis nor virtually any other Black leader
could be brought to accept that the union had at all adequately
defended the interests of Blacks, the UAW had the support of
the CIO, the alliance with which took overriding precedence
for Davis. Davis knew only too well of the level of the anti-
Black feelings being drummed up by some sections of the white
workers. He had witnessed the hurling of racial insults at

Black workers in St. Louis during a strike. He complained to union leaders about the actions taken against the interests of Black workers. But he chose to operate on the premise that the situations of conflict could best be diffused with efforts on both sides. In St. Louis, such a course had been accomplished by measures taken by the local NNC chapter, including recruiting Blacks from other unions to walk on the picket lines. The union, in turn, organized a team of white volunteer organizers to recruit Black workers. Davis viewed the situation as one necessitating extended efforts on both sides for the benefit of all. Whatever the reality, he thought it important to create a good public image for the union among Black workers. Even though the NNC chapter in Detroit reported that Blacks were almost unanimously behind Ford, Davis sought a condemnation from it of Ford's attempt to blame Blacks for physical attacks on union officials.[25]

Davis again defended the UAW at an NAACP conference in Detroit in June, 1937. Local leaders of the NAACP had tried to block the appearance on the program of UAW president Martin and Davis, whose speeches in favor of the UAW stood alone in the midst of praise for Ford. Walter White avoided any favorable comment upon the union, and, in the end, the NAACP refused to take any stand for the UAW. Contrastingly, the NNC had a conference in Detroit around the same time on Black workers and the UAW with Randolph as the main speaker, and it expressed its continued support for the union. The NNC also lent the kind of support it had in the steel campaign, providing the UAW with volunteer organizers and taking it upon itself to contact workers at their homes.[26]

Yet despite the fact that the NNC represented the only Black organization supporting the UAW in its uphill battle, the UAW remained unresponsive to the NNC's offers of cooperation. The UAW was the only CIO union that declined to send delegates to the second National Negro Congress in 1937. By the end of 1937, Davis's strategy had failed to establish a working relationship between the NNC and the UAW.[27]

In the tobacco industry, the chances seemed bright for the CIO and the NNC to conduct a joint campaign to swing another

industry to the AFL rival. That possibility stemmed from
tobacco's nearly 70 percent African-American work force.
Moreover, the predominantly white AFL affiliate, the Tobacco
Workers International Union (TWIU), had exhibited little
interest in organizing Blacks. Even the specter of CIO
competition apparently did not concern union officials. Its
president confided, "Yes I am informed that the C.I.O. is after
the Colored, . . . [but] if they do [organize them] what will they
have if we have the WHITES" (emphasis in original). The
CIO had the field clear if it wanted it.[28]

The NNC found itself involved before it could make any
arrangements with the CIO. Black workers were so
disenchanted with the TWIU that in one plant in Richmond,
Virginia on their own initiative they organized a sit down
strike outside the jurisdiction of the union. The spontaneous
strike was put under the supervision of volunteer organizers
from the NNC. The action won a 33 percent pay increase and
was quickly followed by two more successful strikes in
Richmond. The NNC-supported unions rapidly grew to more
than fifteen hundred members with a 100 percent rate of
affiliation.[29]

Davis thought he saw an opportunity to score a victory for
not only the tobacco workers in Richmond but all Black workers.
He wanted the CIO to establish a national organizing
campaign similar to that in textiles. Tobacco offered the first
opportunity for the CIO to show that its interest went deeper
than preventing the use of Blacks as strikebreakers in
industries in which they represented a significant minority.
Tobacco could provide the first mass organizing campaign under
the CIO in an industry employing mostly African-American
workers. Davis hoped such an arrangement could pave the way
for the CIO to take on domestic and agricultural workers. He
would not see his ambitions realized.[30]

While Davis negotiated an agreement with Brophy for
turning the Richmond unions over to the CIO, the AFL finally
got into the fight for Black workers in self-preservation. The
record of the TWIU would not do much to attract Black workers,
but NNC organizers in Richmond reported that they needed to
be able to give the workers a final answer from the CIO. One of

them wired Davis that it was "imperative [that] the CIO launch [a] real offensive on [the] tobacco front immediately."[31]

Neither Davis's wish for a Tobacco Workers Organizing Committee nor the sought-after extensive action among tobacco workers would come to pass. Within a year the Black organizers hired by the CIO would find themselves unemployed. They struggled to raise the funds to keep their campaign among the tobacco workers of Richmond going. Even the president of the district of the CIO's United Cannery, Agricultural, Packing and Allied Workers of America, which had been given the Richmond tobacco locals, alerted Davis to the "dissatisfaction among the tobacco workers with the CIO," and indicated that Davis would be wise to investigate the causes before jumping to defend the CIO. The NNC did not gain the desired timely action from the CIO despite organizing more than five thousand workers in Richmond, of the total of twenty-five thousand Blacks in the industry.[32]

Davis would also be disappointed with the CIO's decisions regarding agricultural and domestic unions. The complete absence of or severe weakness of trade unions for these workers meant that the impact of the CIO's rapid advances in union membership would never be felt by the majority of African-American workers. The NNC had maintained contacts and offered support to labor activists in these fields, and Davis hoped to have their unions taken on by the CIO. He had endorsed the idea of an Agricultural Workers Organizing Committee. As with tobacco, no such committee would be formed. In July, 1937, the United Cannery, Agricultural, Packing, and Allied Workers was chartered by the CIO, and this same international was given jurisdiction over the tobacco unions organized by the Congress. But the CIO never accorded it, and never intended to, the same status it had the unions in the northern mass production industries and its work amounted to a drop in the ocean of Black farmers and agricultural laborers. Domestic workers would not be even that fortunate. As Davis commented, "We have the field pretty much to ourselves."[33]

Although the joint organizing ventures with the CIO produced mixed results, Davis forged ahead in building an alliance with the political wing of progressive labor from the beginning of 1937. Davis believed that Labor's Non-Partisan League represented not only the leading force among trade unions but in independent labor and radical politics in general, and, as such, the most powerful ally the NNC could win. But at the same time, he professed that "the individuals having leadership in this movement have considered the problem of the Negro people only within the narrow scope of the trade union movement." Davis believed that these limitations applied to all such movements of the time and rendered the Congress' role that much more important. His experiences with the Farmer-Labor coalition in 1936, in which he and Randolph had taken part and in which the progressives played the leading role, had convinced him that the fulfillment of the progressive agenda alone did not bring with it any assurances of the advancement of Black liberation. A chastened Davis had decided that the NNC needed some form of additional leverage. Its relations with the CIO promised just that.[34]

While labor activities were still primary during this period of the NNC, the move to cement a relationship with Labor's Non-Partisan League thrust a legislative agenda into the second position. Davis explained to local leaders that, initially, the NNC would back the League on its current agenda. But Davis explicitly promised that in the future the League would reciprocate with invaluable service on civil rights legislation, notably the Anti-Lynching Bill. He also hastened to point out the importance for Blacks of the legislation the League was emphasizing, which consisted essentially of supporting the Roosevelt administration of which Black radicals had once been so critical.[35]

Yet the NNC retained its political independence and initiative. The major portion of its legislative efforts, like that of the "old guard" NAACP, consisted of support for the Anti-Lynching Bill, which would be stalled in Congress for the entire Depression decade. The NNC also lobbied for the protection of Black interests under the Wages and Hours bill, which was to fulfill something of the same purpose as the NRA. Davis appeared before the Senate and House Committees on Labor and focused on what he perceived to be potential negative effects of the bill for Blacks, asking that changes be made to prevent the traditional discrimination against Black workers in the South. The LNPL, on the other hand, insisted that the question be examined for its impact on most workers, meaning, of course, northern white workers. Davis's independent stance at least proved that he was under no obligation to side with the "labor progressives" on every issue, even one of so great importance to the latter's goals. But the episode also showed with whom "labor progressives" would side every time it really counted, and how little "unity of labor" meant when it threatened white privilege.[36]

IV.

By the time the second National Negro Congress was convened, the progressive unionism honeymoon was officially over. As the illusions of immediate labor solidarity, if not outright liberation, faded, Black radicals such as Davis turned their thoughts and their words back to the "racial politics" that had been so recently denounced. Quite simply, racism in America was not budging, even under the weight of the "progressive" CIO.

The second Congress devoted less attention to the great promise of trade unionism and more to the old standby of working for the reform legislation which Black political organizations like the NAACP had sought for decades without success. In an address on national radio, Davis announced, "We have come because a world at odds with itself has denied us our rights of manhood and citizenship." He placed the passage of the Anti-Lynching Bill at the top of the list of immediate objectives.[37]

But Black radicals hoped that, at the least, their strategy of bringing the CIO, with its millions of organized workers, into the struggle for civil rights would bear fruit. No organized force among whites of nearly such size had ever been heard in support of civil rights for African Americans. And the NNC's efforts did seem to foretell a certain degree of success. The CIO cooperated with the NNC for the first time on something that was not of immediate interest to the former in taking part in preparations of the second Congress. Leading CIO officials, including CIO chief John L. Lewis, SWOC head Philip Murray, and LNPL director E.L. Oliver endorsed the Congress. The CIO's Union News Service gave the event "a good play," and the federation helped obtain the national radio hook-up which carried Davis's speech. This aid was modest, to be sure, but something of a start.[38]

More important, on the surface of things at least, CIO representatives at the Congress seemed to signal a new attitude on the part of organized labor toward the struggle for civil rights. Pennsylvania Lt. Gov. Thomas Kennedy of the United Mine Workers assured the Congress that the struggle for "economic progress . . . can be spread to other avenues and strength can be given to you in your fight" for civil rights. Philip Murray added, "Surely, trade unions . . . have but one service to render--a better distribution of the world's goods, a greater opportunity to improve your status economically, socially and politically."[39]

Even with the CIO's assistance, the second congress did not achieve quite the proportions that Davis had hoped, but it did just about match the first. One thousand one hundred forty-nine delegates packed the general sessions and came to express their views on the same wide range of subjects as at the first convention. Included were two hundred nineteen representatives from labor. In addition, between four and five thousand people filled the Metropolitan Opera House in Philadelphia for each of the three daily sessions. They received the greetings of President Roosevelt, Mayor Fiorello LaGuardia of New York and Governor Elmer A. Benson of Minnesota. John L. Lewis expressed the "CIO's gratitude."[40]

The resolutions reflected the changing emphasis of Congress leaders. Resolutions on labor were fewer. The participants did call for the obligatory "labor unity" between the AFL and CIO and protested the "sad neglect" of domestic workers by organized labor, requesting "an intensive campaign . . . toward organizing [them] throughout the country." But civil rights issues were given a place at the top of the agenda.[41]

The focus on that legislation did not mean the Congress had lost interest in organizing Black workers. Now that it included more experienced labor activists, the Congress established a new apparatus to allow the national office to concentrate on other matters without diminishing its trade union functions. At a meeting of the executive board following the convention, a trade union committee with broad authority was created. The leading Black trade unionists in the Congress were selected to head the new body, which was to include at least twenty-five figures from the AFL and CIO, each representing a different industry. Davis and Randolph were to serve as liaisons to make recommendations to John L. Lewis, and Charles H. Houston of the NAACP was to be the legal adviser.[42]

At the same time, Davis stepped up his efforts to cement the alliance with the CIO, more determined than ever to pull it into the civil rights movement. As instructed, Davis reported to Lewis the decisions of the Congress and the subsequent board meeting. Davis reaffirmed the Congress' support for the CIO and Labor's Non-Partisan League, assuring Lewis that the delegates stood behind the CIO's efforts. He told Lewis that despite past bad relations between the NNC and UAW, the Congress had chosen auto as its next point of concentration and anticipated cooperation from the international. But Davis also conveyed the feeling that the CIO had not strived with sufficient vigor to treat Black workers fairly. Davis transmitted the NNC's desire for the appointment of a Black executive assistant who would seek to protect the interests of African Americans throughout the CIO by ensuring that a uniform policy toward Blacks obtained in each international. Furthermore, Davis repeated his proposal that a Tobacco Workers Organizing Committee be established. Such a development "would have significance far beyond the vitally important tobacco industry," sending a definitive message to Black workers across the country that the CIO took account of their problems.[43]

Having integrated union activists into the Congress' labor activities, the national office turned its attention to the legislative agenda. The executive council meetings were increasingly convened in Washington to facilitate combining them with lobbying, in particular, for the NAACP's Anti-Lynching Bill. NNC leaders believed that gathering all forces in its favor was critical early in 1938 as the Anti-Lynching Bill faced a filibuster by southern senators. Although the Congress of Industrial Organizations had endorsed the bill at its founding convention in late 1937, its words had yet to translate into deeds. Davis began pressing "progressive labor" for immediate measures. His tone changed. He wrote to E.L. Oliver, "A quarter of a million voters in the 1938 Congressional elections will depend on the emphatic display on the part of labor of its intention to give genuine practical aid to the Negro people in every legitimate desire that they have to exercise citizenship." He submitted a statement he had drafted opposing the filibuster to Labor's Non-Partisan League, requesting that Oliver sign it and release it to the press as a League initiative, to which Oliver obliged. Davis also asked for copies to be sent to all senators, which was also done. The same process resulted in a similar statement from John Brophy. Oliver noted that the letters and releases had garnered a lot of publicity and that he immediately began receiving responses from senators.[44]

But Davis remained dissatisfied with the attitude the League expressed toward the Anti-Lynching Bill. Oliver had confided that, although messages had been sent to all senators, he did not think it advisable to judge the "few progressive Senators from the South" on the basis of the their position on the bill. Davis continued to push Oliver to change that stance. At the end of February, after negotiations with Davis concerning "joint action in the coming election campaign," the League agreed to his terms of using the anti-lynching legislation as "one of its tests of the desirability of reelecting a candidate for Congress." The *CIO News* soon announced that the bill was being "vigorously pursued by the League throughout the [current] session" of Congress.[45]

Davis decided to make immediate use of this new development through a national conference on anti-lynching in Washington. Davis set out to rally progressive labor around the bill. The League gave support to the Congress in the various tasks of arranging the conference, and the CIO lent its support. In addition, Davis succeeded in gaining the participation of some subordinate bodies of the AFL, although the federation itself declined invitations to take part.[46]

The joint effort with labor became "the order of the day" for the National Negro Congress. In building for the occasion, lobbying delegations converged on Washington from NNC locals in several states, in cooperation with other organizations seeking passage of the bill. Local NNC councils began featuring the issue to rallies of thousands. In the largest of the events that spring, eight thousand gathered in Union Square, and ten thousand heard Eleanor Roosevelt, one of the leading political figures in the New Deal administration, in Philadelphia. One Congress leader, Henry Johnson, assistant national director of the Packing House Workers Organizing Committee, wrote to Davis that despite intense activity around the unionization campaign in the stockyards, the Chicago council had just concluded a mass meeting of 2,500 featuring the anti-lynching fight and that a city-wide conference on the issue would be held soon thereafter.[47]

On March 19, a total of one hundred thirty delegates from twenty states representing thirty organizations gathered in Washington to promote the anti-lynching legislation. Messages came in from Senator Robert Wagner, author of the bill, in addition to other senators, and from John L. Lewis and Philip Murray. Religious leaders present included Bishop L. W. Eyles of the A.M.E. Zion Church and Rev. V.W. Jernagin representing the National Baptist Convention. Labor groups with official representatives included the CIO, UAW and Labor's Non-Partisan League. The statement drawn up by the conference in the name of the organizations represented included the following statement: "We . . . call on all organizations and anti-lynching committees to vigilantly watch and call for the defeat of all those who voted against this legislation." The resolutions called for joint action by all the organizations represented, specifically requesting that organized labor bodies give the issue special attention.[48]

The events that culminated in the Congress' national anti-lynching conference marked the high-water mark of Davis's program to unite the National Negro Congress and "progressive

labor" around a civil rights agenda. Having built a
relationship with the CIO and Labor's Non-Partisan League,
Davis was finally in a position to influence their policies, at
least to a small extent. He had by no means obtained every
concession that he and Congress leaders had sought from the
organizations, but, viewed from the starting point, the results
were still apparent. Most significant perhaps, the League's
reversal of policy on the Anti-Lynching Bill signified
something approaching the bilateral relations necessary to
have a true alliance. Not only had organized labor entered the
struggle for civil rights for the first time, but it had done so on
terms advanced by a major Black organization. If only in a far
different form than Black radicals had imagined, the Black-
labor alliance was born.[49]

V.

No one could deny that the reality failed to live up to the
expectations. The alliance meant not the liberation of African
Americans from racial oppression which neo-Debsians
envisioned, not an event on the scale of the Civil War, as NNC
youth secretary Ed Strong had prophesied, not the "Magna
Charta for black labor" that Davis promised. It meant little
more than verbal support by white labor for a doomed piece of
mildly reformist legislation.

Changes there were, and these could not be denied. Black
conservative George Schuyler described them:

> Recently I visited 35 industrial centers
> investigating the response of the Negro workers to the
> new labor unionization drive. Almost everywhere
> workers were found to be flocking to both the A.F. of L.
> and C.I.O. unions in unprecedented numbers. They were
> found functioning as officials in literally hundreds of
> unions. . . . In some cases they had formed
> organizations and struck for better working conditions
> before organizers arrived on the scene. Wherever they
> had joined with white fellow workers for mutual

improvement, race relations had vastly changed for the better.

Here at long last were color prejudice and discrimination being effectively attacked through labor associations, organization and education. Here were colored and white workers striving toward a common goal with astonishing *esprit de corps*. . . .

Of course color prejudice and discrimination still obtain in the labor movement in America. . . . But not in fifty years has America witnessed such interracial solidarity.

Still, after the initial euphoria had worn off, even these more modest assessments would be tempered.[50]

When Lester Granger warned African Americans in 1938 not to mistake the CIO for a "militant pro-Negro organization," he could have been speaking to many of its present-day partisans. The "racial egalitarianism" of the CIO has become a "progressive" article of faith that has lasted through every shift in the direction of the "progressive" movement. When, in addition, the civil rights movement of the 1950s and 1960s redefined liberalism, which had traditionally refused to extend its principles to African Americans, it became incumbent upon the new liberalism to find a heritage of "racial egalitarianism" to call their own. Their quest led them to the CIO. It did not lead them, on the other hand, to an acknowledgement that to whatever degree such a label could be remotely applied, African Americans, not "progressive" or liberal ideology, deserved the credit. The debt has never been repaid.[51]

The CIO did not start out as the civil rights advocate it became. While the CIO certainly needed to seek the support of African Americans, that did not mean that it automatically adopted advanced positions on matters of interest to them. The early CIO, although it privately professed the desire to organize African Americans on the "UMW model," did not formulate a clear policy on their behalf. It simply sought to replicate its own position, which John P. Davis had so accurately appraised during the height of his "progressive labor" days: "'We will organize Negro workers to protect the interest of white workers, guaranteeing to them economic privileges." Davis, however, did not appreciate the overwhelming significance of his own words, and did not apply this truth to the campaigns the NNC was to help the CIO carry out.

Moreover, there was nothing within the initial program of the CIO or its constituent internationals to assure African Americans that the new federation would join the struggle for civil rights. Such support was a significant departure from even that of the United Mine Workers, as Black radicals like Davis keenly appreciated. While the UMW had favored racially liberal policies in regard to organizing workers, they had not expressed interest in Black political rights. In that sense they were no more advanced than the AFL, despite having *already* organized large numbers of Blacks.

The leap from that starting point to the CIO's advocacy of civil rights covers the period of the development of the relationship between it and the NNC. The events of the time show that mere coincidence cannot explain the concurrence. CIO leaders did not immediately begin addressing large gatherings of Blacks in support of civil rights. Philip Murray's address to the national steel conference for Black workers was a noteworthy event at the time. Such engagements did not become a frequent activity of CIO leaders until years after the formation of their relations with the NNC. Moreover, as Murray made clear in 1936, some of the CIO leadership, including someone as "racially liberal" as Murray, did not think that Black workers could be organized until after white workers, just as the AFL had always looked upon the question. Such thinking from a leader so high up in the CIO, the future head of the CIO, showed that the CIO did not accept the need to organize Blacks as a matter of course, much less that civil rights formed an integral part of organized labor's agenda.

Ultimately, however, of far greater significance than what the CIO did do was what it did not do. The greatest signal the CIO could have sent African Americans would have been to start a serious national campaign to organize agricultural workers and domestics. No other move could have benefited Blacks more, and none could have given an indication of the CIO's wholehearted concern for their plight. Perhaps the CIO helped initiate a "wave" in race *relations*, but in terms of the *economic conditions* of African Americans it was little more than a ripple, affecting only the small number of Black workers in the predominantly northern industries.

Not only did the Black-labor alliance turn out to be something quite different from Black radicals' expectations, but Black radicalism changed in the process. Early Black radicals had called for a clear departure from the tradition of liberalism in racial matters. Later radicals, like Davis, would help to continue its work. The Southern Conference on Human Welfare in Birmingham, Alabama best indicated the circles in which Davis, the leader of the radicals' project, chose to move by the end of 1938. The twelve hundred participants of this thoroughly liberal organization elected Davis co-president along with several prominent white leaders, including a senator, a congressman, and a governor. From the three hundred Black leaders present, Davis was one of two African Americans chosen for the executive board in company with Mary McLeod Bethune, and ahead of such figures as F.D. Patterson, president of Tuskegee, Charles Johnson of the Urban League, and former New Deal official Forrester Washington.[52]

Moreover, Davis, like many other radicals, adopted a new view of the New Deal. From having perceived it virtually as the enemy, he now thought of the Roosevelt administration as an ally against the bloc of reactionary southern senators. In 1938, the NNC hailed Roosevelt for his "progressive administration." If radicals had once sought to transform liberals into "progressives," they had ended by transforming "progressivism" into liberalism.[53]

Davis, in guiding the organizational expression of 1930s Black radicalism, retreated to a stance more in accord with his JCNR work than with his days as a Black radical champion of progressive laborism/syndicalism. Describing the purpose of the Congress, Davis wrote, in reference to the upcoming special session of Congress in late 1938, "The [National Negro] Congress is here to lobby for Negro participation in these economic plans." He continued to focus on the failure of the federal government to provide for domestic and agricultural workers and the plight of the unemployed. And the experiences of the JCNR years had translated directly at times into tactics for the Congress' work, the best example being the fight for a Black division under the Wages and Hours Bill to safeguard the interests of Blacks. Moreover, he still believed that "we must daily keep in touch with the existing wages and hours, housing and WPA administrations: to keep them alert to the special problems of Negroes."[54]

Davis also rediscovered, to some extent, the Black masses whose advocate he had always believed himself to be. As leader of the NNC, he tried to involve them in its activities. Its mass meetings drew thousands of African Americans. And on one occasion, he cautioned the New York council that by too often speaking at meetings held by other groups, the NNC reached only white audiences. While noting that in of itself that was not bad, Davis suggested that such addresses to whites would "not serve to awaken the Negro masses who never hear our speeches." The latter goal had clearly climbed on Davis's agenda, however much it smacked of "narrow racial politics."[55]

The neo-Debsian philosophy that had launched the NNC faded into the background. Statements in its vein were still to be found, such as that by Max Yergan, then second vice-president, speaking to the second national convention in Philadelphia in 1937. But already there was a different quality to them:

> There is nothing inherently of a narrow racial purpose in the program of the National Negro Congress. To be sure, it is racial in that it calls Negroes to action; it is racial in that it proposes--as it inevitably must--that Negroes strive as Negroes; it is racial in that it is determined that Negroes shall become part of, and shall identify themselves with, the larger struggle in America and the world for a genuinely improved life in every respect. But there need be no apology, and there is none, for this particular emphasis. The cause of the Negro is the cause of democracy.

Most of the 1930s Black radicals who embraced neo-Debsianism would themselves become disillusioned with it and retreat into "narrow racial" politics. Davis himself would become editor of a reference book on African Americans.[56]

The NNC's relationship with organized labor reflects, to some extent, this changing perspective. After its relationship with the CIO and LNPL had developed, the NNC did not assume their priorities. It continued to push the new labor federation to consider the interests of African Americans, including arguing for the formation of a Tobacco Workers Organizing Committee and the appointment of a executive assistant in the CIO to monitor the status of Blacks in its affiliates. Moreover, Davis informed even those in organized labor seeking the cooperation of the NNC on legislation that the NNC was putting all its resources into the "vigorous fight" to secure the interests of agricultural and domestic workers. Davis did not see the alliance with the industrials as antithetical to the interests of the majority of Blacks who labored in agriculture and domestic service. He wrote to a supporter, "there is no inconsistency between the program of the C.I.O. and that of farm unity." He believed that the CIO had the ability to accomplish the organization of agricultural and domestic laborers. And neither did he apologize for pushing the CIO to take up those tasks. He wrote to Revels Cayton, Secretary-Treasurer of the Maritime District Federation in San Francisco, and also an NNC activist, "In the four years of our existence there is hardly one of the 42 CIO internationals who have [*sic*] not been aided by our work."[57]

Still, Davis's legacy lies in another direction. With the NNC, he had built a relationship with progressive organized labor. Its failures would, in large part, be linked to the failures of its alliance partner, the NNC, the outgrowth of 1930s Black radicalism. Unlike other segments of the population, employers in particular, Davis placed his trust in organized labor to adopt policies increasingly favorable to Blacks, in spite of his own recognition that it had traditionally, at best, done no more than seek to guarantee white privilege. By 1938, he had come to realize just how much it needed prodding, but he placed his faith in "a growing sense of class unity in the labor movement [which would help] to break down the color bar." With the CIO having already organized four million workers, it became the largest and best organized force among white groups to campaign for civil rights. But Black radicals had sought more than civil rights. They had stood for the possibility of a fully integrated, non-racial labor movement that would tear up the economic basis of American racial oppression. It did not.[58]

Epilogue

At root, the Black radical consensus program for Black labor of the 1930s, with its neo-Debsian basis, had been founded on the belief that no racial, i.e., national, struggle was necessary for the liberation of African Americans, but that all struggles began and ended with the simple class struggle of workers of whatever kind without distinction. Under the conditions of the Great Depression, they believed, in common with the left in general, that the class struggle centered above all upon the organization of workers into industrial unions, reaching its culmination in the Congress of Industrial Organizations.

For a time, the CIO would seek to organize African Americans where they otherwise constituted an obstacle to the success of mass organization campaigns. But after the moment of crisis passed, after the Depression gave way to renewed prosperity on a scale the labor aristocracy had never dared hoped for, Black workers were forgotten. The much ballyhooed "Operation Dixie," the organizing drive of the early post-World War II years in which the CIO declared its intention of bringing the benefits of industrial unionism to southern workers white and Black, never more than a token, was given up at the first sign of southern white opposition.

Even in its heyday from its formation in 1935 to the passage of the Taft-Hartley Act in 1947, which aimed to root out the "communist influence" in the union movement,[1] the CIO's record with respect to Black workers was far from unblemished. Rhetoric there was in abundance, at least after CIO leaders were made to recognize the militancy of the Black workers

193

within its constituent unions. But the CIO took little action. From its point of view, especially in the South, the "Negro question was a ticklish one," in the words of CIO leader William Mitch. The CIO did nothing to suppress overt manifestations of racism on the part of some of its officers. It appointed few African Americans to staff positions, fewer still to leading roles, although some were elected on the local level where Black workers in the union were in the majority. Far from concluding that the era of interracial union solidarity was at hand, leading Black intellectuals and unionists called for and organized independent Black trade union groups to combat racism in the ranks of labor.[2] Reluctantly, the CIO would be forced by rank-and-file pressure to acknowledge that discrimination remained to be dealt with and to form, in 1942, after seven years of existence, the Committee to Abolish Racial Discrimination (CARD). But, rather than a determined campaign to achieve the lofty aim declared in its title, CARD, according to historian Marshall Stevenson, represented "a bureaucratic approach to institutional racism." Not surprisingly, its accomplishments were modest and inadequate. As one student of Black labor history, former NAACP labor director Herbert Hill, puts it, "The forms of discrimination sometimes changed, but the substance did not."[3]

Moreover, what little the CIO did do, it did not do alone, nor without being pushed to remember "the brother in black," as sociologist Horace Cayton phrased it in 1941. Within the history of the National Negro Congress it becomes clear that the legendary "racial egalitarianism" of the CIO, insofar as there is any substance to it, resulted only from the struggle of African Americans within it. The NNC's constant insistence upon the hiring of Black organizers played an important role in the success of getting and keeping Blacks in unions. That organization played a major, indeed, the crucial, part in bringing forth statements on civil rights from the CIO and turning the words into actions. In some cases, John P. Davis succeeded in getting the CIO and Labor's Non-Partisan League, the political wing of the CIO, to issue his words as their own. Most notably, an agreement between Davis and the LNPL was responsible for the position the League took in support of a congressional bill against lynching, despite the expressed desire of the LNPL head to avoid it. But, of course, the expressed support of organized labor was a long way from even the passage of the bill (which never occurred), let alone the elimination of lynching itself, or, more remote still, the liberation of African Americans from centuries of oppression in the United States.[4]

For its part, the CIO could well be satisfied at the outcome of its alliance with the NNC. The CIO got much-needed help in bringing African Americans into its unions in industries employing them in large numbers. It had access to experienced organizers, sometimes made available at no charge. Within a few years, hundreds of thousands of Black workers were adding to the CIO coffers each month. Their support, financial and physical, made at least some of the CIO's triumphs possible.

But if the impact of African Americans on the CIO and its campaigns was substantial, the reverse cannot be said to be true. As Roderick Ryon has most forcefully pointed out, the CIO rarely conducted campaigns to help large numbers of Blacks without large numbers of whites. The tobacco industry provides the best example. In this industry employing predominantly Black workers, the CIO's early efforts were so half-hearted that the AFL won many battles despite retaining segregated locals. John P. Davis, as head of the National Negro Congress, asked the CIO for a Tobacco Workers Organizing Committee to send out the right message to Black workers everywhere: the CIO would support a predominantly Black union. But the CIO chose to use its resources elsewhere. Especially devastating to the revolutionary aspirations of Black radicals, the CIO and its political backers would refuse to undertake the organization of Black agricultural and domestic workers, who together accounted for two-thirds of African American laborers during the Depression era. Such a development represented a particularly crushing blow for Black women, who were overwhelmingly confined to domestic drudgery. The results remain clearly in evidence today.[5]

"Progressive unionism," then, proved to be perfectly compatible with the continuation of racism, discrimination, and segregation. Apparently class interest was not as simple a

matter as the Black radicals of the 1930s had declared it to be,
since the "end of classes," the prosperity and merger into the
"middle class" of the northern, overwhelmingly white
proletariat could occur even as African Americans, especially,
but not only in the South, remained impoverished, outside of
unions, and continued to form, with other "minorities," the
bottom rung in the American working-class structure. Nor was
the world-wide "slavery" of the people of color brought to an
end. As much of the American, European, and, in general,
basically white proletariat of the world climbed to new
heights of prosperity, proletarians of color (as the working
classes of Africa, Asia and Latin America might be called) sank
to new depths, in both relative and absolute terms. The
"inseparable" class interests of all workers proved to be
separable after all.

Du Bois, capable of profound insight on occasion, had
foreseen all of this in advance. Accurately perceiving the
narrow basis behind the trade union-centered reformism that
Black radicals, all rhetoric aside, had embraced, he warned,
"[W]hen it comes to a minority and disadvantaged group like
that of the American Negro, a restoration of the full power of
the capitalistic system in the United States can mean to them
little more than a restoration of their former unfortunate
condition." And how could a mere alteration of the form of
trade union organization, even the organization of African-
American workers into unions, change the nature of the
American capitalist system? Was it not merely part of the
larger effort at reform designed to help bring about the
restoration of the status quo?[6]

Black radicals cannot be absolved of their share of the
blame. Their convergence around the programmatic outlook of
neo-Debsianism in the mid-Thirties set the stage for just such a
result. Inch by inch they gave up the ground that the ABB
radicals had wrested from the left, at least the communist left.
No longer did Black workers have the right to regard white
workers as only "potential allies." No longer could they base
their alliance with the white workers on the condition that it
aided the liberation struggle of the "Negro people of the
world." Instead, it became their duty to join in the

"progressive" cause, the fight for industrial unions and labor politics (which, ironically, became, World War II, Democratic Party politics--i.e., the party of slavery of old). When the CIO launched its massive organization drives of the late Thirties, Black workers were called upon to join their unions. This cemented the alliance, so labor officials and Black radicals claimed. The common interests of both were served. But what of the majority of the African-American people? The CIO would not even agree to so much as a nod in their direction. And though the NNC did not desist from raising these issues with CIO leaders, it never threatened to cut off relations, leaving the CIO with a virtual free hand. The alliance of joint interest, of "revolutionary duty" and class-consciousness, had degenerated into an alliance of convenience.

Having virtually declared the end of the Black liberation movement, most of the Black radicals of this time would live to see, and many would participate in, its next phase in the Fifties and Sixties. Far from the promised end to the "reactionary politics of race," Black nationalism would flower once again in the Sixties. The 1950s and 1960s would prove, as had sporadic episodes in the Twenties and Thirties, that the potential for mass rebellion among African Americans in the South did indeed exist, and the same period witnessed revolutionary upsurges in Africa, the West Indies, and Latin America.

II.

The understanding of the connection of nationality, or race, and class, then, is not quite so simple. So much is this the case that recently it has become fashionable for those claiming to have learned the lessons of history to speak of "plural identities," of which class and nationality are merely two among many. But the adherents of such mistaken views place nationality and class side by side because they never bother to place them in relation to one another. To start with the question of interpreting Black labor history is to end up inevitably at the question of the relationship of race and class.[7]

Among neo-Debsians, it was the custom to "derive" the "Negro Question" in America from the economic oppression of African Americans. In other words, it was *because* African Americans had been an "oppressed class," indeed, an enslaved class, that they cohered as an especially oppressed group (when this was admitted) in modern capitalist society. But this explanation exactly reversed the history: African Americans were certainly not of African descent because they were slaves, but they were slaves, in their overwhelming mass, because they were of African descent. Nationality can under no circumstances be derived from class, but class is often derived from nationality.[8] Hence, insofar as a slave was a member of a class, and confined to that class, he or she was so confined because of national origin. Class differences, then, to some degree always stood in relation to national differences. As Marx writes, "The discovery of gold and silver in America, the extirpation, enslavement and entombment in mines of the aboriginal population, the beginning of the conquest and looting of the East Indies, the turning of Africa into a warren for the commercial hunting of black skins, signalised the rosy dawn of the era of capitalist production." So, to be African in Africa was to be hunted by European slavecatchers, to be African in America was to be a slave, to be Native American was to be exterminated, to be East Asian was to be a "coolie," and so forth. Native American, African, and Asian all shared this in common (which is, in fact, all they shared in common): They were to be subjected to the encroachment of capitalism, and they became its subjects.[9]

On the other hand, no matter how infinitely oppressed the Russian serf or English, French, or German worker, he or she remained Russian, English, French or German, and did not become, on the basis of class affiliation, Polish, Irish, Algerian, or Turkish. And, while, class distinctions can be obliterated either as a characteristic of an individual, or even in the form of the disappearance of or raising up of whole classes, national distinctions, as they affect whole nations at least, cannot be thrown off so readily. Hence, if the lot of

Russian, English, French and German workers has improved immensely, perhaps so much that they are no longer separable from the middle classes of those nations, the same cannot be said of the nationality of Poles, Irish, Algerians and Turks. These national conflicts continue to rage.

Superficially, this analysis lends credence to the standpoint, which lies at the root of various forms of nationalism, both in the United States and, especially, in the so-called "Third World," which ignores class. It seems that nationality, or race, takes precedence over class in history. Class relations appear more fluid, national more lasting. But if this dominance of nationality seems to hold, it is only because the transformation of nationality into class is thereby ignored, just as this transition is generally ignored in history. When W.E.B. Du Bois said that the "color line" had become the question of the 20th century, he was referring to the enslavement of people of color by the European imperialist powers. Du Bois came to this conclusion from his analysis of the relative position of races (nationalities) in the world. But this analysis he shared with a thinker who came at the question from the point of view of class. Lenin, a European whose first concern was the emancipation of the working class, wrote, "The characteristic feature of imperialism consists in the whole world, as we now see, being divided into a large number of oppressed nations and an insignificant number of oppressor nations." Both Du Bois and Lenin recognized how dependent these European imperialist powers were upon the class exploitation of the workers and peasants in the nations so oppressed, and how they were able on that basis to pay their own workers better, so that the latter constituted what Engels had long ago termed "an aristocracy within the working class."[10]

The whole question, therefore, resolves itself right back into one of class. But it does not do so directly, as with the neo-Debsians. It does so only through the "intermediary" of nationality (race), so that "class" becomes not the "pure" class of Debsianism, but class which preserves its national identity, the class form with national substance, as it were. In general, nationality becomes a characteristic of class, but only because class becomes a characteristic of nationality.

In the realm of theory, the end result can be derived at the moment the analysis is performed. Not so in that of history. There it first appears as a tendency, although this tendency was quite accurately understood by two thinkers as disparate as Du Bois and Lenin, and perhaps, as early as Marx.[11] By the 1990s this trend can be far more precisely proved statistically. It was a cliche in the 1930s to pronounce that the wealth of society rested on the labor of the workers. If this is so, then our present wealth is of "Third World" origin. Rough calculations suggest that within the richest countries of Europe as well as the U.S. and Canada 25% or approximately 125 million people (including dependents) belong to the laboring classes. In the rest of the world, the figures are closer to 90% or around 3870 million people. And the incomes of the latter are an infinitesimal fraction of the former, at a qualitatively entirely different level.[12]

Perhaps this situation is only the confirmation of what the liberal British economist John Atkinson Hobson foresaw nearly a century ago: "There is [among European imperialist powers] . . . the habit of economic parasitism, by which the ruling State has used its provinces, colonies, and dependencies in order to enrich its ruling class and to bribe its lower classes into acquiescence." If this were to continue,

> The greater part of Western Europe might then assume the appearance and character already exhibited by tracts of country in the South of England, in the Riviera and in the tourist-ridden or residential parts of Italy and Switzerland, little clusters of wealthy aristocrats drawing dividends and pensions from the Far East, with a somewhat larger group of professional retainers and tradesmen and a large body of personal servants and workers in the transport trade and in the final stages of production of the more perishable goods; all the main arterial industries would have disappeared, the staple foods and manufactures flowing in as tribute from Asia and Africa.

In short, virtually our own "post-industrial" society, which consumes more commodities and material wealth than ever, and produces an ever-smaller share of it. Hobson continues,

> We have foreshadowed the possibility of even a larger alliance of Western states, a European federation of great Powers which, so far from forwarding the cause of world civilisation, might introduce the gigantic peril of a Western parasitism, a group of advanced industrial nations, whose upper classes drew vast tribute from Asia and Africa, with which they supported great tame masses of retainers, no longer engaged in the staple industries of agriculture and manufacture, but kept in the performance of personal or minor industrial services under the control of a new financial aristocracy.[13]

Whatever we make of the current state of affairs in the world, the statistics quoted above show it to be the case that to be from the "Third World" is to be, almost exclusively, of the laboring classes and poor, whereas to be from the "First World" is to be middle class, and even if a worker, to be of a middle-class standard of living (a member of the "labor aristocracy"). If an exception exists, then it consists of members of national (racial) minorities, who, though they have benefited from the rapid rise in wealth in Western society, have done so far less than members of the ruling nationalities (races). Indeed, both nationality and class remain in the modern world. But more and more they are becoming indistinguishable.

Notes

Introduction

1. Baltimore *Afro-American*, May 25, 1935; "Unemployment Among Negro Male Workers at the End of 1934," Report Prepared for the Joint Committee on National Recovery, May 19, 1935, National Negro Congress Record Group, Box 2, Schomburg Collection of the New York Public Library. That the difference in the unemployment figure for Black workers as opposed to the overall rate seems small by today's standard is a commentary, not upon the extent of racial oppression in the 1930s, but upon the degree to which it has been overcome in the interim.

2. Mary Anderson, "The Plight of Negro Domestic Labor," *Journal of Negro Education*, January, 1936, pp. 66-72; John P. Davis, "A Survey of the Problems Under the New Deal," *JNE*, January, 1936, pp. 8-11.

3. For estimates of the number of Black unionists at various junctures, see Philip S. Foner, *Organized Labor and the Black Worker, 1619-1973* (New York: Praeger Publishers, 1974).

4. For a review of the works that have treated Black radicalism in the 1920s and 1930s, see Keith Griffler, "The Black Radical Intellectual and the Black Worker: The Emergence of a Program for Black Labor, 1918-1939," Ph. D. dissertation, Ohio State University, 1993, pp. 5-23.

5. Paul F. Brissender, *Earnings of Factory Workers, 1899 to 1927: An Analysis of Pay-Roll Statistics*, Census Monographs X (Washington, D.C.: Bureau of the Census, 1929), pp. 53-4.

6. Standing at the forefront of this myth is that eminent
ideologist of imperialism Gunnar Myrdal, in his *An American
Dilemma: The Negro Problem and Modern Democracy*, (New
York: Harper and Row, 1944). Myrdal claims that the CIO
"followed the principle that Negroes should be organized
together with whites" and attempted to gain places for Blacks
"in occupations where they have not been working before and to
demand more equality for them in job advancement." He
continues, the industrial unions "have made a courageous start"
and have consistently tried "to spread the principle of
universal labor solidarity and to combat race prejudice." The
CIO achieved only limited gains in organizing Blacks only
because of the racism of white workers, the resistance of
employers, and the "suspicions" of Black workers--apparently
wholly unjustified (loc. cit., pp. 402-03). It is worth noting that
Myrdal ignored the opinion offered in a manuscript contribution
to the Carnegie-Myrdal undertaking by Ralph Bunche, who
had been in the forefront of the movement to align Blacks with
organized labor through his participation in the founding of
the NNC. Bunche wrote, the AFL *and* the CIO "are both weak,
ridden with factional strife and disputes, controlled by a
narrow-minded bureaucracy of professional labor leaders, and
more often than not, socially unintelligent." In *both*
federations, he believed, leaders "harbor intensive racial
prejudices" (quoted in John Kirby, *Black Americans in the
Roosevelt Era: Liberalism and Race* (Knoxville: The
University of Tennesee Press, 1980), pp. 210-11). For a review of
the remaining pertinent literature, see Griffler, loc. cit., pp.
324-31.

Chapter 1

1. Karl Marx, *Capital: A Critique of Political Economy*,
Vol. 1 (Chicago: Charles Kerr, 1906), p. 329; see Engels in Karl
Marx and Frederick Engels, *Collected Works*, Vol. 25 (New
York: International Publishers, 1987), p. 98; Philip Foner,
*American Socialism and Black Americans: From the Age of
Jackson to World War II* (Westport, Ct: Greenwood Press, 1977).

2. Foner, *American Socialism and Black Americans*, p. 343; Philip Foner and Ronald L. Lewis, eds., *The Black Worker: A Documentary History from Colonial Times to the Present*, vol. 6 (Philadelphia: Temple University Press, 1981), pp. 385-6.

3. Foner and Lewis, eds., *The Black Worker*, vol. 5, p. 530; Foner, *American Socialism and Black Americans*, p. 355.

4. V.I. Lenin, *Collected Works*, volume 26, (Moscow: Progress Publishers, 1965), p. 168; *Lenin on the United States* (New York: International Publishers, 1970), pp. 303-307, 115-205, 453-459; Philip Foner and James S. Allen, eds., *American Communism and Black Americans: A Documentary History, 1919-1929* (Philadelphia: Temple University Press, 1987), pp. xii-xiv. According to Theodore Draper (*American Communism and Soviet Russia: The Formative Period* (New York: Viking Press, 1960), pp. 321, 325), Lenin also wrote to the American party in 1921 demanding to know why they had initiated no work among African Americans. This may or may not be true, but it is now known that Lenin had by that time already met Black communist Otto Huiswoud, a member of the CP, which makes this assertion seem less likely. To be sure, Draper is wrong to conclude that ABB communists were only recruited into the CP in 1921. At least a few of them had been in it, in fact, since its inception in 1919.

Draper may well be correct that Lenin's reference to African Americans in a speech at the second Comintern congress was prefaced by the words "dependent nations and those without equal rights," rather than "subject" or "underpriviledged" (pp. 337-9). But Draper can conclude nothing on this basis. For he takes it out of its context of a discussion on *imperialism* and its effects upon people's subject to its peculiar forms of oppression. And here there can be no doubt that Lenin deliberately meant to include African Americans. For Draper it is merely a question of words, as though this were Biblican text rather than intellectual, which leads Draper to conclude that "We can only speculate" as to what Lenin meant. In fact, we can do more. We can refer to his other writings. It is clear from the quotation provided in the text that Lenin, at least, saw the parallel between foreign workers (sometimes euphemistically called "guest" workers) in European nations and African American workers in the U.S. For Lenin, then, a subject people and a people "without equal rights" were the same (for the fact that members of such groups of people without rights on the basis of their national, or, if it is preferred, racial affiliation is precisely the definition of "subject" people). Draper has evidently caught an example of poor translation, but it does not support his conclusions.

5. Alan Adler, ed., *Theses, Resolutions and Manifestos of the First four Congresses of the Third International* (Atlantic Highlands, NJ: Humanities Press, 1980), pp. 27-36.

6. Claude McKay, *The Negroes in America* (Port Washington, NY: Kennikat Press, 1979), xv-xviii, 6-10; *International Press Correspondence*, vol. 3, no. 10 (March 15, 1923), pp. 158-9; Negro Worker, May, 1935.

7. Robert Hill, "Introduction" to the reprint edition of the *Crusader* (New York: Garland Publishing Inc., 1987), p. xxvi; Domingo quoted in McKay, *Negroes in America*, pp. 38-40; interview with Hall in Foner and Lewis, *The Black Worker*, p. 434; Cyril Briggs later wrote in the *Liberator*: "It was Lenin who laid the basis for that whole-hearted support which Communist parties throughout the world have given to the nationalist movements in . . . [the] oppressed countries, as well as for a free black republic of South Africa, self-determination for the Negro people of the Southern United States and complete racial, social, and political equality for the Negro, north and south" (January 18, 1930).

8. Foner and Allen, loc. cit., pp. 5-8.

9. Quoted in McKay, loc. cit., pp. 38-40; for Haywood's attitude to the Russian revolution, see his articles in *The Liberator* in 1919 and 1920.

10. Foner and Lewis, *The Black Worker*, vol. 5, pp. 523-532, vol. 6, pp. 411-22.

11. Robert Minor, *The Liberator*, August 1924.

12. Scott Nearing, *Black America* (New York: International Publishers, 1929); Nearing, *The Making of a Radical: A Political Autobiography* (New York: Harper and Row, 1972), p. 148.

13. Nearing, Black America, pp. 7, 70, 126, 132, 219, 261.

14. *Ibid.*, pp. 6, 106, 130, 132, 214, 262; for the circumstances surrounding his resignation/expulsion from the party, see his *Political Autobiography*.

15. Briggs, "How Garvey Betrayed the Negroes," *Negro Worker*, August 15, 1932, pp. 14-15, Briggs lists as the earliest members of the ABB, along with himself, Richard B. Moore, Otto Huiswoud, W.A. Domingo, and "Hubert Harrison before his degeneration"; Harry Haywood, *Black Bolshevik: Autobiography of an Afro-American Communist* (Chicago: Liberator Press, 1978), pp. 122-31; Haywood confirms that Briggs was the founder and leader of the ABB.

16. McKay, *Negroes in America*, p. 38; similar statements can be found by Richard B. Moore, Otto Huiswoud, Lovett Fort-Whiteman, and others. See Foner and Allen, loc. cit.

17. Quoted in McKay, *Negroes in America*, pp. 38-40.

18. Foner and Allen, loc. cit., pp. vii-ix.

19. Hill, loc. cit., pp. v-xlviii.

20. Robert Hill, introduction to the Garland reprint of *The Crusader*, xvii, xlvi, lxvii-lxx.

21. *Crusader*, Sept. 1918, pp. 1-4, 10; Oct. 1918, p. 7; Dec. 1918, pp. 3, 5-6; Jan. 1919, pp. 3-4, 7, 14; Feb. 1919, p. 6; April 1919, p. 8; June 1919, p. 6.

22. *Crusader*, Sept. 1918, pp. 1-4, 11; Nov. 1918, p. 1, 7-8; March 1919, pp. 22-3; May 1919, p. 3.

23. *Crusader*, Nov. 1918, pp. 5-6, 12-14. Even after Briggs gave up, in mid-1920, the plan of "a free Negro State [in] the territory now included in the United States" as "unsatisfactory both to the Negro and the white man" and "too vulnerable for permanent independent existence," he continued to advocate "autonomy ('government of the Negro, by the Negro and for the Negro')," or what he sometimes called "self-determination" for the people of African descent (*Crusader*, July 1920, p. 5). It is unclear when, or, indeed, if, this aspect of Briggs' thinking ceased to be important to his outlook on the "Negro Question."

24. Hill, introduction to *The Crusader* reprint, p. xxvi.; *Crusader*, April 1919, p. 10; May 1919, pp. 4-5; June 1919, pp. 3-4.

25. *Crusader*, June 1919, p. 7.

26. *Crusader*, April 1921, pp. 8-9, 10-11; May 1921, pp. 29-30.

27. "Program of the African Blood Brotherhood," in Foner and Allen, loc. cit., pp. 16-23; Harry Haywood to Cyril [Briggs], October 26, 1961, Harry Haywood Papers, box 1, Bentley Library, University of Michigan, Ann Arbor.

28. "Program of the African Blood Brotherhood," p. 23.

29. *Ibid*. Implicit in this statement and the programmatic outlook of the ABB is the notion that class-consciousness, a term which white radicals used to indicate an orientation to class struggle on the part of workers, included also the understanding on the part of workers of the importance of the "Negro Question" and that it required separate solution. As such, the ABB program calls into question, to some degree, the class-consciousness of the vast majority of white Americans, and also, perhaps, puts over its own claim as the "vanguard" of the American revolutionary workers, at least until the CP accepted its program. This same use of the term can be found in the writing of W.A. Domingo, who wrote that the Bolsheviks under Lenin were "imbued with class consciousness" because they championed the cause of the nationally oppressed peoples of the world (quoted in Claude McKay, *The Negroes in America*, p. 39).

30. McKay, *Negroes in America*, pp. xv-xviii. McKay would always retain a special feeling of love for rural life that he drew from this heritage. It gave his brand of communism a special, somewhat unusual flavor. He wrote in 1921, "For my part I love to think of communism liberating millions of city folk to go back to the land" (*The Liberator*, June 1921).

31. *The Liberator*, August, 1922; *The Negroes in America*.

32. *Ibid.*, pp. xi, 23, 38-40.

33. *Ibid.*, p. xvii-xviii, 5, 23; *The Liberator*, June, 1921.

34. Haywood, loc. cit.; Foner and Allen, loc. cit., p. 70; James Jackson [Fort-Whiteman], "The Negroes in America," *Communist International*, No. 8, 1925, pp. 50-52.

35. Foner and Allen, loc. cit., p. 96.

36. *Crusader*, April 1921, p. 10; May 1921, pp. 29-30; Foner and Allen, loc. cit., p. 37.

37. Moore was born on the Caribbean island of Barbados in 1893. In 1909, he arrived in New York with his family, determined to secure their existence. The recipient of a brief

education, he had embarked upon gainful employment at the age of eleven, and he continued his assortment of odd working-class jobs in Harlem. He quickly took his place in Black radical circles, where his fame as an orator quickly spread. In 1918, he joined the Socialist Party, and soon after, the ABB and Communist Party, probably in 1919. From there, he quickly rose to become, along with Briggs, one of the two leading Black members of the CP in the mid-1920s; Richard B. Moore, *Caribbean Militant in Harlem: Collected Writings, 1920-1972* (Bloomington: University of Indian Press, 1988), pp. 19-68.

38. Moore, *Caribbean Militant in Harlem*, pp. 143-55.

Chapter 2

1. *New York Times*, Dec. 26, 1922; McKay, *Negroes in America*, pp. 38-40; the veracity of this incident is confirmed by Cyril Briggs, who adds that it was given wide publicity in the Black press ("Our Negro Work," *Communist*, September, 1929, p. 496.

2. Cyril Briggs, "Our Negro Work," pp. 495-96.

3. Haywood, *Black Bolshevik*, pp. 121-22, 218-244; William L. Patterson, *The Man Who Cried Genocide: An Autobiography* (New York: International Publishers, 1971), p. 97.

4. Harry Haywood to Cyril [Briggs], October 26, 1961, loc. cit.; Foner and Allen, loc. cit., pp. 25-27.

5. Lenin, "Preliminary Draft Theses on the National and Colonial Questions. For the Second Congress of the Communist International," in *Selected Works in Three Volumes*, vol. 3 (New York: International Publishers, 1967), pp. 422-7.

6. Foner and Lewis, eds., *Black Worker*, pp. 453, 454.

7. Cyril Briggs, "Our Negro Work," *Communist*, September, 1929, pp. 494-501; Lenin, "Preliminary Draft Theses," loc. cit.; Foner and Allen, loc. cit., pp. 28-30.

8. Ibid.; McKay, *Negroes in America*, p. 7.

9. Foner and Allen, loc. cit., p. 37.

10. Otto Hall interview, in Foner and Lewis, *Black Worker*, p. 434.

11. Briggs, "Our Negro Work," p. 496.

12. *Ibid.*, pp. 434-5; James Jackson [Fort-Whiteman], "The Negroes in America," *Communist International*, No. 8, 1925, pp. 50-52; "Editorial Comment," p. 53.

13. Foner and Allen, loc. cit., pp. 109-23; *Harlem Liberator*, September 2, 1933.

14. Foner and Allen, loc. cit., p. 182.

15. W.E.B. Du Bois, *Selections from the Crisis*, vol. 2, ed. by Herbert Aptheker, (Millwood, New York: Kraus-Thomas Organization Limited, 1983), p. 456, 495; Foner and Allen, loc. cit., p. 14.

16. Du Bois, *Selections from the Crisis*, p. 495.

17. *Ibid.*, pp. 458-60, 491.

18. *Ibid.*, pp. 458-60, 461.

19. *Ibid.*, pp. 480-84; McKay, *Negroes in America*, p. 49.

20. *Crusader*, May 1919, p. 3; Du Bois, *Selections from the Crisis*, pp. 495, 509-10, 530, 565.

21. *Ibid.*, p. 456.

22. Abram L. Harris, Jr., "Lenin Casts His Shadow Upon Africa," *The Crisis*, Vol. 31 (April 1936), pp. 272-5.

23. Ibid.; Abram L. Harris, *Race, Radicalism, and Reform, Selected Papers*, ed. by William Darity, Jr., (New Brunswick, NJ: Transaction Publishers, 1989), p. 166.

24. Harris, "Lenin Casts His Shadow Upon Africa," p. 275.

25. The document in question is Harris's "Black Communists in Dixie," in *Race, Radicalism, and Reform*, pp. 140-48; Darity suggests that the story, in which Harris describes events of two students, is autobiographical (p. 127), and his conclusion seems entirely warranted.

26. *Ibid.*, pp. 63, 129.

27. *Ibid.*, p. 138.

28. Alma Rene Williams, "Robert C. Weaver: From the Black Cabinet to the President's Cabinet," Ph.D. dissertation, Washington University, 1978; Davis is quoted on p. 24.

29. Davis, "The Black Man's Burden," *Nation*, January 9, 1929, p. 44.

30. Ralph J. Bunche to Dr. Du Bois, May 11, 1927 in Herbert Aptheker, ed., *The Correspondence of W.E.B. Du Bois*, vol. 1

(Amherst: University of Massachusetts Press, 1973), pp. 353-354.

31. See, for example, the unsigned editorials in *The Messenger* of May 1925, p. 196; and September 1925, pp. 324-5; see also Philip Foner, *American Socialism and Black Americans*; and John Howard Seabrook, "Black And White Unite: The Career of Frank R. Crosswaith," Ph.D. dissertation, Rutgers University, 1980.

32. Foner and Lewis, *The Black Worker*, vol. 5, pp. 521-27.

33. *Ibid.*; vol. 6, pp. 385-6, 290; Moore, *Caribbean Militant*, p. 147.

34. *Messenger*, September 1925, pp. 324-5; Jervis Anderson, *A. Philip Randolph: A Biographical Portrait* (New York: Harcourt Brace Jovanovich, Inc., 1972), especially pp. 113-119, 168-172; Hughes quoted p.138.

35. William Harris, *Keeping the Faith: A. Philip Randolph, Milton P. Webster, and the Brotherhood of Sleeping Car Porters, 1925-37* (Champagne: University of Illinois Press, 1982), pp. 104-14, 153; Harris concludes, "it is difficult to understand just how Randolph felt about a strike in the early spring of 1928," citing mainly personal reasons for his opposition to the strike; Manning Marable, "A. Philip Randolph, A Political Assessment," in *From the Grassroots: Essays Toward Afro-American Liberation* (South End Press, Boston, 1980), p. 75; Foner, *Black Workers*, p. 184-6; Harris, *Harder We Run*, p. 88.

36. Seabrook, loc. cit., pp. 29, 90-134.

37. *Ibid.*

38. Ibid., p. 172.

39. *Ibid.*; Foner and Lewis, *Black Worker*, vol. 6, pp. 217, 220, 387, 388-91.

40. *Ibid.*

41. *Messenger*, August 1925, pp. 296-7.

42. *Ibid.*

43. *Messenger*, June 1925, p. 228, July 1925, p. 261; on the BSCP, see Harris, *Keeping the Faith*, and Anderson, *Randolph*; on the ANLC, see Haywood, *Black Bolshevik*, pp. 143-6, 164; and James Ford, *The Negro and the Democratic Front* (New York: International Publishers, 1938), p. 82; as well as the

voluminous writings on the "Negro Question" of 1928-1929 in
the *Communist* and other CP organs.

44. Harris, *Keeping the Faith; Messenger*, June 1925, p. 228,
July 1925, p. 261; and August 1925, p. 303.

45. *Ibid.* It is possible that Harris himself was one of those
who attended Brookwood College. Certainly, he did during
this period strike up a significant connection with it,
participating in at least one symposium on Black workers and
organized labor, that proved crucial to the course of his
Depression-era career. Very likely it was through his contact
with the Brookwood school that Harris became a convert to
A.J. Muste's Conference for Progressive Labor Action, which put
Harris on the road to the development of his program for Black
labor.

46. *Ibid.*

Chapter 3

1. "The Communist International Resolution on the Negro
Question in the U.S.," Foner and Allen, eds., *American
Communism and Black Americans*, pp. 189-96.

2. *Ibid.*, pp. 191-92.

3. For background on its drafting, see Harry Haywood,
Black Bolshevik.

4. "Communist International Resolution on the Negro
Question," pp. 189-96.

5. John Pepper, "American Negro Problems," *Communist*,
October 1928, pp. 628-38.

6. "Theses and Resolutions Adopted by the Sixth World
Congress," Foner and Allen, loc. cit., pp. 196-98. The difference
between the Sixth Congress resolution and the later resolution
on the same topic by the Comintern Executive Commitee cannot
be explained, as in Foner and Allen, by the claim (p. 189) that
the CI resolution took account of the discussion, for the purport
of the two resolutions run in opposite directions. What is much
more likely is that the Congress had given some meaning to the
whole question which the hacks on the Comintern executive
could not quite grasp.

7. Pepper, "American Negro Problems."

8. *Ibid.* The treatment of the "Negro Question" by the Sixth Congress as a part of the "colonial question" was different from that at the Second Congress, where it had been within the "*National* and Colonial Questions," and where African Americans had been called a "subject nation" within a larger nation (Allan Adler, ed., *Theses, Resolutions and Manifestoes of the First Four Congresses of the Third International*, pp. 76-81).

9. *Ibid.*

10. Jos. Prokopec, "Negroes as an Oppressed National Minority," *Communist*, March 1930, pp. 239-45.

11. *Ibid.*

12. *Ibid.*

13. *Ibid.*, pp. 242-3, 244.

14. M. Rubinstein, "The Industrialization of the South and the Negro Problem," *Communist*, February 1930, pp. 148-53.

15. Myra Page, "Inter-Racial Relations Among Southern Workers," *Communist*, February 1930, pp. 144-45.

16. "Draft Program for the Negro Farmers in the Southern States," *Communist*, March 1930, pp. 246-56.

17. *Ibid.*

18. Page, "Inter-Racial Relations Among Southern Workers," p. 163.

19. "Resolution on the Negro Question in the United States. Final Text, Confirmed by the Political Commission of the E.C.C.I.," *Communist*, February 1931, pp. 153-167.

20. *Ibid.*, pp. 153, 160, 161.

21. *Ibid.*, p. 158.

22. *Ibid.*, pp. 163, 164, 167.

23. *Ibid.*, pp. 154, 156, 161-62, 166, 167.

24. *Ibid.*, pp. 157, 166-67. Browder's claim that Black workers must free themselves of distrust of white workers is a clear departure from the Comintern principles set down at the Second Congress, when it was stated that such "distrust" on the part of the workers of oppressed nations was entirely justified. Indeed, Lenin declared, "National hatred will not disappear so quickly. This hatred will be quite justified on the part of the oppressed nation. It will be overcome only after the victory of

Socialism and after the final establishment of complete
democratic relations between nations." (Quoted in N. Nasonov,
"Against Liberalism in the American Negro Question,"
Communist, April 1930, p. 304).

   25. *Ibid.*, p. 153. The context of the Comintern's praise for
the American CP, followed as it is by a polemic against the
"Lovestoneites," suggests that the Comintern wanted to give
them no room to criticize the faults of the American party. The
resolution seeks to imply that any difficulties in the area of
the "Negro Question" resulted from "the gross opportunism of
the Lovestoneites." At any rate, having accomplished its
purpose, and being free to move back to the right, the Comintern
under Stalin had no more need to hold the "Negro question"
over the heads of the American Communist Party.

   26. Jim Allen, "Some Rural Aspects of the Struggle for the
Right of Self-Determination," *Communist*, March 1931, pp. 249-
55.

   27. *Ibid.*, pp. 249, 255.

   28. Earl Browder, "For National Liberation of the Negroes!
War Against White Chauvinism," *Communist*, April 1932, pp.
295-309. Browder claimed further, "Our task is to bring this
struggle for national liberation under the leadership of the
proletariat, defeating the influence of the bourgeoisie which
can lead it only to betrayal. This is precisely the central point
of Lenin's program on the national question, which is the
instrument for unifying these two main forces for common
struggle against imperialism" (p. 309). Actually, in his
"Report of the Commission of the National and Colonial
Questions" at the Second Comintern Congress, Lenin said,
"What is the cardinal idea underlying our theses? It is the
distinction between oppressed and oppressor nations. . . . [W]e
emphasize this distinction" (Lenin, *Selected Works*, p. 456).
Browder sought to obliterate it.

   29. B.D. Amis, "For a Strict Leninist Analysis of the Negro
Question," *Communist*, October 1932, pp. 944-49.

   30. James S. Allen, *The Negro Question in the United
States* (New York: International Publishers, 1936).

   31. *Ibid.*, pp. 1-11.

   32. *Ibid.*

33. *Ibid.*, pp. 12-183.

34. *Ibid.* Allen specifically refers to the era of the Civil War and Reconstruction as an "unfinished revolution" and places the question of the social and economic status at the center of the epoch. This interpretation, under the guise of something new and profound, has been revived in Eric Foner's celebrated volume on the subject (*Reconstruction: America's Unfinished Revolution, 1863-1877*, New York: Harper & Row, 1988). That he does not acknowledge the source, or at least the precedent, for this view, is a sad commentary on the academy, which is capable of only the most narrow standpoint on what it qualifies as previous knowledge, and constantly appropriates without acknowledgment the thought of others outside its confines. It would be wrong, however, to qualify Allen's view as an original contribution. Such an outlook was quite common among those calling themselves "Marxists" in the 1930s, particularly those of the communists' "Popular Front." It is interesting that at a time when "Stalinism" is universally condemned that scholars such as Foner should return to its favorite historical formulas, and that their worth and originality should be so widely praised.

35. *Ibid.*

36. *Ibid.*, 148-9.

37. Abram L. Harris, Jr., "Lenin Casts His Shadow Upon Africa," *The Crisis*, vol. 31 (April 1926), pp. 272-5; John P. Davis, "The Black Man's Burden," *Nation*, January 9, 1929, p. 44; Ralph J. Bunche to Dr. Du Bois, May 11, 1927 in Herbert Aptheker, ed., *The Correspondence of W.E.B. Du Bois*, vol. 1 (Amherst: University of Massachusetts Press, 1973), pp. 353-354; Ralph J. Bunche, *A World View of Race*, Bronze Booklet Number 4 (Washington, D.C.: The Associates in Negro Folk Education, 1936).

38. *Ibid.*, pp. 1-36.

39. *Ibid.*, pp. 38-65.

40. *Ibid.*, pp. 67-87.

41. *Ibid.*, p. 84.

42. *Ibid.*, p. 82, 89.

43. *Ibid.*, pp. 90-96.

44. Foner and Allen, loc. cit., pp. 189-198.

Chapter 4

1. Haywood, *Black Bolshevik*, pp. 218-244; Foner and Allen, eds., *Communism and Black Americans*, pp. 161-200; Briggs, "Our Negro Work," pp. 496.

2. *Ibid.*, pp. 181-4.

3. *Ibid.*, p. 182.

4. James Ford and William Wilson [William L. Patterson], "On the Question of the Work of the American Communist Party Among Negroes (Discussion Article)," in Foner and Allen, loc. cit., pp. 166-172.

5. Foner and Allen, p. 182.

6. *Ibid.*, pp. 203-208, 166-172, 181-186. For charges of the CP view of African Americans as a "reserve of reaction," see also Haywood, *Black Bolshevik*, and Cyril Briggs, various articles in the *Communist* of 1928.

7. Foner and Allen, p. 172, 181.

8. *Ibid.*, pp. 161-200; Hall's quote is found on p. 186.

9. *Ibid.*, pp. 166-72, 203-208.

10. *Ibid.*, pp. 203-08.

11. Cyril Briggs, "Our Negro Work," *Communist*, September 1929, pp. 494-501.

12. Cyril Briggs, "Further Notes on Negro Question in Southern Textile Strikes," *Communist*, July, 1929, pp. 391-394; the article containing the "misprint" was Cyril Briggs, "The Negro Question in the Southern Textile Strikes," *Communist*, June, 1929, pp. 324-328.

13. Cyril Briggs, "The Negro Press as a Class Weapon," *Communist*, August 1929, p. 459.

14. Otto Huiswoud, "The Negro and the Trade Unions," *Communist*, December 1928, pp. 770-75.

15. Briggs, "The Negro Question in the Southern Textile Strikes," pp. 324-28.

16. *Ibid.*, pp. 325-6; Briggs, "Further Notes on Negro Question in Southern Textile Strikes," pp. 392-93.

17. *Ibid.*, pp. 391-93. Further evidence that such an approach was both viable and warranted is provided in Robin D.G. Kelley, *Hammer and Hoe: Alabama Communists during the Great Depression* (Chapel Hill, N.C.: University of North Carolina Press, 1990). The efforts of Alabama communists led

to the organization of the Sharecroppers' Union, which only got its start at the inititiative of Black sharecroppers themselves at a time when the Party believed only industrial workers could be organized. However, even here the new sensitivity to Black issues was crucial. Having heard of a sharecroppers' uprising in Arkansas, the Birmingham-based Alabama party issued a call to action by sharecroppers in Alabama. This call met with an enthusiastic response and the makings of an organization soon came together. The Party pursued the question with full attention to its anti-racist campaign, including an insistence upon interracialism, which immediately cost it the support of its white contacts. See Kelley, pp. 34-56. Such actions were contrary to the party's policy of only a couple of years in the past (cf. Solomon, loc. cit., pp. 160-220).

Kelley writes, "As local leaders, blacks were encouraged to criticize their white comrades, a practice unheard of in any other Southern organization of its time" (113). It also was not a regular practice in the national Party until Briggs and others began to take it upon themselves to make it a regular practice. Arguably, then, this evidence from the South shows the profound effect Black leaders had on the position of Blacks within the organization, within the context of the Comintern's insistence on the importance of work among Blacks. Perhaps Kelley's most interesting finding is that, unlike the national Party, the Alabama Party reached its apex before the Popular Front period, and declined with the new emphasis on reform. This finding suggests that the militant program of the internationalists, with its program up to and including armed self-defense, was the best means for inroads in the Black Belt South.

18. Briggs, "Our Negro Work," p. 498.

19. Marc Solomon, "Red and Black: Negroes and Communism, 1929-1932," Ph.D. dissertation, Harvard University, 1972, subsequently published in 1988 as part of the Garland series of Harvard dissertations, with a new preface by the author, under the title, *Red and Black: Afro-Americans and Communism, 1929-1935* [sic]; *The International Negro Workers Review*, January, 1931.

20. *Negro Worker,* April-May, 1931, pp. 15-22; for an account of Foster's views on race, see Haywood, *Black Bolshevik.*

21. *Negro Worker,* March, 1932, pp. 19-36.

22. *Liberator,* September 20, 1930.

23. *Liberator,* February 1, 1930; March 8, 1930; September 20, 1930.

24. *Liberator,* February 21, 1931; March 28, 1931; *Harlem Liberator,* April 29, 1933.

25. *Liberator,* June 1, 1932; October 20, 1932; *Harlem Liberator,* May 27. 1933.

26. *Negro Worker,* February-March, 1933; *Harlem Liberator,* May 27, 1933.

27. *Negro Worker,* August-September, 1933; *Negro Worker,* May, 1934; Huiswoud went under the pseudonym Charles Woodson; for evidence of Padmore's evolution away from his earlier internationalism, see *Negro Worker,* April-May, 1933; August-September, 1933; Padmore, "Ethiopia Today," in Nancy Cunard, ed., *Negro: An Anthology* (London: Wishart, 1934); Padmore, "Europe Kills Animals and Men in Africa," Baltimore *Afro-American,* March 24, 1934; for vilification of Padmore, see the series of articles in the party press and *Negro Worker,* summer, 1934; *Harlem Liberator,* September 23, October 7, 1933; May 19, 1934; for biographical information on Maude White, see Haywood, *Black Bolshevik,* p. 217.

Unraveling the circumstances of Padmore's expulsion may not be possible at this late date. Padmore claimed that he was not expelled but resigned "as the only honorable and decent thing a self-respecting man could do" in "protest against [the] base betrayal of my people" by the Comintern, which Padmore maintained had silenced his attacks of British imperialism in the interests of Soviet diplomacy. Subsequently, he charged, the Comintern invented the story of his expulsion to cover its tracks ("Open Letter to Earl Browder," *The Crisis*). Making the whole episode difficult to trace is the fact that neither side said a word until Padmore first aired his charges almost a year after his removal as Negro Worker editor. In fact, his name remained on the list of contributing editors of the *Harlem Liberator* until April of 1934. When Padmore published his

last editorial in the Negro Worker of September 1933, he ended
it with a section entitled "Au Revoir":
> It is with deep regret that I must announce that with
> this issue, I relinquish my position as Editor of the
> *Negro Worker*. However, like Tennyson's "Brook," it is
> hoped that the magazine will go on for ever.

He concluded with an appeal to the "Black toilers of the
world" to "Help the new editor" in his work. In the next issue,
in May of 1934, the cessation of publication was blamed on Nazi
terror, the same explanation that was given in the *Harlem
Liberator* (May 26, 1934). No reference to Padmore was made,
save a vague mention of "editorial shortcomings" in the May,
1934 *Negro Worker*. It is true that the journal had been
published in Hamburg and that Padmore had been arrested and
later expelled from Germany. But, subsequently, it had
resumed publication in Copenhagen (*Negro Worker*, April-May
1933), so the explanation does not lie there.

The most likely explanation is that Padmore was told,
prior to September, 1933, that he was to be reassigned, and was
left in limbo by the Comintern until the spring of the next year
while the Comintern decided what to do with him (which
probably occurred in April of 1934, at which point the *Negro
Worker* was restarted to take away Padmore's angle of attack.
The Comintern claimed [*Negro Worker*, June 1934] its decision
was made in February, but it only announced it in June). During
that period, the Comintern, whether or not through Padmore's
own complaints, surmised that he was discontented with the
developing Comintern policy, and so grabbed at the pretexts
closest to hand to expel him, which consisted of a combination
of outright slander, deliberate "confusion" of Padmore with a
Liberian reformist of the same name, and some genuine "black
chauvinist" (as his biographer calls it [James R. Hooker, *Black
Revolutionary* (New York: Praeger Publishers, 1970)]) elements
that had crept into his thinking. Padmore, for his part,
probably said nothing until his expulsion was handed down (or,
alternatively, knowing that expulsion was to be the outcome,
resigned at the last moment). An astute political observer,
Padmore, in turn, had probably divined the Comintern's reasons
for suppressing the journal after his editorship was terminated.

In forming this impression, Padmore may have gleaned hints from directives issued to him. It seems unlikely, although far from impossible, that he was told directly to cease criticizing British and French imperialism, both because such criticisms, albeit far milder, continued for a time when the *Negro Worker* resumed publication, and because the secretive Comintern hierarchy would not likely have confided in such an outsider as Padmore.

As for the charges, Padmore was accused, first, of refusing to break off relations with two "exposed provocateurs," one of whom was a Kenyan communist associated with the *Negro Worker* and a fierce opponent of British imperialism who was expelled at the same time as Padmore. Actually, Padmore's closest "associate" at this point was Nancy Cunard, a white British patroness of avante garde art, who had taken an interest in people of African descent and taken up Padmore upon his expulsion to England. She, however, was very close to the communists; her book *Negro: Anthology Made by Nancy Cunard, 1931-1933* was published by the party press in England, and its contributors included such "orthodox" communists with impeccable credentials as James Ford.

Second, Padmore was charged with spearheading a swindle to raise a million dollars for Liberia. Padmore denied these charges, and, indeed, the author could find no evidence to back them up. Hooker, in his critical biography, asserts that George Padmore was being deliberately confused with a Liberian Padmore, who may have initiated just such a scheme.

Finally, Padmore was accused of "lay[ing] the path for unity with the Negro bourgeois exploiters and their agents," or "petty bourgeois nationalism," as it later came to be called by the American party in its accusations against various Black communists. This was the only charge with some legitimate basis. But almost all of Padmore's Black nationalist writing of the Du Bois type appeared after his expulsion. And many of the explicit charges, which began to appear in the summer of 1934 in the party and Comintern press, were outright fabrications, such as Padmore's alleged advocacy of Japanese imperialism. In short, Padmore's drift toward, if not "Du Boisism" then perhaps something very close to Briggs's early

Crusader days, seems to have had little to do with his expulsion.

Whatever the truth behind the episode may have been, it caused a tremendous amount of excitement in the Black press in the summer of 1934. Articles appeared in several Black papers (Baltimore *Afro-American*, June 16, 1934; Pittsburgh *Courier*, June 23, 1934; New York *Amsterdam News*, June 16 and July 28, 1934), both by Padmore and about him, and in response the communist press went after the "betrayer" and "enemy" Padmore, with a zeal that recalled the crusade against Trotsky in the 1920s.

28. Mark Naison, *Communists in Harlem during the Depression* (Urbana, Ill.: University of Illinois Press, 1983), pp. 95-111, quotes are found on p. 98.

29. Earl Browder, "For National Liberation of the Negroes! War Against White Chauvinism," *Communist*, April 1932, pp. 295-309; Naison, p. 99; for evidence of Briggs' feelings toward Ford, see the letter of Briggs to Richard B. Moore quoted in Moore, *Caribbean Militant*, p. 68.

30. Naison, p. 102.

31. *Ibid.*, p. 108; on Moore's personal hardships, see Joyce Moore Turner, "Richard B. Moore and His Works," in Moore, *Caribbean Militant*, p. 58; Moore quoted p. 59.

32. New York *Amsterdam News*, June 16, 1934, July 28, 1934; Padmore further alleged that Huiswoud was the Comintern's "tool" in the whole enterprise, and further remarked, "[D]espite every effort to discuss these most important issues, . . . some of the most and devoted and capable Negro comrades are just being systematically reduced to the status of marionettes"; he further declared, "[T]he real question invoked is one affecting the fundamental rights of the Negro peoples in their relationship to the revolutionary movement and therefore one of vital importance not only to the twelve million Negroes in the United States, but to the 250,000,000 blacks in Africa and other colonial lands" (*ibid.*, June 16, 1934).

For his part, Briggs's response to the charges against Padmore was harsher than that of Otto Hall to the accusations against Moore in 1928. Then, Hall had at least questioned the validity of the charges against Moore, and declared that even if they were true, "this comrade . . . should be corrected [rather than expelled]. I say that we should bring this comrade here to Moscow because he is the official leader of the American Negro Labor Congress and I believe that he can be saved for the Party" (Foner and Allen, p. 183). Of course, for Padmore, being recalled to Moscow at a time when party functionaries from all over the world were being put into internal exile there would have been the last thing he needed. Nevertheless, Briggs all too readily accepted Padmore's expulsion. He could at least have argued that, if departure from Lenin's policy meant expulsion, then the leaders of the American party who were reviving the positions Briggs himself had fought so hard to overcome were far more deserving of this fate than Padmore. Instead, Briggs borrowed their argument in accusing Padmore of adopting an imperialist outlook. He helped pave the way for the full-scale war on the "nationalist deviation" of which he would himself become a victim.

The denunciation of Padmore in the communist press after the controversy erupted over his expulsion sent a clear message of what the future of the "Negro Question" was to be. An article in the *Negro Liberator* of July 21, 1934 stated, "There cannot be any separation of the struggles of the white toilers for the betterment of their conditions from the struggles of the oppressed Negro peoples." Anyone who witnessed the barrage of criticism launched at the pariah Padmore was likely to think twice about any statement that smacked of such "Padmorism."

33. See the *Negro Worker* of 1935-1937; Briggs, *Crusader*, August 1912, p. 7. With bitter irony at the post-World War I campaign proclaiming Germany "unfit to govern colonies," and giving them, therefore to England and its allies, Briggs had further remarked in 1919 (*Crusader*, January 1919, p. 152):

The British Secretary of State for Colonies, Walter Hume Long . . . announced that "although he had no desire to enlarge the British Empire, he saw no alternative to the solution of the problem (!) of the German colonies save by their inclusion in the empire."

British statesmen have "never wanted to enlarge the empire," but somehow or other it has suffered constant enlargement. We suppose the world should sympathise with these "unwilling" builders of empire who, despite their "sincere" desires to the contrary have always been loaded down with the lands and territories of other peoples. It is by accident that so vast a portion of the globe is painted RED--with the British red and the red of martyred patriots. It was by accident that such proclamations were issued as the one of February 3, 1848, relating to certain districts of South Africa, and described by Sir Godfry Langden, K.C.M.G., as "denying profusely any desire to extend the Queen's dominions or deprive chiefs of their hereditary rights, it annexed at a sweep a vast tract of country, with the sole view, as stated, of affording protection and establishing good relations between the miscellaneous people dwelling within it." . . . And how British hearts must bleed at the necessity for shooting down Indians, Egyptians, Bantus and Irishmen, who are so indiscreet as to want to govern themselves and develop their countries for their own interests.

34. Briggs, "Our Negro Work"; cf. Padmore, note 32; Hall's self-defense was appended by the editors of the *Communist* to Briggs' article "Further Notes on Negro Question in Southern Textile Strikes," p. 394. Hall maintained that, far from advocating segregated locals, he had charged the local party organizers with the task of organizing a local of the ANLC among the African Americans in the area who were not eligible to sign up with the union, since they were not workers. He implied that his position had been deliberately misrepresented by the white functionaries ("Note," *Communist*, July 1929, p. 394).

35. *Harlem Liberator*, April 7, 1933; see the *Negro Worker* of 1935-37 (Huiswoud went under the pseudonym of Charles Woodson).

36. *Harlem Liberator*, November 4, November 18, 1933; April 7, 1934; Naison, pp. 99-100.

37. *Harlem Liberator*, April 26, 1934. Briggs also expressed no objection to the demotion of Moore. Indeed, the party left it to him, in an article in his former paper the *Harlem Liberator*,

to announce that Haywood was succeeding Moore, who, Briggs loyally repeated, "tendered his resignation on account of ill health" (April 26, 1934). Joyce Moore Turner more accurately notes that party assignments "had taken their toll on Moore's health, but that it was also his political health that was suffering" (in *Caribbean Militant*, p. 63).

38. Haywood, *The Road to Negro Liberation*, copy in Haywood Papers, box 1; Haywood, notes from an unidentified speech, Haywood Papers, box 2.

39. Haywood, *The Road to Negro Liberation*; Naison, pp. 108-09; the *Negro Liberator* ceased publication in 1935, the *Negro Worker* in 1937.

40. *Harlem Liberator*, October 14, November 4, November 18, 1933, January 27, April 26, May 19, 1934. The drift toward the dominance in Black communist circles during this period of middle-class intellectuals was unmistakable. The old generation of West Indies workers-turned-radicals and African Americans at home in the workrooms and factories was being replaced by those with a different sort of entree. In the *Harlem Liberator* of June 9, 1934, Harry Haywood, already an "old timer," decried the political leadership of African Americans and asked, "Where are the Negroes to look for . . . new leadership?" Although he answered, "among the Negro workers," the same issue of the paper provided what had long since become the CP's answer. Under the title "Countee Cullen Accepts Bid to 'Lib' Banquet," the *Harlem Liberator* noted that Cullen was a former "classmate of Ben Davis at Harvard." The party had once prided itself on its working-class roots. It now touted a different sort of credential: an Ivy League education or its equivalent (Ben Davis, John P. Davis, William Patterson) or artistic renown (Hughes, Cullen, Arna Bontemps, Richard Wright). Naison (*Communists in Harlem*) refers to the appointment of Hughes as LSNR head as a "public relations coup" (p. 42). He fails to note that it also represented a takeover of another kind.

41. Naison, pp. 101-02.

42. Ibid., pp. 100-108; Berry quoted in Moore, *Caribbean Militant*, pp. 67-8; on Briggs' and Moore's expulsions, see Haywood, *Black Bolshevik*, p. 492; the same source provides

the best account of his own expulsion; see also Moore, loc. cit., pp. 66-69.43. Domingo quoted in McKay, *Negroes in America*, pp. 38-40.

Chapter 5

1. Fitzgerald quoted in William K. Klingman, *1929: The Year of the Great Crash* (New York: Harper & Row, 1989), p. 338; Harvey Klehr and John Earl Haynes, *The American Communist Movement: Storming Heaven Itself* (New York: Twayne Publishers, 1992), p. 67; signers of the manifesto, according to Klehr and Haynes, included John Dos Passos, Sidney Hook, Matthew Josephson, Granville Hicks, Edmund Wilson, Malcolm Cowley, Sherwood Anderson, Theodore Dreiser, Lincoln Steffens, and Langston Hughes; Peter Fearon, *Origins and Nature of the Great Slump, 1929-1932* (Atlantic Highlands, NJ: Humanities Press, 1979), p. 35; League of Nations, *Statistical Year-Book of the League of Nations, 1931-32* (Geneva: League of Nations, 1932), p. 68; see also note 1 to the Introduction.

2. A.J. Muste, "Sketches for an Autobiography: Historical Essays, 1891-1960" in Nat Hentoff, ed. *The Essays of A.J. Muste* (New York: The Bobbs-Merrill Company, Inc., 1967), p. 134; *Harlem Liberator*, May 27, 1933.

3. On the IWW, see Melvyn Dubofsky, *We Shall Be All: A History of the Industrial Workers of the World* (New York: Quadrangle, 1969).

4. On the UMW, see Melvyn Dubofsky and Warren Van Tine, *John L. Lewis, A Biography* (Urbana: University of Illinois Press, 1986).

5. *Ibid.*; Muste, loc. cit., p. 101.

6. *Ibid.*, pp. 84-123.

7. Dubofsky and Van Tine, *Lewis*, pp. 162-204; Muste, loc. cit., pp. 126-140.

8. *Ibid.*, p. 132; *Harlem Liberator*, September 2, 1933.

9. Harris, *Keeping the Faith;* Foner, *Organized Labor and the Black Worker*, pp. 177-87; *Report of Proceedings of the Convention of the American Federation of Labor*, 1933, p. 193.

10. Seabrook, "Crosswaith," pp. 29, 90-134; Foner, *Socialism and Black Americans*, pp. 338-364.

11. *Ibid.*

12. *Ibid.*; Du Bois criticized the refusal to organize Blacks and whites together in the South: "For the most part [the SP's] theoretical attitude has never been put to a practical test. . . . The question of segregated Locals in the South is of tremendous practical importance . . ." (p. 357).

13. *Ibid.*; Seabrook, "Crosswaith," pp. 134-136.

14. Ibid., 136-144; Frank Crosswaith, "Trade Unionism--Our Only Hope," *The Crisis* June 1935, pp. 166-7, 187.

15. Seabrook, "Crosswaith," pp. 134-144.

16. Du Bois, *Selections from the Crisis*, pp. 509-10, 526, 531, 544, 564-565; Du Bois, *Against Racism: Unpublished Essays, Papers, Addresses, 1887-1961*, edited by Herbert Aptheker (Amherst, Mass: The University of Massachusetts Press, 1985), pp. 103-158; [Cyril Briggs], "A.N.L.C. Repudiates Statements of Du Bois of Similarity of Programs," *Liberator*, March 29, 1930. On Du Bois's struggles inside the NAACP, see Manning Marable, W.E.B. Du Bois, *Black Radical Democrat* (Boston: Twayne, 1986).

17. Herbert Aptheker, ed. *The Correspondence of W.E.B. Du Bois* (Amherst: The University of Massachusetts Press, 1973), pp. 470-73.

18. Harris, "Brookwood's Symposium on Negro Labor," *The Crisis*, September 1927, p. 226; Sterling D. Spero and Abram L. Harris, *The Black Worker: The Negro and the Labor Movement* (New York: Columbia University Press, 1931).

19. Harris, "The Negro Worker: A Problem of Progressive Labor Action," *Labor Age*, XIX (February 1930), pp. 5-9; reprinted in *The Crisis*, March 1930, pp. 83-85; for the editorial board of the *Labor Age*, see January, 1930, p. 29; Spero and Harris, *The Black Worker*, p. 405.

20. Harris, *Race, Radicalism and Reform*, pp. 167-9.

21. *Ibid.*, p. 429.

22. Francille Wilson (loc. cit.) points out Harris's preference for independent socialist groups.

23. Ernest Rice McKinney, "The Reminiscences of Ernest Rice McKinney," Columbia University Oral History Collection,

Part II, No. 123.; Ernest Rice McKinney, "The Negro's Road to Freedom" *Labor Age*, September 1932, pp. 12-13, 29.

24. *Ibid.* When McKinney followed Muste in the merger with the American Trotskyists, and became a member of its national and political committees, it, too, adopted neo-Debsianism as its outlook. Trotsky, however, evidently did not agree with this course by his American followers. He commented, "It is very disquieting to find that until now [1939] the party has done almost nothing in this field." In 1939, Trotsky and his most important Black disciple, C.L.R. James, yet another West Indian communist (born in Trinidad), discussed the "Negro Question" in America. James expressed the view that "No one denies the Negro's right to self-determination. It is a question of whether we advocate it." James recommended that the Trotskyists not advocate self-determination, on the grounds that African Americans preferred assimilation, had no nationalist ambitions nor characteristics of a national group, and that "it is the surest way to divide and confuse the workers in the South." Black self-determination in the South would be "asking too much from the white workers." James did add that Trotskyists must still announce themselves in favor of the right of self-determination and support African Americans if they raised the demand.

Trotsky, for his part, continued in his belief that the "Negro Question" rested in the domain of "internationalism." He rejected any notion that Black self-determination would be "reactionary," but insisted that "self-determination" not be imposed. Let African Americans decide themselves. At any point present or future, the Trotskyists would support their movement for independence. He disagreed with James in the latter's belief that African Americans exhibited no characteristics of a nation. The difference between the West Indies and "situation of Negroes in the States" was "not so decisive." Trotsky did disagree, however, with the "CP's attitude of making an imperative slogan of it. . . . It was a case of the whites saying to the Negroes, 'You must create a ghetto for yourselves.'" ("Discussions with Trotsky" in C.L.R. James, *At the Rendezvous of Victory, Selected Writings* (London: Allison and Busby, 1984), pp. 33-51. Trotsky also remarked,

"The characteristic thing about the American workers' parties, trade union organizations, and so on, was their aristocratic character. It is the basis of opportunism. The skilled workers who feel set in the capitalist society help the bourgeois class to hold the Negroes and the unskilled workers down to a very low scale. Our party is not safe from degeneration if it remains a place for intellectuals, semi-intellectuals, skilled workers, and Jewish workers who build a very close milieu which is almost isolated from the genuine masses [Trotsky, of course, was himself Jewish]." In contrast, he called African Americans, as the "most oppressed part of the working class," "a vanguard of the working class" and insisted upon their recruitment in large numbers into the Trotskyist Socialist Workers Party "if it is [to be] capable of finding its way to the most oppressed part of the working class" [pp. 46-7]. This, he declared, was to constitute a major reorientation of the party away "from the most aristocratic workers' elements to the lowest elements" [p. 49].)

One exception to the general Trotskyist rule in America was Albert Weisbord, who split with Trotsky over questions of theory but remained close to him politically. In his two volume opus, *The Conquest of Power* (New York: Convici Friede Publishers, 1937), Weisbord writes,

[T]he failure to give [the "Negro Question"] its proper due, the failure to work out a Marxist line for the thirteen million Negroes in the United States, is the best sort of proof that the communist movement is yet immature and unrooted in American life. . . . The communist movement must bring to life the true history of the American Negro, must live in the closest communion with Negro society, must become part of the very heart of the struggles of the Negroes for their emancipation. Here is an acid test of whether the communist party is becoming americanized. A genuine communist organization must demand that its members live with the Negro people and intermingle their activities with those of the oppressed Negro masses in every possible way. An American Communist Party that numbered more Negroes than whites would be far better than a party with more foreign-born than natives in its midst. We shall be able to judge the communism of an organization, indeed, precisely by the yardstick of how many Negroes are in its ranks, how many have been developed as militant fighters. (p. 1168)

Weisbord considered African Americans a "national minority" and advocated a positive program of the right of self-determination, "the right to govern themselves independently and to set themselves up as a separate nation" as necessarily "one of the principal slogans for Negro liberation." Like the Comintern, Weisbord advocated that this be carried out in the Black Belt. But he added that Black workers had the additional duty of struggling to turn such a republic (evidently possible, in his mind, while the U.S. remained capitalist) into a "Soviet Republic." The working class, he asserted, had to hold to such a position as "the best way to prove to the national minority composed of Negroes that the working class fights for their liberation and against the oppressive policy of the white ruling class" (p. 1169). Only with the cooperation of white workers could self-determination for Blacks be achieved. Like the ABB communists, he linked the struggle in America to that in Africa and the West Indies.

25. Langston Hughes, *The Big Sea: An Autobiography* (Thunder's Mouth Press, New York, 1940, p.235-7.

26. Davis, "The Black Man's Burden," *Nation* January 9, 1929, p. 44.

27. John P. Davis, notes for a speech, no date [1934?], National Negro Congress Record Group, Box 1.

28. Ralph J. Bunche, "A Critique of New Deal Social Planning As It Affects Negroes," *Journal of Negro Education* 5 (January 1936), pp. 59-65.

29. Davis, notes for speech, no date [1934?]; McKinney, "The Negro's Road to Freedom."

30. Alma Rene Williams, "Robert C. Weaver: From the Black Cabinet to the President's Cabinet," Ph.D. dissertation, Washington University, 1978, pp. 11-18; John B. Kirby, *Black Americans in the Roosevelt Era: Liberalism and Race* (Twentieth Century America Series; Knoxville, Tenn.: The University of Tennessee Press, 1980), 155-6; Davis, "Negro

Industrial League," no date, National Negro Congress Record Group (Hereafter NNC RG), Box 1; Davis, "What Price National Recovery," *The Crisis*, XL, (December, 1933), p. 272.

31. T. Arnold Hill, "An Emergency is On!" *Opportunity*, XI, (September, 1933), p. 281.

32. William E. Leuchtenburg, *Franklin D. Roosevelt and the New Deal, 1932-1940* (Harper and Row, New York, 1963) p. 64-71; Raymond Walters, *Negroes and the Great Depression: The Problem of Economic Recovery* (Greenwood Publishing Co., Westport, Conn., 1970), p. 110.

33. Davis, "Negro Industrial League"; Davis to Walter White and T. Arnold Hill, July 10, 1933, NNC RG Box 1; Davis to Henrietta Buckmaster, November 15, 1938, NNC RG Box 12.

34. Davis to Walter White and T. Arnold Hill, July 10, 1933.

35. "Black Labor and the Codes," *Opportunity* (August, 1933); Kirby, *Black Americans*, p. 157; Wolters, *Negroes and the Great Depression*; Manning Marable, *W.E.B. DuBois: Black Radical Democrat* (Twentieth-Century American Biography Series; Boston: Twayne Publishers, 1986), p. 136-42; Mark Naison, *Communists in Harlem During the Depression*, pp. 82-87; White to George F. Haynes, September 14, 1933, quoted in Kirby, *Black Americans*, p. 158-9f; White apparently feared the possibility that the Joint Committee could have become a rival to the NAACP from its beginning; Abram Harris, in his report to the NAACP, suggested bringing the Joint Committee under NAACP control to prevent that; Wolters, *Negroes and the Great Depression*, p.333.

36. Davis to Fraternal Council of Negro Churches, no date, NNC RG, Box 3; Report of the Executive Secretary of Joint Committee on National Recovery, February, 1935, NNC RG, Box 3; report of the Executive Secretary of JCNR, December 15-16, 1933, NNC RG, Box 3; manuscript of speech by Davis, 1935, NNC RG Box 3; the twenty-four member organizations of the Joint Committee were: AME Church; AME Zion Church; Alpha Kappa Alpha Sorority; Alpha Phi Alpha Fraternity; Colored Methodist Episcopal Church; Delta Sigma Theta Sorority; Improved Benevolent and Protective Order of Elks of the World; National Association for the Advancement of Colored

People; National Association of Colleges for Colored Youth; National Association of Colored Women's Clubs; National Baptist Convention of the United States; National Catholic Interracial Federation; National Council Protestant Episcopal League; National Housewives League; National Medical Association; National Negro Bar Association; National Negro Business League; National Technical Association; Negro Industrial League; Omega Psi Phi Fraternity; Public Affairs Committee of the National Young Women's Christian Association; Race Relations Department of the Federal Council of Churches of Christ in America; Women's Auxiliary of the National Baptist Convention; Women's Parent Mite Missionary Society. Davis to selected Negro leaders, April 18, 1935, NNC RG, Box 1.

37. Hill, "An Emergency is On!" p. 280. Weaver, "Wage Differential." Davis, "What Price National Recovery," p. 272.

38. Baltimore *Afro-American*, December 16, 1933; press release, NNC RG, Box 1; Robert C. Weaver, "A Wage Differential Based on Race," *The Crisis*, XLI, p. 237; Hill, "An Emergency is On!" p. 280; Wolters, *Negroes and the Great Depression*, p. 112-3; William H. Harris calls the Joint Committees work on the codes a "success" and writes that it "led the agitation that convinced the NRA that the government could not sanction different wage and hour standards for blacks and whites"; *The Harder We Run: Black Workers Since the Civil War* (New York: Oxford University Press, 1982); see also Kirby, *Black Americans*, p. 155-61.

39. Davis, "What Price National Recovery," pp. 271-2; Davis, "Blue Eagles and Black Workers," *New Republic*, LXXXI, (1934), pp 7-9; Davis charged, "wherever the predominant labor supply of a geopgraphical section is Negro, that section is called 'South' amd given the lowest [wage minima]"; Berglund and Others, "Labor in the Industrial South," University of Virginia, 1930, NNC RG, Box 1.

40. Davis, "Report of the Executive Secretary of JCNR," October 11, 1933, NNC RG, Box 3; Davis, press release, May 8, 1934, NNC RG Box 1; Davis, "Report of the Executive Secretary of JCNR," June 1, 1934, NNC RG, Box 3; *Opportunity*, September, 1933, p. 262; Davis to Elmer F. Andrews, July 18,

1938, NNC RG Box 12. It is not certain at what point Davis joined the CP. In 1934 Harry Haywood was still denouncing him and his JCNR (see chapter 4). But by 1937, Davis was, according to a Communist party document in the National Negro Congress records, definitely in the party, and had apparently been for some time; "Minutes of the Committee on Legislation held on February 22, 1937, at 8:30 p.m."; NNC RG, the context makes it clear that this is a party document; Davis is identified as "Danman," and clearly reveals his identity as the head of the National Negro Congress.

Despite Davis's left-wing views, he has been charged with being Republican, a charge that has stuck. In 1934, a series of charges appeared in the Black press labeling Davis a paid agent of the Republican Party. The reports alleged that Dr. Gustav Peck, executive director of the NRA Labor Advisory Board, had made the charge, adding that Davis was attempting "to confuse the colored [sic] group and hamper the Roosevelt Administration." Because Davis was in the hospital following a major operation, he was unable to respond quickly, seemingly imparting legitimacy to the charges. Within a couple of weeks Davis sent an open letter to the Black press in which he exposed the campaign as the concoction of two Black Democrats, Lieut. Oxley and Rienzi Lemus. Davis included excerpts from a letter from Peck denying having made the allegation. Peck also noted that he considered Davis a thoughtful critic of the New Deal and that he could "understand agitation from the 'Left' for something more radical than the New Deal." Press release, July 31, 1934, NNC RG, Box 3; Davis, "Open Letter to the Negro Press," July 11, 1934, NNC RG, Box 3; for some reason, the charge of Davis being a Republican seems to have remained; Wolters labeled him Republican based on his own "specualtion" and Kirby followed suit; Wolters, *Negroes and the Great Depression*, pp. 373, 381; Kirby, *Black Americans in the Roosevelt Era*, p. 155. Interestingly, Oxley had been the representative to the Joint Committee from Omega Phi Psi. Davis to Oxley, December 11, 1933, NNC RG, Box 1.

41. Davis, manuscript, 1934, NNC RG, Box 2; Davis, "Blue Eagles and Black Workers," p. 9; Davis, "Report of the

Executive Secretary of the Joint Committee on National Recovery," January, 1934, NNC RG Box 3; Davis, unidentified draft of a speech, (1935?), NNC RG Box 1.

42. Davis, "The Negro in Labor Struggles Since the New Deal," 1935, NNC RG Box 1; Davis, "Report of the Executive Secretary of the JCNR," March 14, 1934; Report of the Committee on Continuation, April 13, 1934, NNC RG, Box 3.

43. Wolters, *Negroes and the Great Depression*, pp. 331-34.

44. Davis, manuscript, 1934, NNC RG, Box 2; Davis, "Report," November 6, 1933; Davis, "Report," March, 16, 1934; Davis, "Report," June 1, 1934, NNC RG, Box 3; Davis, "Report," June 1, 1934, Davis, "Report," April, 1934; Davis, "Report," December, 1934, NNC RG, Box 3; a copy of the "Harris Report" can be found in the convention material for 1934, Papers of the NAACP, microfilm edition, series 1, reel 14; for an account of the events in the NAACP surrounding the report, see Wolters, *Negroes and the Great Depression*. Davis contributed a militant speech for the occasion, denouncing capitalism and political conservatism; Davis, speech delivered to NAACP Convention, June, 1934, manuscript, NNC RG, Box 2.

Chapter 6

1. The call for a National Negro Congress from the Communist Party appeared in the *Negro Liberator*, throughout the spring of 1935. According to communist Harry Haywood, the idea for a National Negro Congress arose in the Party in mid-1934 as part of the Popular Front strategy. See Haywood, loc. cit.

2. Davis, "Report of the Executive Secretary of the Joint Committee on National Recovery," December 14, 1934, February 9, 1934; NNC RG Box 3; form letter from Davis and Bunche, (1935), NNC RG Box 1.

3. Davis, "A Black Inventory of the New Deal" *The Crisis*, May 1935; form letter from Davis, April 18, 1935, NNC RG Box 1. "Draft Proposal for a Discussion of the Program of a National Congress for Negro Rights," NNC RG, Box 5.

4. Davis to T. Arnold Hill, May 4, 1935, NNC RG Box 3;
Powell to Davis, May 7, 1935, Randolph to Davis, May 3, 1935,
Carter to Davis, May 10, 1935, NNC RG Box 4.

5. Smith to Davis, May 8, 1935, Moore to Davis, (May,
1935), Miles to Davis, April 29, 1935, NNC RG Box 3.

6. Baltimore *Afro-American*, May 25, 1935.

7. "Tentative Program for National Conference," NNC RG
Box 3; *Afro-American*, May 25, 1935; Eleanor Ryan, "Toward a
National Negro Congress," *New Masses* XV June 4, 1935;
"Editorial Comment: The National Conference on the Economic
Crisis and the Negro," *Journal of Negro Education* (hereafter
JNE), January, 1936.

8. Davis, "A Survey of the Problems of the Negro Under
the New Deal," *JNE*, January, 1936, pp. 8-11.

9. Bunche, "A Critique of New Deal Social Planning As It
Affects Negroes," *JNE*, January 1936, pp. 59-65.

10. Dorsey, "The Negro and Social Planning," *JNE*, January,
1936, pp. 105-109. Dorsey had previously teamed up with
Davis to attack the New Deal and put forward the radicals'
program at a conference under the auspices of the Brotherhood
of Sleeping Car Porter, during the summer of 1934; Baltimore
Afro-American, July 28, 1934.

11. DuBois, "Social Planning for the Negro, Past and
Present," *JNE*, January, 1935, pp. 110-125; Dorsey, "Negro and
Social Planning," pp. 107-109; Mary Anderson, "The Plight of
Negro Domestic Labor," *JNE*, January, 1936, pp. 66-72; Olive
Stone, "The Present Position of the Negro Farm Population: the
Bottom Rung of the Farm Ladder," *JNE* January, 1936, pp. 29-30.

12. Randolph, "The Trade Union Movement and the
Negro," *JNE*, January 1936, pp. 54-58; Hill, "The Plight of the
Negro Industrial Worker," *JNE*, January, 1936, p. 45-47. At this
time (1934-37), Hill served as the acting executive director of
the National Urban League. Under him, the National Urban
League moved to implement its pilot program to facilitate the
unionization of Black workers. Its "Workers' Councils,"
however, never became a significant force in the unionization of
Black workers. They did, however, accord better with the
mood among local Urban League leaders than did the League's
traditional pro-business conservatism (see Jesse Thomas Moore,

Jr., *A Search for Equality: The National Urban League, 1910-1961* (University Park: Pennsylvania State University Press, 1981), pp. 80-85); and Nancy J. Weiss, *The National Urban League, 1910-1940* (New York: Oxford University Press, 1974), pp. 281-97). But even Eugene Kinckle Jones, the permanent executive secretary whom Hill temporarily replaced and warred with, was not immune to the spirit of the times brought about by, as he put it, the "class-controlled, profit-mad, caste system which in 1929 collapsed." Thus he wrote in 1934, "If white workers are to be protected in their struggle for the rights of men who toil, there must be equal protection for all of the workers of every minority group in our land and towards this end we must work" (*Opportunity* 12 (May 1934), pp. 141-44).

13. Baltimore *Afro-American*, May 25, 1935; Myers, "The Negro Worker Under NRA," *JNE*, January, 1935, pp. 49-52. Granger would become head of the National Urban League in 1941 and steer a mainstream (for the conservative Urban League) course. At this time, however, Granger, who was graduated from Dartmouth College and had an advanced degree in social work from the New York School of Social Work, was the director of the League's "Workers' Councils" and a full-fledged member of the radical consensus grouping. HUAC deemed him worth keeping track of, and he was described by associates as a "weekend Communist" (Moore, loc. cit., pp. 80-81; Weiss, loc. cit., pp. 284-85). He would take an active role in the National Negro Congress.

14. Baltimore *Afro-American*, May 25, 1935; Davis, "Survey of Problems," p. 12; "Tentative Program"; James W. Ford, "The Communist's Way Out for the Negro," *JNE*, January, 1936, pp. 88-95; Ernest Rice McKinney, "The Workers Party's Way Out for the Negro," *JNE*, January, 1935, pp. 96-9; Norman Thomas, "The Socialist's Way Out for the Negro," *JNE*, January, 1935, pp. 100-04.

15. Ford, "The Communist's Way Out," pp. 88-95; *Afro-American*, May 25, 1935.

16. McKinney, "The Workers Party's Way Out," pp. 96-99.

17. Thomas, "The Socialist's Way Out," pp. 100-04; James Ford, "The National Negro Congress,"*Communist*, April 1936, p. 322.

18. DuBois, "Social Planning for the Negro," pp. 110-25; Dorsey, "Negro and Social Planning," pp. 105-09.

19. *Afro-American*, May 25, 1935.

20. Ibid., DuBois, "Social Planning for the Negro," pp. 110-25.

21. *Afro-American*, May 25, 1935; Dorsey, "The Negro and Social Planning," *JNE*, loc. cit., pp. 105-9; "Harris Report," loc. cit. James Ford, writing in the *Communist* (April, 1936, p. 318), praised the "decidedly growing clarity on the class problems and the Negro" witnessed at the Howard Conference. He said the proceedings testified to "a broader outlook, and a desire for united actions in the solution of the problems of the Negro people." For their part, by virtue of sticking to their old position, the socialists fit ideologically if not organizationally into the new consensus. SP leader Norman Thomas argued "for recognition by the Negro of the fact that his hope must lie in the glory and comradeship which a society of workers irrespective of race can achieve" (*The Crisis*, October 1936, p. 294). And Black socialists Frank Crosswaith and Alfred Baker Lewis (loc. cit.) reasoned, "At the bottom, the Negro question is a labor question."

22. Ralph Bunche, "The Programs, Ideologies, Tactics and Achievements of Negro Betterment and Interracial Organizations," MSS prepared for Carnegie-Myrdal study, June 7, 1940, pp. 32; *Negro Liberator*, June 1, 1935; Davis, "Need for a National Negro Congress," Negro Liberator, August 1, 1935.

23. Miller, "Turning to the Left," *Richmond Planet*, June 1, 1935; Davis, "Need for a National Negro Congress," *Negro Liberator*, August 1, 1935.

24. Foner, *Organized Labor and the Black Worker*, pp. 64-81, 158-188, 202, 211; Foner concludes on the AFL's attitude toward Blacks in 1935: "The history of the black working class and of the labor movement since the turn of the century had produced not the slightest alteration in the attitude of the AF of L leadership"; Harris, *The Harder We Run*, p.73-4, 89; W.E.B. DuBois; "Postscript," *The Crisis*, December 1933, p. 292;

Davis, "Report of the Executive Secretary of the Joint Committee on National Recovery," December 15, 1933, NNC RG, Box 3.

It must be kept in mind that opposition to the AFL craft leadership under Green was a far different matter from opposition to the labor movement in general. It is true, however, that, in this respect, the Black radicals tended to be more vocal in their criticism than mainstream "progressive unionists," a fact which emphasizes their relative independence from it even as they accepted its basic tenets.

25. Foner, *Black Workers*, pp. 204-6; Harris, *Harder We Run*, p. 89.

26. Foner, *Black Workers*, pp. 204-6; Harris, *Harder We Run*, p. 89.

27. Foner, *Black Workers*, pp. 206-8; Harris, *Harder We Run*, 89-90; "The Urban League and the A.F. of L.: A Statement on Racial Discrimination," *Opportunity*, August, 1935; Federated Press Report, "A.F. of L. Committee Hears Negroes Tell of Discrimination," July 9, 1935, NNC RG, Box 1.

28. Federated Press Report, "Committee Hears Negroes"; Foner, Black Workers, pp. 206-8; "The Urban League and the A.F. of L."

29. Foner, *Black Workers*, pp. 208-11; Harris, Harder We Run, 90-92.

30. Dubofsky and Van Tine, *Lewis*, pp. 162-80; Foner, *Black Workers*, pp. 212-13.

31. Dubofsky and Van Tine, *Lewis*, pp. 162-80; Foner, *Black Workers*, pp. 213-14; A. Philip Randolph, "The Trade Union Movement and the Negro," *JNE* V (January 1936), pp. 54-5; Horace R. Cayton and George S. Mitchell, *Black Workers and the New Unions* (Chapel Hill: University of North Carolina Press, 1939),pp. 198-201; Spero and Harris, *The Black Worker*, pp. 352-82.

32. DuBois, "Postscript," *The Crisis* (December 1933), p.292; "The Negro and Union Labor," *The Crisis*, June, 1935, p. 183. White quoted in Foner, *Black Workers*, pp. 211-12.

33. Foner, *Black Workers*, p. 213; Cayton and Mitchell, *New Unions*, p. 201; Davis to M.T. Wermell, October 5, 1936, NNC RG, Box 8.

34. Davis to Miss Arna Bogue, December 11, 1935, NNC RG, Box 4; Langston Hughes, press release, February 1, 1936, Bontemps to Davis, February 7, 1936; Houston to Davis, May 7, 1935, NNC RG, Box 3; Davis to White, December 20, 1935, and January 20, 1936, White to Davis, September 13, 1935 NNC RG Box 3; White to Davis, December 31, 1935, NNC RG Box 8.

35. Davis, *Let Us Build a National Negro Congress,* (Washington, 1935), NNC RG, Box 2.

36. Davis to Miss Anna Bogue, December 11, 1935, NNC RG Box 4; Randolph, "Introduction" to Davis, *Let Us Build;* Anderson, *Randolph,* p. 234; Harris, *Harder We Run,* p.111; John Fitzpatrick to Davis, February 6, 1936, Davis to Fitzpatrick, February 29, 1936, NNC RG, Box 5; Davis to Randolph, December 18, 1936, NNC RG, Box 7.

37. Davis to The Officers and Members of All Trade Unions Affiliated to the American Federation of Labor and to the Railroad Brotherhoods (1936?), NNC RG Box 5, Davis to Mr. Hall, January 6, 1936, Box 5; Davis to Clifford McLeod, January 8, 1936, NNC RG Box 6; Randolph to Davis, January 31, and February 4, 1936, NNC RG Box 7.

38. Davis to John L. Lewis, January 16, 1936, telegram, Brophy to Davis, February 3, 1936, NNC RG, Box 4; Davis to John Fitzpatrick, February 29, 1936, NNC RG Box 5.

39. Telegram, Davis to Brophy, February 4, 1936, NNC RG, Box 4; Davis to Mr. Lanzy, Secretary of Local 87 Amalgamated Meat Cutters and Butcher Workmen of North America, (January?, 1936), NNC RG Box 6.

40. *Official Proceedings of the National Negro Congress,* Washington, D.C. 1936, NNC RG Box 2; letters expressing a desire to attend but a lack of funds preventing it are too numerous to cite, but see, for example, Tom Burke to Davis, December 28, 1935, NNC RG Box 4; Lester Granger, "The National Negro Congres - An Interpretation," *Opportunity,* XIV (May 1936), 151-52; Davis, *Let Us Build* and numerous press releases, NNC RG, Box 5.

The Congress also declared itself behind African-American small businessmen, a point which drew criticism from the *Nation* as an inconsistency. This stance, however, was only an effort to pay lip service to the CP's "Popular Front" strategy.

Davis said nothing about it in his call. James Ford, writing in the *Communist* (Ford and A. W. Berry, "The Coming National Negro Congress: A New Phase in the Liberation Struggles of the Negro Peoples" Communist, February 1936, pp. 140-41), was responsible for putting it on the agenda of the Congress. But it never got off the paper it was written on.

41. Granger, "The National Negro Congress," pp. 151-52; James W. Ford, "The National Negro Congress," *Communist* XV (April 1936), pp. 324-25.

42. Ford, "The National Negro Congress," p. 324; *Official Proceedings of the National Negro Congress.*

43. In "Minutes of the Committee on Legislation," loc. cit., of the Communist party, Davis (identified as "Danman") responded as follows when asked to get Randolph's approval for a joint letter in the name of the Congress: "This is not necessary. I could not get agreement from Philip Randolph on sending out a joint letter. He would say 'You do yourself. You draft [the] letter which you send out to all Council members and release to [the] press stating that you have addressed all members with the following proposal."

44. Ralph Bunche, "Triumph? Or Fiasco?" *Race* I (Summer 1936), pp. 93-6.

45. *Race* I (Winter 1935-36), p. 3.

46. Granger, "Old Guard v. A.F. of L." *Race* I (Winter 1935-6), pp. 46-47; Hughes, "Too Much of Race," *The Crisis*, 44 (September 1937), p. 272.

47. *Ibid.*

Chapter 7

1. Davis's fellow radicals became disillusioned with the CIO and the working out of their labor program at various times and for various reasons which are hard to discern. Lester Granger was the first to experience second thoughts, warning of the dangers of too deep a belief in the CIO as early as January of 1936 (see "Industrial Unionism and the Negro," *Opportunity*, January 1936, pp. 29-30). Granger, however, continued to work with the NNC, at least for a time. Ralph Bunche and his

Howard Colleagues, including Emmett Dorsey and Abram Harris, had nothing further to do with the NNC, and by the time Bunche wrote his research memorandum for the Myrdal study (loc. cit.), he was thoroughly disillusioned with it and critical of the very organizational form he had once helped to shape.

2. Davis to M.T. Wermell, October 5, 1936, NNC RG, Box 8; for discussions of the CIO's early attitude towards Blacks, see Harvard Sitkoff, *A New Deal for Blacks: The Emergence of Civil Rights as a National Issue: The New Deal Era* (New York: Oxford University Press, 1978), pp.198-225; August Meier and Elliot Rudwick, *Black Detroit and the Rise of the UAW* (New York: Oxford University Press, 1979), pp. 22-29, William H. Harris, *The Harder We Run*, pp. 95-123, and Philip Foner, *Organized Labor and the Black Worker*, pp. 215-237.

3. Davis to M.T. Wermell, October 5, 1936.

4. *Ibid.*

5. *Ibid.*

6. Davis, speech to Convention of Social Workers, Atlantic City, N.J., May 25, 1936, NNC RG, Box 90.

7. Davis to M.T. Wermell, October 5, 1936.

8. Davis to Mrs. Eleanor Rye, March 24, 1936, NNC RG Box 7; Davis to Lester Granger, (April?, 1936), NNC RG Box 5; Press Release, "McDonald Stirs Federation of Labor on Jim-Crow Policies and Rules. 'National Negro Congress Must Live On'" (March 15, 1936), NNC RG Box 7; Eleanor Rye to Davis, May 13, 1936, NNC RG Box 7; Davis to Randolph, June 7, 1936, NNC RG Box 7; Davis to Frank Crosswaith, June 8, 1937, NNC RG Box 4.

9. Davis to James H. Baker, August 18, 1936; Davis, Report of the National Secretary of the National Negro Congress, Cleveland, Ohio, June 19-20, 1936, NNC RG Box 7; the SWOC was founded June 4, 1936 with the conclusion of an agreement between the CIO and the AFL union in steel; Walter Galenson, "The Unionization of the American Steel Industry," p. 15; Davis's first written proposal to the SWOC came less than a week later, meaning the NNC's relationship with the SWOC had been established at the very beginning.

10. Davis, Report of the National Secretary, June 1936; Davis, "'Plan Eleven'--Jim-Crow in Steel," The Crisis, September, 1936, p. 262; Davis to Charles W. Burton, July 22, 1936, NNC RG Box 4.

11. Davis, "Proposed Plan for Organization of Negro Steel Workers in Youngstown, O.: Submitted by the National Negro Negro Congress to Steel Workers Organizing Committee of the Committee For Industrial Organization," June 10, 1936, NNC RG Box 2.

12. Davis to James H. Baker, August 18, 1936, NNC RG Box 4; Davis, Report of the National Secretary, June 1936; Maude White to Davis, July 13, 1936, NNC RG Box 8.

13. Davis, "Plan Eleven," loc. cit.

14. Speech of Ed Strong (National Chairman of Youth Section of NNC), SNYC [Southern Negro Youth Congress] conference, February 13-14, 1937, Richmond, Va., NNC RG Box 2; Davis, "Plan Eleven," loc. cit.

15. Davis to Randolph, June 6, 1936, NNC RG Box 7; Davis, "Plan Eleven"; Davis to Randolph, July 10, 1936; NNC RG Box 7; Davis to Arthur Fauset, July 22, 1936, NNC RG Box 5; Davis to Charles W. Burton, July 22, 1936, NNC RG Box 4.

16. Davis to Charles W. Burton, July 22, 1936, NNC RG Box 4; correspondance between Davis and Philip Murray, Van A. Bittner, William Mitch, and others, too voluminous to cite here, NNC RG Boxes 4-8; Davis to Randolph, July 22, 1936, NNC RG Box 7; Davis form letter, July 10, 1936, NNC RG Box 4; Murray quoted in Meier and Rudwick, *Black Detroit and UAW*, p. 25-6n; Davis, "Plan Eleven." p. 276. Those commentators who, following the leaders of that federation, have cited the CIO as a paragon of racial liberalism, ignore the attitude of CIO officials toward the organization of Black workers. Murray, who later headed the federation when John L. Lewis jumped ship, repeats here the viewpoint that had always characterized organized labor. Otto Huiswoud quoted in Chapter 4.

17. Davis quoted from a letter to Randolph, September 5, 1936, NNC RG Box 7.

18. See the correspondence between Davis and SWOC officials, cited in note 16; Davis to Bertram M. Gross, April 29,

1938, NNC RG Box 10; Davis to Simon Carson, January 16, 1937, NNC RG Box 9; Davis to Charles W. Burton, January 14, 1937, NNC RG Box 9; Clinton Golden to Davis, January 28, 1937, NNC RG Box 10; Alexander Jones and others to All Trade Unions, Church Organizations, Fraternal, Club and Veteran Oraganizations, Friends of the Negro People, May 19, 1937, NNC RG Box 10; Davis to Gross, April 29, 1936, NNC RG Box 10; Joe Cook to Davis August 2, 1937, NNC RG Box 9.

19. See Griffler, loc. cit., pp. 267-70; Davis to Philip Murray, March 31, 1937, NNC RG Box 11; Murray to Davis, April 5, 1937, NNC RG Box 11; Wittner, "The National Negro Congress," p. 893-4; Cayton and Mitchell, *Black Workers and the New Unions*, p. 202-6.

20. Davis to Solomon Barkin, April 13, 1937, NNC RG Box 9; Davis to Sidney Hillman, June 16, 1937, NNC RG Box 10; Solomon Barkin to Davis, April 7, 1937, NNC RG Box 9; Tecia Davidson to Davis, June 18, 1937, NNC RG Box 9; Davis to Harry Bridges, September 24, 1937, NNC RG Box 9; Davis to Revels Cayton, September 24, 1937, NNC RG Box 9; Davis to Cayton, September 30, 1937, NNC RG Box 9; Revels Cayton, "Maritime Union Planned," NNC RG Box 90; Wittner, "The National Negro Congress," p. 895; Davis to Jacob Baker, June 1937, NNC RG Box 9. The ILGWU employed Frank Crosswaith as an organizer in New York. Nothing better highlights the difference in the approaches of Crosswaith and Davis (and other young radicals) than the fact that it was Davis, and not Crosswaith, who put forward this demand and got the desired result. Crosswaith, having finished his work inside the Socialist Party, and apparently valuing his job with the ILGWU, chose to keep quiet on its shortcomings. Indeed, he did more. He extolled, through *The Crisis*, the union's "traditionally sound position regarding the rights of Negroes." He added, with much exaggeration, "It is a well-known fact that the Negro workers in the I.L.G.W.U. enjoy every privilege and share every responsibility with their white fellow members" ("Trade Unionism--Our Only Hope," *The Crisis* June 1935, pp. 166-7, 187).

21. Meier and Rudwick, *Black Detroit and the UAW*, pp. 3-29; Davis to Robert J. Evans, July 29, 1936, NNC RG Box 5; Davis

to Robert Evans, August 10, 1936, NNC RG Box 5; Ben Allen to Davis, November 10, 1936, NNC RG Box 4; Davis to Allen, November 26, 1936, NNC RG Box 4; Dred Scott Newsome to Davis, January 1, 1937, NNC RG Box 11.

22. Meier and Rudwick, *Black Detroit and the UAW*, pp. 18; Davis to Wyndam Mortimer, April 3, 1937, NNC RG Box 11; Davis to Francis A. Ransom, September 17, 1937, NNC RG Box 11; Davis to Walter Hardin, September 28, 1937, NNC RG Box 10; Davis to Merrill Work, April 15, 1938, NNC RG Box 15; Davis to John L. Lewis, October 19, 1937, NNC RG Box 11.

23. Davis to Wyndam Mortimer, April 3, 1937, NNC RG Box 11; Meier and Rudwick, Black Detroit and the UAW, p. 38.

24. Davis to Walter Hardin, October 6, 1937, NNC RG Box 10.

25. Davis to Wyndam Mortimer, April 3, 1937, NNC RG Box 11; Davis to Dred Scott Neusom, June 1, 1937, NNC RG Box 11; Detroit Council [NNC] to Davis, no date, NNC RG Box 9; Dred Scott Neusom to Davis, June 23, 1937, NNC RG Box 11; Paul Kirk to Davis, July 6, 1937, NNC RG Box 10.

26. Meier and Rudwick, *Black Detroit and the UAW*, p. 55-8; Davis to Hardin, October 6, 1937.

27. Davis to Homer Martin, September 13, 1937, NNC RG Box 11; Francis A. Hanson to Davis, September 15, 1937, NNC RG Box 10; Davis to Hanson, September 17, 1936, NNC RG Box 10; Martin to Davis, September 23, 1937, NNC RG Box 11; Davis to Walter Hardin, September 28, 1937, NNC RG Box 10, Davis to Wyndam Mortimer, NNC RG Box 11; Walter Hardin to Davis, October 4, 1936, NNC RG Box 10; Davis to Hardin, October 6, 1937, NNC RG Box 10; Mortimer to Davis, October 7, 1937, NNC RG Box 11.

28. Davis to John Hayes, June 15, 1937, NNC RG Box 10; Stuart Bruce Kaufman, *Challenge and Change: The History of the Tobacco Workers International Union*, (Distributed by the University of Illinois Press, no place of publication, 1987),p. 94; Davis, Memorandum to John Brophy, "Proposal for Initiation of National Organizing Campaign for Tobacco Workers," NNC RG Box 9.

29. Davis to Frank B. Crosswaith, April 12, 1938, NNC RG Box 12; Davis, memorandum to Brophy.

30. Davis, memorandum to Brophy.

31. Davis to Congressman John T. Bernard, May 19, 1937, NNC RG Box 9; Davis to John Brophy, May 18 and May 20, 1937, NNC RG Box 9; telegram, Christopher Columbus Alston to Davis, May 21, 1937, NNC RG Box 9.

32. James E. Jackson to Davis, April 29, 1937, NNC RG Box 13; Davis to Jackson and Francis Grandison, April 30, NNC RG Box 13; Leif Dahl to Davis, February 25, 1938, NNC RG Box 12.

33. Davis to C.J. Coe, September 12, 1937, NNC RG Box 9; Davis to R.B. McKinney, April 9, 1936, NNC RG Box 6; Clyde Johnson to Davis, May 15, 1936; NNC RG Box 6; Davis to John F. Moors, June 9, 1937, NNC RG Box 6; Davis to J.R. Butcher, September 27, 1937, NNC RG Box 9; telegram, E.B. McKinney to National Negro Conference, October 17, 1937, NNC RG Box 11; Davis to W.M. Martin, April 12, 1937, NNC RG Box 11; Foner, Black Workers, p. 228; locals of the NNC, particularly in Washington, D.C. and Chicago, where Congress activists were union leaders, got heavily involved in the organizing efforts among domestics; Davis to Frank Crosswaithe, April 12, 1938, Box 12; Davis to Neva Ryan, September 2, 1936, NNC RG Box 7; Ryan to Davis, September 8, 1936, NNC RG Box 7; Davis to Florence Barnes, February 17, 1937, NNC RG Box 9; Ryan to Davis, May 14, 1938, NNC RG Box 14; Lillie Brewer to Davis, no date, NNC RG Box 9.

34. Davis to M.T. Wermell, October 5, 1936, NNC RG, Box 8; Davis to Randolph, May 29, 1936, NNC RG Box 7; Davis to Randolph, June 6, 1936, NNC RG Box 7; Randolph to Davis, June 10, 1936, NNC RG Box 7; Randolph to Howard Y. WIlliams, June 12, 1936, NNC RG Box 7; Howard Y. Williams to the National Executive Council of the National Negro Congress, NNC RG Box 8.

35. Davis to Arthur Huff Fauset, March 11, 1937, NNC RG Box 10; "Proceedings of the Second National Negro Congress," Washington, D.C., 1937; NNC RG Box 11; Davis to Charles Wesley Burton, April 1, 1937, NNC RG Box 9; Davis to Jett Lanck, March 6, 1937, NNC RG Box 11.

36. Davis, "Testimony before the Senate and House Committees on Labor, Washington, D.C. on Wednesday, June 9, 1937; the Committees were considering the Black-Connery

Wages and Hours Bill and entitled 'Fair Standards Act of 1937,'" NNC RG Box 90.

37. *Proceedings of the Second National Negro Congress* (Washington, 1937), NNC RG Box 11 Radio Address of John P. Davis, Executive Secretary of the National Negro Congress, Columbia Broadcasting System, Sunday, October 17, 1937, NNC RG Box 90.

38. Davis to Officers and Members of International Unions, Central Labor Unions, State Federations of Labor and Local Unions, (Summer 1937), NNC RG Box 9; John T. Bernard to Davis, May 11, 1937, NNC RG Box 9; Davis to John L. Lewis, August 15, 1937, NNC RG Box 11; Ralph Hetzel, Jr. to Davis, August 27, 1937, NNC RG Box 10; Len De Caux to Davis, September 30, 1937, NNC RG Box 9; De Caux to Davis, September 11, 1937, NNC RG Box 9; Davis to Ralph Hetzel, September 13, 1937, NNC RG Box 10; Davis to Gardner Jackson, September 13, 1937, NNC RG Box 10; Davis to Frank J. Bender, September 21, 1937, NNC RG Box 9; Hetzel to Davis, September 16, 1937, NNC RG Box 10; Ben Careathers to Davis, October 2, 1937, NNC RG Box 9; Philip Murray to Davis, October 2, 1937, NNC RG Box 11; Davis to Arthur Fauset, no date, NNC RG Box 10.

39. *Proceedings of the Second National Negro Congress.*

40. *Proceedings of the Second National Negro Congress*; Lewis to National Negro Congress, NNC RG Box 11; Roosevelt to Davis, October 14, 1937, NNC RG Box 2.

41. *Proceedings of the Second National Negro Congress.*

42. Esther McNeill to Henry Mayfield, December 9, 1937, NNC RG Box 11; report of the Meeting of the Executive Board of the National Negro Congress, Held at 10:00 A.M. in Philadelphia, Monday October 18, 1937, NNC RG Box 10; Manning Johnson to Davis, October 20, 1937, NNC RG Box 10.

43. Davis to Lewis, October 19, 1937, NNC RG Box 11.

44. Davis to Senator Ernest Lundeen, November 12, 1937 NNC RG Box 11; Randolph to the National Officials, Regional Directors, State Directors, Local Councils and Officials, December 7, 1937, NNC RG Box 7; Davis to James E. Baker, January 28, 1938, NNC RG Box 12; *CIO News*, March 26, 1938; Davis to Randolph, January 21, 1938, NNC RG Box 14; Davis to

Len De Caux, January 24, 1938, NNC RG Box 12; Davis to De Caux, January 25, 1938, NNC RG Box 12; CIO press release, January 25, 1938; Davis to E.L. Oliver, January 21, 1938, NNC RG Box 14; Oliver to Davis, January 25, 1938, NNC RG Box 14; Oliver to individual Senators, January 22, 1938, Labor's Non-Partisan League press release, January 24, 1938, NNC RG Box 14.

45. Davis to Randolph, January 21, 1938, NNC RG Box 14; Oliver to Davis, January 25, 1938, NNC RG Box 14; Davis, report of the executive secretary of the National Negro Congress, [Spring, 1938], NNC RG Box 15; *CIO News*, February 26, 1938.

46. Davis to Members of the National Executive Council, February 16, 1938, NNC RG Box 14; Davis to Kathryn Lewis, February 17, 1938, NNC RG Box 13; Davis, memorandum to Oliver, February 17, 1938, NNC RG Box 14; Davis to Randolph, March 14, 1937, NNC RG Box 14; John L. Lewis to Davis, March 17, 1938, NNC RG Box 13.

47. Charles Wesley Burton to Davis, March 8, 1938, NNC RG Box 12; Dasis to Gadys Stoner, April 15, 1938, NNC RG Box 15; Davis to DeWitt Alcorn, April 15, 1938, NNC RG Box 12; Davis, memorandum to member of the national executive council, February 16, 1938, NNC RG Box 14; Randolph to Davis, March 12, 1938, NNC RG Box 14; Randolph to Davis, April 2, 1938, NNC RG Box 14; Davis to Randolph, April 7, 1938, NNC RG Box 14; Henry Johnson to Davis, March 16, 1938, NNC RG Box 13.

48. NNC press release, "Mass Organizations Rally Behind NAACP in Effort to Re-Open Fight for Passage of Anti-Lynching Bill in this Session of Congress," NNC RG Box 90; Statement of Gardner Jackson of Labor's Non-Partisan League, representing E.L. Olvier, Exec, Vice-President, at National Negro Congress conference, Washington, D.C. (Whitelaw Hotel), Saturday, March 19th, NNC RG Box 90; Statement to the Public Adopted at National Negro Congress Conference on Anti-Lynching Legislation, NNC RG Box 90; Resolution on Program of Action-- Anti-Lynching Conference, March 19, 1938, Washington, D.C., NNC RG Box 90.

49. Sitkoff, in his chapter on the contribution of organized labor to civil rights, notes that in the early Thirties, organized labor seemed an unlikely partner for the Black rights organizations; he gives the events under NNC sponsorship as the earliest entrance of the CIO into civil rights, even quoting Brophy's "speech" to the Anti-lynching conference [actually a prepared statement read for him]; he fails to acknowledge the Congress' role, *Emergence of Civil Rights*, p. 222-3.

50. George S. Schuyler, "Reflections on Negro Leadership," *The Crisis*, November 1937, p. 328.

51. Granger cited in Marshall F. Stevenson, Jr., "Challenging the Roadblocks to Equality: Race Relations and Civil Rights in the CIO, 1935-1955," Center for Labor Research, Ohio State University, Working Paper 6, p. 9. The importance of the CIO's role in civil rights has been documented by Harvard Sitkoff, among others, who writes that the CIO "created a wave in race relations" in the late Thirties. But like his predecessors, Sitkoff fails to analyze adequately the origins of that current in the work done by Black organizations themselves, especially the National Negro Congress. He attributes the CIO's position to the influence of the Left, particularly communists, within the federation, to the fight between the craft and industrial forms of organization, and to nothing more than the necessity of winning Black support for unions. He subsumes the efforts of Blacks and the NNC under the rubric of the Left. As an example of CIO work, Sitkoff cites the "Negro Division" attached to the Wages and Hours Bill as a CIO "battle" (*Emergence of Civil Rights*, pp. 198-224). The CIO, however, was only first alerted to the desirability of such an addition to the legislation by Davis in July, 1938. In response to Davis's letter, Brophy wrote, "I am passing on your letter regarding the establishment of a colored [sic] division within the Wage-Hour setup to Mr. Sidney Hillman, president of the Amalgamated Clothing Workers of America, . . . for his information and such attention as he may think practical to give." The idea for the division was actually a Davis initiative that, as he pointed out, had grown out of his experiences during the NRA. Davis actively campaigned for the section to safeguard Black interests, writing to the

appointed administrator of the law, Elmer F. Andrews, even before he arrived in Washington to take his post. (Davis to Brophy, July 18, 1938, Brophy to Davis, July 22, 1938, Davis to Andrews, 1938, NNC RG Box 12.)

52. Davis to Max Yergan, November 26, 1938, NNC RG Box 15.

53. Eastern Regional Conference of the National Negro Congress to President Roosevelt, NNC RG Box 14.

54. Davis to Albert Dent, November 30, 1938, NNC RG Box 12.

55. Davis to Max Yergan, November 18, 1938, NNC RG Box 15.

56. *Proceedings of the Second National Negro Congress.*

57. Davis to Leo Allen, December 10, 1938, NNC RG Box 12; Davis to C.J. Coe, September 15, 1937, NNC RG Box 9; Davis to Cayton, October 3, 1939, NNC RG Box 16.

58. Davis to Charles H. Houston, October 5, 1937, NNC RG Box 10.

Epilogue

1. The passage of the Taft-Hartley Act in 1947, which effectively barred communists in the ranks of the state-regulated unions, brought to an end the first period of the CIO, during which the left played a leading role. For the effects of the passage of this act upon African Americans in unions, see Kaufman, *History of the Tobacco Workers International Union*, p. 108; Foner, *Organized Labor and the Black Worker*, loc. cit., pp. 274-87; Martin Halpern, *UAW Politics in the Cold War Era* (Albany: SUNY Press, 1988); see also Dennis C. Dickerson, *Out of the Crucible: Black Steelworkers in Western Pennsylvania, 1875-1980* (Albany: SUNY Press, 1986); although he does not mention the act, the year 1948 stands out in his account as the period during which the position of African Americans in the steelworkers union began to erode rapidly.

2. The idea of an independent Black trade union federation was opposed by John P. Davis in 1941 as "reactionary," perhaps as a legacy of neo-Debsian thought, perhaps in fear of

competition for his NNC, perhaps at CP insistence; Stevenson, loc. cit.

3. Ibid.; Herbert Hill, "Race and Ethnicity in Organized Labor: The Historical Sources of Resistance to Affirmative Action," *The Journal of Intergroup Relations* 12 (Winter 1984), 5-6.

4. Cayton quoted in Stevenson, loc. cit.

5. Ryon, "An Ambiguous Legacy, Baltimore Blacks and the CIO, 1936-1941," *Journal of Negro History* 65 (Winter, 1980), 18-33.

6. W.E.B. Du Bois, *Against Racism*, ed. by Herbert Aptheker (Amherst, Mass.: University of Massachusetts Press), p. 138.

7. See, for example, Ernesto Laclau, *New Reflections on the Revolution of Our Time* (London: Verso, 1991). For a critique of other analyses of the question, see Griffler, loc. cit., pp. 313-15, 378-81.

8. Call it race or whatever, from the point of view of theory, the distinction is without a difference. In the 19th century, it was the custom to refer to nations as races.

9. Marx, *Capital*, volume 1, p. 823.

Ultimately, nationality is itself a product of natural variation, and the accidents by which mankind was distributed on the planet, accidents including the myriad of migrations, wars, conquests, and so forth. In fact, the latter especially resulted in Europe's accelerated development. Civilization, of course, first appeared in Asia and Africa, while Europe was the "backwoods." Precisely for this reason Europe was subjected to wave after wave of invasion that shook European society to its very foundations, remade it over and over, and accelerated its development. In addition, Europe was the beneficiary of the advances of Eastern society: the horse, gunpowder, the alphabet, all Asian; Arabic numerals, algebra, and the spirit of investigation from Africa. Europe was thereby transformed from backwardness into the "advanced outpost" of civilization, and in its turn, revolutionized social relations in the rest of the world by means of invasion. It was only natural that, as Rudolf Hilferding already understood in 1909, "Since the subjection of foreign nations takes place by force--that is, in a perfectly natural way--it appears to the ruling nation" [i.e., that nation announces] "that this domination is due to some special natural qualities, in short to its racial characteristics.   Thus there emerges . . . racist ideology, cloaked in the garb of natural science...." (*Finance Capital: A Study of the Latest Phase of Capitalist Development*, translated by Morris Watnick and Sam Gordon (Boston: Routledge & Kegan Paul, 1981), p. 335.

10. Lenin, *Selected Works*, volume 3, p. 456.

11. The tendency of Marx's thinking pointed in that direction.   Evidence can be found throughout Marx's last writings; some of this is compiled by R. Palme Dutte, *Problems of Contemporary History*, (New York: International Publishers, 1963); see also, Lenin's *Notebooks on Imperialism*, and *Imperialism, The Highest Stage of Capitalism*,   in his *Selected Works*, volume 3, p. 761.

12. World Bank, *World Development Indicators*, (Washington, D.C.: World Bank, 1988).

13. J.A. Hobson, *Imperialism: A Study* (London: George Allen and Unwin, Ltd., 1938), pp. 194, 314, 364.

Bibliography

Manuscript Collections:

National Negro Congress Record Group, Schomburg Branch, New York Public Library.

Federal Bureau of Investigation File on the National Negro Congress [microfilm] Wilmington, Del.: Scholarly Resources, 1987.

Harry Haywood Papers, Bentley Library, University of Michigan, Ann Arbor.

Columbia University Oral History Collection.

Papers of the NAACP [microfilm].

Newpapers:

Baltimore Afro-American
CIO News
Harlem Liberator
Liberator
Negro Liberator
New York Amsterdam News
New York Times
Pittsburgh Courier
Richmond Planet

Journals:
Communist
Communist International
The Crisis
Crusader
International Press Correspondence
Journal of Negro Education
Labor Age
Liberator
Messenger
Nation
Negro Worker (originally, *The International Negro Workers Review*)
New Republic
New Masses
Race

Unpublished Works:

Bunche, Ralph J. "The Programs, Ideologies, Tactics, and Achievements of Negro Betterment and Interracial Organizations." Unpublished Manuscript prepared for the Carnegie - Myrdal Study, 1940, Schomburg Branch, New York Public Library.

Richards, Alma Rene. "Robert C. Weaver: From the Black Cabinet to the President's Cabinet." Ph.D. dissertation, Washington University, 1978.

Seabrook, John Howard. "Black and White Unite: The Career of Frank R. Crosswaith." Ph.D. dissertation, Rutgers University, 1980.

Stevenson, Marshall F., Jr. "Challenging the Roadblocks to Equality: Race Relations and Civil Rights in the CIO, 1935-1955." Center for Labor Research, Ohio State University, Working Paper 6.

Solomon, Mark Ira. "Red and Black: Negroes and Communism, 1929-1932." Ph.D. dissertation, Harvard University, 1972.

Wilson, Francille. "The Segregated Scholars: Black Labor Historians, 1895-1950." Ph.D. dissertation, University of Pennsylvania, 1988.

Published Works

Adler, Alan, ed., *Theses, Resolutions and Manifestos of the First Four Congresses of the Third International*. Atlantic Highlands, NJ: Hamanities Press, 1980.

Allen, James S. *The Negro Question in the United States*. New York: International Publishers, 1936.

Anderson, Jervis. *A. Philip Randolph: A Biographical Portrait*. New York: Harcourt Brace Jovanovich, Inc., 1972.

Aptheker, Herbert, ed. *The Correspondence of W.E.B. Du Bois* (Amherst: University of Massachusetts Press, 1973.

Brissender, Paul F. *Earnings of Factory Workers, 1899 to 1927: An Analysis of Pay-Roll Statistics*, Census Monographs X. Washington, D.C.: Bureau of the Census, 1929.

Bunche, Ralph J. *A World View of Race*. Bronze Booklet Number 4. Washington, D.C.: The Associates in Negro Folk Education, 1936.

Cayton, R. and George S. Mitchell. *Black Workers and the New Unions*. Chapel Hill: The University of North Carolina Press, 1939.

Cunard, Nancy, ed. *Negro: An Anthology Made by Nancy Cunard, 1931-33*. London: Wishart, 1934.

Davis, John P. *Let Us Build A National Negro Congress*. Washington, 1935.

Draper, Theodore. *American Communism and Soviet Russia: The Formative Period*. New York: Viking Press, 1960.

Dubofsky, Melvyn. *We Shall Be All: A History of the Industrial Workers of the World*. New York: Quadrangle, 1969.

Dubofsky, Melvyn, and Warren Van Tine, *John L. Lewis, A Biography*. Urbana: University of Illinois Press, 1986.

Du Bois, W.E.B. *Against Racism: Unpublished Essays, Papers, Addresses, 1887-1961.* Ed. by Herbert Aptheker. Amherst, Mass.: The University of Massachusetts Press, 1985.

_____*Selections from the Crisis,* ed. by Herbert Aptheker. Millwood, New York: Kraus-Thomas Organization Limited, 1983.

Dutte, R. Palme. *Problems of Contemporary History.* New York: International Publishers, 1963.

Fearon, Peter. *The Origins and Nature of the Great Slump, 1929-1932.* Atlantic Highlands, NJ: Humanities Press, 1979.

Foner, Philip S. *American Socialism and Black Americans: From the Age of Jackson to World War II.* Westport, Ct.: Greenwood Press, 1977.

_____*Organized Labor and the Black Worker, 1619-1973.* New York: Praeger Publishers, 1974.

Foner, Philip S., and James S. Allen, eds., *American Communism and Black Americans: A Documentary History, 1919-1929.* Philadelphia: Temple University Press, 1987.

Foner, Philip S., and Ronald Lewis, eds., *The Black Worker: A Documentary History from Colonial Times to the Present,* Vols. 5 and 6. Philadelphia: Temple University Press, 1981.

Ford, James W. *The Negro and Democratic Front.* New York: International Publishers, 1938.

Galenson, Walter. "The Unionization of the American Steel Industry." *International Review of Social History,* 1956.

Harris, Abram L. *Race, Radicalism and Reform, Selected Essays.* Ed. by William Darity, Jr. New Brunswick, NJ: Transaction Publishers, 1989.

Harris, Abram L. and Sterling D. Spero. *The Black Worker: The Negro and the Labor Movement.* New York: Columbia University Press, 1931.

Harris, William H. *Keeping the Faith: A. Philip Randolph and the Brotherhood of Sleeping Car Porters.* Urbana: University of Illinois Press, 1977.

_____*The Harder We Run: Black Workers Since the Civil War.* New York: Oxford University Press, 1982.

Haywood, Harry. *Black Bolshevik: Autobiography of an Afro-American Communist.* Chicago: Liberator Press, 1978.

Hentoff, Nat, ed. *The Essays of A.J. Muste.* New York: The Bobbs-Merrill Company, Inc., 1967.

Hilferding, Rudolf. *Finance Capital: A Study of the Latest Phase of Capitalist Development,* trans. by Morris Watnick and Sam Gordon. Boston: Routledge & Kegan Paul, 1981).

Hill, Herbert. "Race and Ethnicity in Organized Labor: The Historical Sources of Resistance to Affirmative Action." *The Journal of Intergroup Relations,* 12 (Winter 1984).

Hobson, John Atkinson. *Imperialism, A Study.* London: George Allen & Unwin, Ltd., 1938 ed.

Hooker, James R. *Black Revolutionary.* New York: Praeger Publishers, 1970.

Hughes, Langston. *The Big Sea: An Autobiography.* New York: Thunder's Mouth Press, 1940.

James, C.L.R. *At the Rendezvous of Victory, Selected Writings.* London: Allison and Busby, 1984.

Kaufman, Stuart Bruce. *Challenge and Change: The History of the Tobacco Workers International Union.* Distributed by the University of Illinois Press, 1987.

Kelley, Robin D. G. *Hammer and Hoe: Alabama Communists during the Great Depression.* Chapel Hill, N.C.: University of North Carolina Press, 1990.

Kirby, John B. *Black Americans in the Roosevelt Era: Liberalism and Race.* Knoxville: University of Tennessee Press, 1980.

Klehr, Harvey, and John Earl Haynes. *The American Communist Movement: Storming Heaven Itself.* New York: Twayne Publishers, 1992.

Klingman, William K. *1929: The Year of the Great Crash.* New York: Harper & Row, 1989.

Laclau, Ernesto. *New Reflections on the Revolution of Our Time.* (London: Verso, 1991).

League of Nations. *Statistical Year-Book of the League of Nations.* Geneva: League of Nations, 1932.

Lenin, V. I. *Collected Works.* Moscow: Progress Publishers, 1965.

_____*Lenin on the United States*. New York: International
Publishers, 1970.

_____*Selected Works in Three Volumes*.   New York:
International Publishers, 1967.

Leuchtenburg, William.   *Franklin D. Roosevelt and the New
Deal, 1932-40*. New York: Harper and Row Publishers,
1963.

Marable, Manning.   "A. Philip Randolph: A Political
Assessment." In his *From the Grassroots, Essays Toward
Afro -American Liberation*. Boston: South End Press, 1980.

_____*W.E.B. DuBois: Black Radical Democrat*. Boston:
Twayne Publishers, 1986.

Marx, Karl. *Capital: A Critique of Political Economy*, Vol. 1.
Chicago: Charles Kerr, 1906.

Marx, Karl, and Frederick Engels, *Collected Works*, Vol. 25.
New York: International Publishers, 1987.

McKay, Claud.   *The Negroes in America*. Port Washington,
NY: Kennikat Press, 1979.

Meier, August and Elliott Rudwick.   *Black Detroit and the Rise
of the UAW*. New York: Oxford University Press, 1979.

Moore, Jesse Thomas, Jr. *A Search for Equality: The National
Urban League, 1910-1961*. University Park: Pennsylvania
State University Press, 1981.

Moore, Richard B. *Caribbean Militant in Harlem: Collected
Writings, 1920-1972*. Bloomington: University of Indiana
Press, 1988.

Myrdal, Gunnar. *An American Dilemma: The Negro Problem
and Modern Democracy*. New York: Harper and Row, 1944.

Naison, Mark. *Communists in Harlem during the Depression*.
Urbana: University of Illinois Press, 1983.

Nearing, Scott. *Black America*. New York: International
Publishers, 1929.

_____*The Making of a Radical: A Political Autobiography*.
New York: Harper and Row, 1972.

Official Proceedings of the National Negro Congress.
Washington, 1936.

Patterson, William L. *The Man Who Cried Genocide: An
Autobiography*. New York: International Publishers, 1971.

Proceedings of the Second National Negro Congress. Washington, 1937.

Report of the Proceedings of the Convention of the American Federation of Labor, 1933.

Ryon, Roderick. "An Ambiguous Legacy, Baltimore Blacks and the CIO, 1936-1941." *Journal of Negro History* 65 (Winter 1980), 18-33.

Sitkoff, Harvard. *A New Deal for Blacks: The Emergence of Civil Rights as a National Issue; Volume I: The Depression Decade.* New York, Oxford University Press, 1978.

Weisbord, Albert. *The Conquest of Power.* New York: Convici Friede Publishers, 1937.

Weiss, Nancy J. *The National Urban League, 1910-1940.* New York: Oxford University Press, 1974.

World Bank. *World Development Report.* New York: Oxford University Press, 1988.

Wolters, Raymond. *Negroes and the Great Depression: The Problem of Economic Recovery.* Westport, Connecticut: Greenwood Publishing Corp., 1970.

Index

African Blood Brotherhood
(ABB), 13, 36, 47-48,
51-2, 55, 63-65, 68, 85,
118, 124, 129, 139, 149-
50, 164, 196, 295, 207-
9, 229
  foundation of, 25-6
  program, 29-34
  relations with
    Communist Party, 40-
    46, 79, 89-112
Amalgamated Clothing
Workers of America,
116
American Federation of Labor
(AFL), 20, 39, 47, 114-
115, 117, 146, 157-159,
163, 169, 178, 182-183
  and African Americans, 5,
  6-7, 10, 22, 46, 49, 55-
  61, 119-121, 123, 126,
  128, 145, 151-6, 160-1,
  172, 185, 188, 195, 204,
  237
  as representative of the
  labor aristocracy, 6-9
Africa, 19, 27-28, 31, 35-37,
46, 48, 86, 93, 98-99,

102-103, 107, 196-198,
200-201, 206, 210, 215,
218, 221, 223, 229, 249
Agricultural workers, 46, 150,
178-179, 188-189
Allen, James S., 78-84, 212,
215
Amis, B.D., 79-80, 89, 214
American Negro Labor
Congress (ANLC), 46-
47, 50, 59-61, 94, 98,
101-102, 105, 123, 211,
223
Anti-Lynching Bill, 180-181,
184, 186
Anti-Lynching Conference of
NNC, 246-247
Berry, Abner, 112, 224, 239
Bethune, Mary McLeod, 189
Black liberation struggle, 18,
69, 78
Bolshevik Revolution, 11, 17,
21-22, 27, 39
Bontemps, Arna, 157, 224, 238
Briggs, Cyril, V., 20-22, 25-
35, 41, 48-49, 62-63,
80, 84, 89, 92, 95-99,